HEAT TREATMENT

By the same author

Novels

Paradise For Hire
Mortadella

Reference

The Dictionary of Biographical Quotation
(with Richard Kenin)
Makers of Modern Culture
Makers of Nineteenth Century Culture
The Dragon's Almanac
A Dictionary of Arabic and Islamic Proverbs
(with Paul Lunde)

Other

Fun Art Bus
(with Ed Berman)
The Pied Pipers
(with Emma Fisher)
Your Eyes And Their Care
(with Montague Ruben)

HEAT TREATMENT

Travels beyond the Orient
from Bangkok
to the Solomon Islands

JUSTIN WINTLE

J. M. Dent & Sons Ltd
LONDON

First published 1988

© Justin Wintle 1988

This book is set in 11/13 pt Sabon
by Deltatype Ltd, Ellesmere Port
Printed in Great Britain by
Butler & Tanner Ltd
Frome and London

for
J. M. Dent & Sons Ltd,
91 Clapham High Street, London SW4 7TA

British Library Cataloguing in Publication Data

Wintle, Justin, 1949–
Heat treatment.
1. East & South-east Asia. Description &
travel
I. Title
915'.04428

ISBN 0-460-07012-6

Contents

Author's Note

Several brief passages in this book have previously appeared, in different form, in *The Times, The Financial Times, Punch* and *Discovery*. Of the many people who helped me during my journey I am especially indebted to Faisal and Pitim Helabi, to Lucy and Norbert Dass, and to Tom and Non Palaskas for their hospitalities in Bangkok, Sitiawan and Port Moresby. In the Solomon Islands the two resident British diplomats, John Noss and George Anderson, made me wonder whether I had not already returned home. Sir Raymond Firth, Merlynna Hashim and Peter Yapp offered helpful thoughts on the manuscript. Mr Issherwood at Fuji Film Laboratories kindly donated a supply of colour stock, most of which was misused. My literary agents, Michael Sissons and Pat Kavanagh at A. D. Peters, were as indispensable as ever. My final thanks would be to Peter Shellard, Bill Neill-Hall and Ginny Iliff at J. M. Dent & Sons were not an even greater gratitude owing to my wife Kimiko, who understood why I had to go. I can't promise it won't happen again.

J. W.

Illustrations

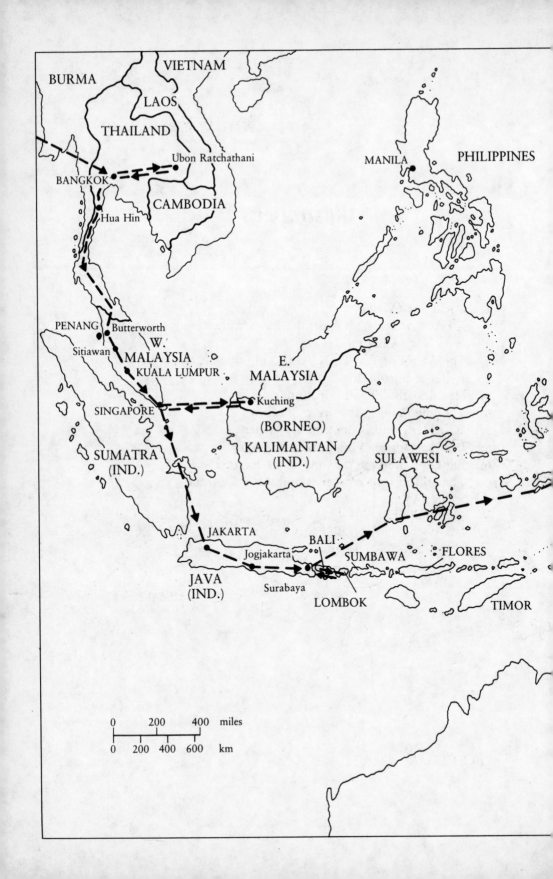

South East Asia

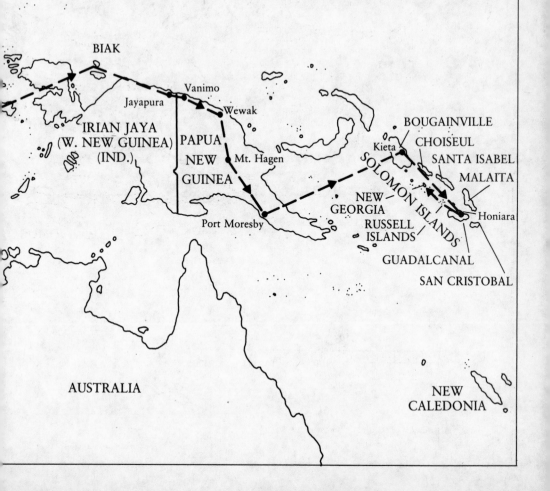

BIAK

Vanimo

Jayapura

Wewak

IRIAN JAYA
(W. NEW GUINEA)
(IND.)

PAPUA

NEW

GUINEA

Mt. Hagen

BOUGAINVILLE

CHOISEUL

Kieta

SANTA ISABEL

MALAITA

SOLOMON ISLANDS

Honiara

NEW
GEORGIA

RUSSELL
ISLANDS

Port Moresby

GUADALCANAL

SAN CRISTOBAL

AUSTRALIA

NEW
CALEDONIA

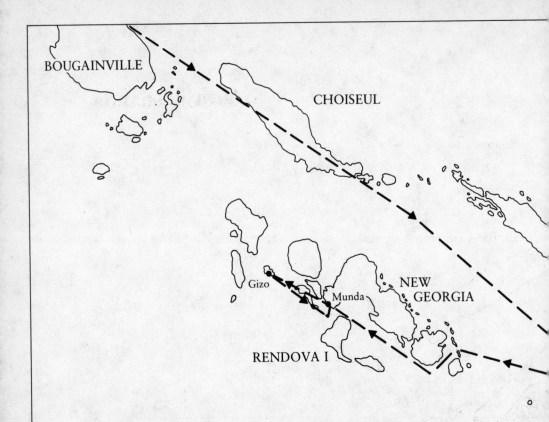

BOUGAINVILLE

CHOISEUL

Gizo

Munda

NEW
GEORGIA

RENDOVA I

Solomon

Sea

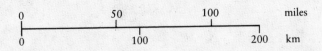

| 0 | 50 | 100 | miles |
| 0 | 100 | 200 | km |

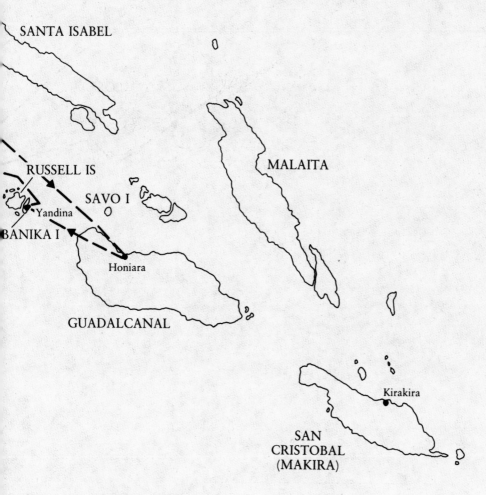

Solomon Islands

South Pacific
Ocean

SANTA ISABEL

RUSSELL IS

SAVO I

Yandina

BANIKA I

MALAITA

Honiara

GUADALCANAL

Kirakira

SAN
CRISTOBAL
(MAKIRA)

BELLONA I

RENNELL I

for William & Noriko Horsley

It is the idea of *Merdeka* that has got them, though it is hard to find out exactly what they think this *Merdeka* – Freedom – will mean. Naked, potbellied children stand along the roadside and pipe '*Merdeka*', raising their clenched fists in salute. Coolies put down their loads and say '*Merdeka*', as you would say 'Hi, Mac'. Neat, pretty Javanese young ladies, selling subscriptions for nonexistent newspapers in the cafés, smile and say '*Merdeka*' politely, like saying 'Good-bye' or 'Delighted to have met you'. It is an immensely successful word. It sounds cheerful and appeals to everyone.

'What are you going to do, once you've got *Merdeka*, Johnny?' someone asked. You do find yourself peevishly wishing the Indonesians would be practical. 'How are you going to make your country run?'

'Oh I see,' said Johnny, still happy as a lark. 'As soon as we have our freedom, we will let the Dutch stay and help us.'

Martha Gellhorn, *Java Journey* (1946)

Part One

MICROPHONE CAN MEAN ANYTHING

ONE

Ten yards of calico

It had been a good day, one of the best. Thanks to Mrs Williams's Immodium my stomach was for once untroublesome. In the morning I'd interviewed the Anglican Archbishop, Norman Palmer, and in the afternoon Sir Peter Kenilorea, until just recently the Solomon Islands' Prime Minister. Then in the evening there was a reception given by the British High Commissioner at his villa high on one of the ridges overlooking the tiny capital Honiara. It also overlooked Savo, an island volcano anchored eighteen miles away at the bottom end of the Slot. Fittingly, for a largely expatriate gathering, the sun was setting; one of those painterly sunsets that do much to enhance the image of the tropics. A lurid splash of orange, two lurid splashes of green, a large vermilion bruise to the north and a general suffusion of damask. What more could anyone want? One day Savo would blow. That was the prediction. Another Krakatoa. Its top was waiting. Sometime in the next ten thousand years. Could be next week, could be tonight. And up there on the ridge, at the High Commissioner's Residence, was the place to see it. A perfect spot to witness a cataclysm. Like the gods at Covent Garden.

I moved from group to group intimating that I had got my hands on a really good story, no, *two* really good stories as a matter of fact. 'What about?' people asked, curious to have a journalist in their midst. 'Malaita, of course,' I replied.

'Malaita, you say? Now I could tell you a thing or two about that lot!'

So little by little I began accumulating a trove of Malaita stories. It was the oldest ruse in the world and it worked. Upon arriving in the Solomon Islands the first thing I had learned was that nearly all the best stories emanate from the island of Malaita. Now I homed in on them as though my life depended on it.

A steady trickle of Cinzano oozed down my gullet, punctuated by dry-roasted peanuts – two luxuries I had long been without. Because of my stomach troubles the Cinzano was the first alcohol I had taken in several weeks, and straightaway it trebled my serendipity. Altogether I was on a high. The last diplomatic function I had attended in Honiara, staged by the Americans, had ended in ignominious disaster. Barely had I made my entry than I had to be carried off again, to a chorus of 'It looks like malaria'. But the same wasn't about to happen on (so-to-speak) home territory. I felt almost well. From time to time I gave Dr John Edge, who the day before had examined me, and who tonight was advising me to go easy on the Cinzano, a look of defiance.

And so it went on until, an hour after the do was supposed to finish, George Anderson, the indispensable Second Secretary, and the best man in Honiara, began rounding up the carless. These included myself, Dr Edge, a man from the embassy in Bangkok who specialized in property, and a gaggle of Overseas Development Administration officials on a visit from their South Pacific headquarters at Suva in Fiji. George herded everyone into a mini-bus, skilfully winged a rival diplomat's limousine as he backed down the drive, laughed like a cavalier, finally got the vehicle facing in the right direction, and brought us all safely down to the coast.

When we arrived at the Mendana Hotel my companions scattered to their rooms. All except a not-very-thin woman in her mid-to-late thirties whom I had imagined to be wived to one of the local expat worthies. We found ourselves facing each other in a deserted lobby with approximately the same question on both our tongues: Have you eaten yet?

'Quick!' said I. 'It's now or never.'

It was almost too late. The kitchen had started to close and by the time we sat down it had closed. But a kindly Malaitan – perhaps the only kindly Malaitan – rustled up two plates of cold meat and some bread.

In the mood I was in I would have liked anybody that hour, but I particularly liked the woman I now found myself opposite. She was not, it transpired, wived to an expat. Rather she, too, was a member of the ODA team. Her name was Penelope Key, and her provenance was health. Before joining the ODA she had worked as a doctor on all manner of medical aid programmes around the world. She had trained as a gynaecologist and her first posting had been to a hill station in New Guinea. Her first solo duty there had involved running down the hill to assist a woman who was giving birth to quads in a canoe.

'It's what you might call being thrown in at the deep end,' she said.

'I know what you mean,' I replied. 'Though I've only ever come across canoes on a quad.'

Dr Key smiled gently, and continued with her story. When she returned to the hill station a man appeared asking her to help kill some baby crocodiles. He didn't want to shoot them, or stick his knife in, because that would have meant leaving a nasty hole in somebody's handbag. What he needed was a measure of chloroform.

Reluctantly Dr Key agreed. She was not terribly disposed toward the slaughter of crocs, young or old, but as a newcomer she could not afford to distance herself from the people she'd come to succour. Getting their trust was all-important. Further, the Papuan could clearly do with the money the skins would fetch in Hong Kong or Singapore – or rather the few dollars he'd be paid by some Australian intermediary. Therefore, having attempted dissuasion, she at last allowed him to put the animals in a drum and poured in what she gauged to be a sufficiently lethal dose.

Next morning she arrived a little late for work. The crocs were gone. The man must have been back to collect them. She was wrong. As she sat writing reports at her desk she suddenly caught sight of three far from soporific long-tailed reptiles snapping their jaws and mincing across the floor in the general direction of her feet, which they had clearly mistaken for a late breakfast.

'But that was nothing compared to what happened later,' Dr Key sighed.

Although her brief was chiefly to deliver babies, much of her work centred on removing spears and other weapons from the shoulder-blades of wounded warriors. The tribes were still fighting each other – and still are. Regularly Penelope Key would get a message not to shut up shop that night as another joust was scheduled for the afternoon.

5

Eventually it all got a bit much. Dr Key told the neighbourhood chiefs that if they wanted her to go on patching up their wounded they must so rearrange matters that casualties were delivered during and not after normal surgery hours. This caused colossal resentment. It was an unpardonable interference, on Dr Key's part, with local customs – or rather Custom, of all concepts the dearest to a Melanesian's heart. Soon some of the warriors (spearsmen, axemen, hacksmen) started threatening her with physical violence, and a police escort had to be organized for her protection. But the tribesmen were not so easily deterred. They were smarter than that. They realized that the way around Dr Key's bodyguards was to send in their womenfolk.

So the tribeswomen went in. One party distracted the police, another assaulted the hapless Dr Key. 'The worst of it was the only guard who didn't desert his post stood back and watched while I was rather badly mauled. When I asked him afterwards why he hadn't come to my rescue he grinned and said he thought it was just another Mary fight.'

That was Papua. After New Guinea she worked in other places in the Pacific, then in S.E. Asia, then in South America. Her tales got better and better, though she wouldn't talk about the horrors she had witnessed in Cambodia. Finally, after Margaret Thatcher, she was the first woman to be flown into the Falklands following the British victory. Cruising the altitude in a Hercules with seventy Tommies, she said, had been no joke either. The soldiers in question had missed out on the action, and behaved accordingly.

'Seventy of them!' she exclaimed. 'You've no idea . . .'

Dr Key finished by objecting strongly to the amount of money the ODA had been obliged to spend in the South Atlantic. Then she asked me the question I knew must be coming and utterly dreaded.

'And what do you do?' she said.

When I told her, her face briefly lit up – 'I've often thought of writing a book myself' – and then promptly collapsed again: 'But I don't think I could.'

'Piffle!' I cried. 'You've got a head-start on all the so-called professionals. You've lived a life, you've got something to write about, and that's the only thing that matters. Or the only thing that *should* matter.'

Dr Key returned my stare with more than a little suspicion.

'Well,' she began cautiously. 'I've always sent long letters to my mother, telling her everything I've been up to. But nobody else in my family seems remotely interested.'

'Of course not,' I objected. 'They're all jealous of you, that's why. A family, particularly an English family, hates it when one of its members *does* anything. There's always a huge envy present, which as often as not is articulated in silence.'

'Do you think so?'

'I'm sure so. And those letters to your mother – what treasure, what gold! Let them be your archives. Probably you won't need anything else. I expect you could even publish them as they stand.'

'But I've read some books by women overseas, and the majority of them are horribly dull.'

'You mean Memoirs of A Consul's Wife or Reminiscences of The Missionary's Cook, that sort of thing?'

Dr Key nodded.

'Then there you are. You're not a diplomatic consort, nor a missionary's pantry girl. You're the real McCoy, the real Miss McCoy, and you must do it.'

'But I'm still not sure I could. I mean, I might not have the skill.'

'Skill!' I shrieked. 'SKILL?'

And I was off. You don't need skill to write a book, I insisted, unless you have nothing to say in the first place. The surfeit of apparent skill in today's books is nothing but a mask for the typical modern author's crushing lack of experience, of involvement. Your average modern author is (a) over-educated, and (b) monumentally empty. His products are all small beer masquerading as tequila sunrise. Nothing but coquetry. Nothing but make-up. Craft paraded as content where none exists . . .

Then I really began hamming it. I made half-a-dozen unsavoury remarks about Truman Capote – I'd just finished reading *Music for Chameleons* – and paid the usual bloated homage to Messrs Conrad, Orwell and Greene. It was all the fault of the universities, I said, for permitting themselves to run literary faculties. Why, I even knew somebody who had done three years' research into whether Shakespeare was a Jew, and all at the taxpayer's expense!

But, I persisted, the climate at last was changing. People were getting sick of dreams and fantasies. There was a renewed interest in Real Stuff writing, preferably with a moral lining. And as far as I could judge, Penelope Key MD was just the sort of person to provide it. The climate wouldn't change just like that. The climate had to have something to work on, to get its teeth into. The climate needed a shove in the right place.

In this importunate vein I must have waxed a good half hour. The thought occurred to me that perhaps I'd gone berserk, but I couldn't stop. I just went on and on, as if something awful was clawing at my innards.

Eventually, though, I did run out of wind. Dr Key was staring at me with a deal of bemusement on her face.

'Anyway,' I said, 'what about it?'

'I might,' Penelope replied. 'Perhaps I will.'

*

I slept very well that night. At last my journey was beginning to take the shape I had wanted it to take when I left London three months before.

Notoriously, travelling oscillates between two extremes: tight itineraries with no let-up, a kind of glorified appointment-keeping, and its subjective opposite, total free fall. The secret of good travel, I suspect is to establish and maintain a balance. On my way to the Solomons, however – through Thailand, Malaysia, Indonesia and New Guinea – there had been far too much free fall. Most days I was overcome with vertigo from the moment I woke up. Now Guadalcanal, thank goodness, presented opportunities for a more impersonal fulfilment.

I had been to the Far East several times before, mainly for rather touristic/romantic reasons. This trip I wanted to be different. As well as seeking to satisfy a perennial craving to discover how the other 99.9% lives I wanted to challenge the complacency that too easily besets a writer cossetted in the comforts and security of a European democracy. Specifically, I wanted to test and extend my range. Most of my professional life had been spent compiling reference books, editing other people's manuscripts and penning book-reviews. True, I had also written a somewhat seedy novel about Thailand, and another even seedier novel about Bologna, but these, compared to the rest of my output, had been blithe anomalies. Somewhat late in the day it dawned on me that my activities were unnecessarily, even unnaturally limited.

The itch began in 1985, when I paid my first visit to Tokyo. There my host and cicerone was the BBC Japan correspondent, William Horsley. At the Foreign Correspondents' Club in Yurakucho, surrounded by writers whose primary interest was in the world, not the word, I fell prey to the documentary muse. The desire to try my hand at journalism, and especially foreign reportage, took hold.

This in part explains the diatribe I inflicted on poor Penelope Key. But my bombast was also an expression of fear: fear that my journey might after all end as it had started; in failure. In the South-East Asian countries I had come down through I had had plenty of lively, even topical, experiences; but these experiences had somehow remained distanced from the histories of those countries. As a would-be journalist what I had wanted to experience, in however small a way, was a fusion, a coming-together of the subjective and the objective. In other words I wanted to witness history in the making, or, if not in the making, then at least as it came piping hot out of the oven.

That ambition was finally, if somewhat strangely, realized in my encounters with, of all persons, the former Governor of Wandsworth Prison, encounters that took place in the days that immediately followed my dinner with Dr Key. But until I met Bill Guinan it was, to use a phrase, touch and go all the way.

But why the Solomons?

In the post-Tokyo mood I was in the odds were I would have taken off for some remote corner sooner or later. But the precise destination was suggested, as it nearly always is suggested, by chance. I would never have set off for the South Pacific in the winter of '86 unless in the winter of '85 I hadn't first journeyed to Hong Kong.

As they say, one travel begets another . . .

*

It was mid-October and I was still brooding about Tokyo when, early one morning, the phone rang. On the line from the other side of the world was Maurice, whom in my entire life I had met perhaps twice. How would I like to come out to Hong Kong and work there?

'You want to see China, don't you? Well, now's your chance. Bring your binoculars and you can see China every day of your life.'

Maurice was looking for someone to edit a magazine. This wasn't my line at all, but when an annual salary of £25,000 was hinted at I quickly saw the logic of not saying no at once.

9

'You're not the only candidate,' Maurice added quickly. 'There's another man in Gambia who's in with a very strong chance. But it would do no harm to talk.'

'Fine,' I said. 'I'm listening. When can I expect you?'

'You can't. We're expecting you. The Big White Chief wants to meet you face to face. We'll pay the fare of course.'

'With a hotel thrown in?'

'With a hotel thrown in.'

Without further ado I packed my hold-all, arguing to myself that perhaps magazines were an area of publishing I should get acquainted with. The magazine in question sounded pure gloss, but one had to start somewhere. And hadn't my motto always been that life's worthless unless you do a lot of different things with it?

From Hong Kong I'd be able to to visit Tokyo and Seoul and Singapore and Manila and Surabaya and Sulawesi and a dozen other choice places as often as I liked. Some of them I had been to before, some of them I hadn't: but, with a modicum of luck, soon they'd all be just a stone's throw away!

I boarded Cathay Pacific's newly introduced non-stopper at Gatwick in a state of rare elation. When the first meal was served the somewhat winsome Chinese girl beside me asked whether I wanted her scrambled egg. She didn't want it, she said, because she didn't see how the eggs could possibly be fresh.

'What do you mean? Don't you know that on a jumbo they keep live chickens up in the cockpit! Eat your omelette. It's probably the freshest you'll ever taste.'

The girl pecked at the square yellow lung on the square yellow tray in front of her. Soon the omelette had disappeared.

'How was it?'

'Fine,' said the girl.

'Then have mine, too.'

But matters took a downturn when the plane landed at Kai Tak airport.

At Kai Tak one waits an age to clear immigration. Then you go through customs into a tolerably air-conditioned and relatively empty hall. The exit proper is at the end of this vestibule. Beyond the glass doors are usually about a million people waiting to greet their friends and relatives. There's also a pong which must be piped straight through from the sewers of Canton sixty miles away.

Realizing only now that I hadn't had any sleep for at least twenty-four hours I stumbled out into the late afternoon heat. Jostled on all sides I did my best to pick out Maurice amid a sea of bubbling faces. At last I espied him. Maurice hadn't made it any easier. He was several times larger than the last time we had met, and he had further camouflaged himself behind a luxuriant beard. Had he not called out my name I would have walked straight past him.

'You made it,' Maurice greeted me, oddly wanting enthusiasm. 'We'd better take a cab. There are a couple of things I have to tell you.'

Maurice turned leadenly on his heels and ploughed towards the taxi rank, leaving in his wake a litter of badly trampled Chinese women and their children. I followed as best I could, shouldering my hold-all to avoid causing further mutilation.

The taxi-driver, who wore spectacles thick enough to burn a hole in each eyeball within two seconds if he ever looked at the sun, drove like a distraught whippet. But that, as I later discovered, was par for the course. Ninety per cent of Hong Kong taxi-drivers are severe myopics. It's a job you take if you can't sign up as a steward on one of the airlines and haven't enough capital to open a shop.

The car shot forward, braked, and shot forward again.

'I'm putting you up at the Luk Kwok down on the old waterfront in Wanchai,' Maurice began. 'That should ensure you get at least something out of your trip. The Luk Kwok's the hotel they used for *Suzy Wong*. It's not what it used to be, but the place is surrounded by bars. As soon as we've checked you in we'll try a few. Though I must say straightaway that I'm not sure it's a good idea your being here.'

'Oh?'

Maurice shifted uncomfortably in his seat.

'Yes. There are a couple of things I must tell you,' he repeated. 'But let's discuss it over a beer, shall we?'

It was easy to see why Maurice didn't want to hang about at the Luk Kwok. In fact the hotel probably hadn't changed an iota since the '50s, down to and including the staff. The corridors were lined with alopecic geriatrics who stared at me as though I'd come from another planet. And the peeling paintwork was all of the same vintage.

The bar in the street behind the Luk Kwok on the other hand was distinctly snazzy. The employees were considerably younger and barely possessed a full suit of clothes between them.

'I like that one,' said Maurice, pointing at a girl who promptly

11

stepped forward and introduced herself as Matilda. 'Trouble is, in a place like this and at this time of the day they're so damned expensive. Mama-san has to nip off to the labour exchange and find a replacement. Beer?'

Afraid of the consequences alcohol might have on my already ballooning jet-lag I shook my head. Orange juice was fine.

'You were going to tell me,' I prompted, 'why it's not such a good idea my being here.'

'Was I?'

'In the taxi.'

'Oh yes, I suppose I was.'

Maurice blinked twice at a long-haired rubberized thing called Dorothy and drew a breath. 'Yes yes. You see, there are a couple of things I should tell you. Like for instance, right now, I'm suspended by the company.'

'Oh,' I said.

'Quite,' gravelled Maurice. 'Oh.'

Bit by bit the story came out. The evening before, at roughly the time I was setting off for Gatwick, Maurice had slipped into the Foreign Correspondents' Club for a quick noggin before going home. And because the FCC was the colony's premier watering hole it was some time before Maurice thought about leaving.

'I was just sitting there, chatting to a colleague, when the glass I was holding took flight and made a bee-line for this other fellow's face. I don't know how it happened, but chaos ensued instamatically. There were a load of other glasses on the table and I used them as ammunition. Purely to defend myself, you understand, though that's not how anybody else saw it. The long and the short of it is I managed to get through about a hundred quid's worth of the things before somebody had the good sense to restrain me.'

At this point Maurice glared at me savagely.

'Of course,' he accused, 'it's all your fault. I admit I was drunk. But then I nearly always am drunk. However I don't usually fling beer-mugs around the place. The reason is I was just so damned glad you were coming. That's why. If you hadn't been on your way I wouldn't have been so excitable and nothing untoward would have happened.'

'So?'

'So now I've got to appear before the Club's Committee. And until the outcome of that is known I'm suspended at work. Officially that is.

Unofficially I'm still at my desk. That's because someone's got to do my job and it might as well be me because nobody else would know how. But the Big White Chief has to do something to preserve his standing with the other Club members. Hong Kong is still like that, I'm afraid. So, if the Club decides to expel me then I'm also for the chop as far as the company is concerned. If not, I'll keep my job. Right now, though, I'm persona non grata. You see what a mess you've got me into? And you're persona non grata as well, because you're a friend of mine. Otherwise you wouldn't be 'here, would you? It's all a question of extension. Starts in the Club, extends to the office, and now you're feeling the draft as well.

'It's even more complicated than I've outlined. There's background you see. I've been working for the company for seven years and I'm still not a director. I was in at the beginning and it's me that's built the whole thing up. But the Big White Chief is a touch possessive about these things. On the other hand without me there's a fifty-fifty chance the operation would disintegrate. Last week I asked him again. When are you going to make me a director? I said. But now I'm back to where I was. My antics at the FCC are the perfect excuse for keeping me pinned down. And I have to concede he's got a point. I mean he can't go round shelling out directorships to bar-room brawlers, can he? And by the same token now is not the time for me to offer my services elsewhere in Hong Kong – at least not for the level of remuneration I'm accustomed to. Looks like I'm stuck for the while. Got my wheels firmly in the mud. As far as you're concerned, though, it's hopeless. The last thing the Big White Chief wants is for me to pack his staff with my supporters.'

'But he has agreed to pay my expenses, hasn't he?'

'Oh yes. I spoke to him about that this morning. That's the problem, you see. He's not what you'd call an all-out shit. The Big White Chief, being a somewhat insecure character, likes to appear open-handed. By all means, if you know someone you think can do the job let's have a look at him. That sort of thing. But afterwards he'd say; "Are you out of your mind? That friend of yours couldn't turn a pitchfork." '

'As bad as that?'

'Yes. And no. The problem is I'm just not sure. As I've said he pays me well enough. He's like all paranoids. You never really know where you are with him.'

While Maurice had two more beers we talked about such generalities as mutual acquaintances, wives and the weather, which in Hong Kong is even more a topic of conversation than it is in England. Then it was time to go. Maurice said goodbye to Susan and Alice as well as to Matilda and Dorothy and I led him back into the street outside. It was getting dark now, and the go-go clubs were beginning to shimmer.

'Want to try The Hunter?' Maurice asked. 'It's a very good place. It's just down there.'

'Maybe after I've eaten.'

Maurice suddenly grabbed my arm and squeezed it tightly.

'Don't worry,' he said, 'I'll make sure he sees you, and I'll back you all the way. A hundred per cent. My word.'

We left Wanchai and went to Maurice's sixteenth-floor apartment halfway up the Peak.

For those who have never been there the Peak is a large hill in the middle of Hong Kong island. If Christ had been Chinese Satan would certainly have taken him to the top of it for the third temptation. 'Whereabouts on the Peak do you live?' is the standard euphemism for establishing somebody's social position. The very rich have dwellings on the top, the plain rich just below, then come the would-be rich, the ordinary wealthy, the affluent, and so on down the scale. The great mass of the population lives across the water on mainland Kowloon. Besides Hong Kong itself there are 150 other islands belonging to the colony, a fact that seems little known to the outside world. Most of these are only partially inhabited. 'Living in the islands' is for those who either fancy themselves as eccentrics, or have decided that the upper tiers of the Peak are permanently beyond their reach. They have settled instead to live comfortably in surroundings of incomparable beauty. Modern communications being what they are this is hardly the hardship it sounds. Just recently some of the plain rich and the would-be rich have taken up residence on Lantau. They are among the luckiest people on the planet.

While Maurice fixed drinks I surveyed Hong Kong proper from his balcony. The city, both parts of it, Hong Kong Central and Kowloon, was spread out below me like an illuminated tablecloth. Nearer were the other apartment blocks, a host of tall modernist salt-cellars impossibly balanced on the hillside. It was a vast, exhilarating yet somehow lifeless panorama, with precisely the quality of an ektachrome photograph. Then I remembered. In Hong Kong nobody is allowed to install any neon that flashes or flickers, in case it disorientates incoming aircraft. Incoming aircraft fly right over the heart of Kowloon after negotiating some very steep mountains on the landward side. Therefore the entire conurbation is covered with neon that doesn't so much as blink. From where I was it looked like a well-guarded jewellery store. The blazing night had been stopped dead in its tracks.

'So how do you like the golden egg?' Maurice asked, pushing into my hands a glass the size of a rose-bowl. In it a few ice-cubes floated lonesomely on top of a small lake of whisky.

I took my first cautious sip.

'It is mildly breath-taking, I must admit.'

'Oh come on,' said Maurice. 'You can do better than that. You're a writer for God's sake. What's your first impression?'

'Very well then. My first impression, if that's what you want. Of Hong Kong. Of the Peak. The Peak is not a mountain. It's an artificial kidney machine, the biggest ever made. It's what keeps all the money-diggers alive.'

It was Maurice's turn to groan.

'Oh bloody hell,' he expostulated. 'If that's your attitude then you'd better not see the Big White Chief after all.'

'It's not my attitude,' I smiled, covering at the double. 'It's my impression. My first one. I'm sure I'll have others.'

'You'd better have. Any more bullshit like that and I won't pay your hotel bill.' And then: 'When you come here you'll appreciate soon enough just how important the occasional drink is. Do you realize, at the rate I'm going I'll only just be a sterling millionaire by the time I retire?'

Dinner was served. Without in any way becoming less unsober Maurice transformed himself into an altogether different person. He became, to all intents and purposes, the striving, solicitous family man. In front of his wife and children he mused out aloud what would be the best course of action to square their somewhat disparate ambitions. His son wanted them all to go back to England, where he could enrol at a proper university. The wife wanted to stay put. The daughter was thinking creatively about America. From what was said it was clear that Maurice's tussles with the Big White Chief not only stretched back into the dawn of time, but were also central to everyone's deliberations. If his family were agreed on one thing it was that none of them wished to hear the B.W.C.'s name spoken ever again.

I was soon of a similar opinion. Three days later a message reached me at the Luk Kwok that the Big White Chief was prepared to grant an audience, at ten o'clock on Thursday morning. In the meantime Maurice strove hard to keep his guest amused. Generally this meant prolonged after-hours drinking at the Ladies' Recreation Club on the same level of the Peak as his apartment. At the weekend I was ferried across to Lantau to meet a selection of the new-breed millionaires at a lunchtime barbecue. 'I wonder what became of the best of us?' pondered a 23-year-old advertising tiger who owned a yacht, a Porsche, a Rolls Royce, a house in Tokyo and a park in Adelaide. But because, unofficially, Maurice was still working, Maurice had sometimes to go to bed, and then I was left to my own devices. These consisted in the main of imbibing whisky at the Makati Inn and listening to the conversations of the Filipina amahs. My excuse was I was researching 'The Diary of a Filipino Housemaid' which, if I ever got round to writing it, would provide the last word in the satiric deconstruction of Thatcherite Britain. Each night I tried to sleep, but sleep simply wouldn't come. I was too excited, and soon too exhausted.

I did, however, finally manage to fall asleep at eight o'clock on Thursday morning. And I remained asleep until well past eleven. Ringing through my apologies I arrived at the Big White Chief's office only two hours late. The B.W.C., a pocket-sized Australian, indicated a chair and proceeded to gaze through the window as though Don Bradman were outside shaping up for the next delivery. In an unseemly rush I divulged my various plans for rejuvenating what was already a highly viable magazine. Then I, too, fell silent. The next delivery never came. The B.W.C. continued staring through the window, and after another five minutes I conceded that I was on a hopelessly sticky wicket.

So much for that, I said to myself. All that remained was to get on the first flight back to London.

But it was not to be.

On my way out of the B.W.C.'s office I ran into Maurice.

'How did it go?'

'I don't think it went at all.'

'Oh come on. It's far too soon to say that. The man from Gambia doesn't arrive until tomorrow. Perhaps his plane will crash. I'll treat you to a lunch at the Correspondents' Club. I'll introduce you to Philip Smiley.'

'But . . .'

'I know. But I can still take you in. The Committee hasn't met yet.'

Philip Smiley was the most disgustingly healthy-looking person I had clapped eyes on in a long while. His face shone with vitamins. He was also the brother of Xan Smiley, for whom, as one of the better Africa correspondents around, I nurtured an unbounded admiration. Even in the deep torpor of my sleeplessness Philip couldn't help but make an impression on me. Everyone else in Hong Kong seemed in terrible need of a hospital.

Maurice parked me at Philip's table and disappeared before anyone could give him the bum's rush. Having made polite enquiries about Xan, I congratulated Philip on his appearance. He was at least seven years older than he looked.

'So tell me,' I asked, 'where have you been to keep your youth so immaculately preserved?'

Full of haliborange candour Philip replied:

'For the last few years, here. I've become a stock-broker. Before that though I was in the Solomon Islands, with the Service.'

'I've heard of the Solomons. What are they like?'

Philip paused before he answered. Then he pronounced:

'Sheer paradise. All you need is four poles and ten yards of calico for a house and – sheer paradise!'

*

Four poles and ten yards of calico! For six months I tried to put the idea out of my head. The Solomon Islands were simply too far away, in every sense, to merit the effort. But all the while my yearning to be up and away militated against my better judgement, so that eventually I started converting the cons into pros. The great advantage of the Solomons, I began reasoning to myself, was that it was highly improbable that any other journalist, unseasoned or otherwise, would make the same trek at the same time. I could cut my teeth in isolation, unaffected by the competitiveness which, I had observed in Tokyo, seemed a pre-condition of the correspondent's calling.

Thus a whim hardened into a resolve. But no sooner had I made up my mind than I began hedging my bets. It was entirely possible that as well as being devoid of other journalists the Solomons would also be devoid of any 'news', in which case I would be badly out of pocket. To make sure the trip didn't completely destroy my finances I elected to write a travel book as well; and to make sure the travel book didn't fall into the same trap I considerably broadened my itinerary.

I sat down and cobbled together just enough information about my destination to bait my agent's line.

'As all the world knows,' my outlined breezed, 'the Solomon Islands were formerly a British Protectorate, and are now a member of the Commonwealth. There are about 500 of them, stretching in two chains a distance of 900 miles just below the Equator to the East of New Guinea. They were first discovered in the sixteenth century by Alvaro de Mendaña de Neyra. This Spaniard gave the Solomon Islands their name on account of the natural treasures he expected to find among them. Soon afterwards the legend started that King Solomon's hoard was hidden somewhere among the atolls and volcanoes that comprise the basic terrain. In fact small quantities of gold have been extracted ever since, but mainly the Solomons are famous for tuna, copra, palm oil and timber. There is a lot of malaria, and the rainfall is measured in yards rather than inches. The people are a complete mix: Melanesians, Micronesians, Polynesians, plus of course European and Chinese traders.' And then, after a short paragraph about Philip Smiley, came the killer blow. 'The provisional working title for my book is *Beyond The Orient*. Once in the Solomons I shall make it my task to report on whatever is afoot. But I shall not travel there directly. Rather I shall fly first to Bangkok, then head down to Jakarta via Kuala Lumpur and Singapore. From Jakarta on to Port Moresby (Papua New Guinea), and then either by boat to Honiara, or by plane from Brisbane (Air Pacific flies twice weekly to Guadalcanal).'

Thanks to Hong Kong the Lure of the Orient had caught up with me again, and any prospective publisher would have been forgiven for thinking the Solomons merely a pretext for a joyride through S.E.Asia. Yet incredibly, in no time at all, the firm of J.M.Dent & Son agreed to give me a contract. Not of course that it was quite as simple as that. There was still a question of money. Although the offer Dent's came up with was handsome enough, a shortfall was likely. I spent the next several days on the telephone abasing myself before the editors of divers newspapers and magazines – a necessity I was wholly unused to, and which I found intensely distasteful. Having successfully cleared the decks of a seemingly infinite bodyguard of secretaries and personal assistants, I would give my name and the editor would say I'm sorry but can you repeat that please? Further, the positive results (yes, we'll read anything you care to send) were as daunting as the negative (sorry mate, our travel columns are booked solid for the next ten years, or we already have our stringers in all the places you've mentioned). When the responsive editors got down to particulars the frightening prospect dawned; much graft was what was expected. Usually they wanted pieces on places not quite on my schedule, so that obliging them would substantially reduce what profit margins there were.

Step by step, however, I committed myself to going. Contracts were signed, and agreements reached. Family and friends were told, tickets bought. Soon it would have cost me more to withdraw from the project than stick with it. Yet just what sort of corner I had so deftly painted myself into only became apparent when I returned to the library to see what else I could discover about the Solomon Islands.

At first my findings were auspicious – at least from the point of view of an author on the make. Remarkably the only Distinguished Writer who appeared to have set foot in the archipelago was Jack London, and his sojourn there, described in *The Cruise of the Snark* (1911), had been brief enough. Otherwise zilch, which left the way open for me to do for the Solomons what R.L. Stevenson and Herman Melville had done for Samoa and the Marquesas. Hooray! Quel stroke of bonne chance! But then, as I began actually to read London's chapterette, my heart skipped a beat. There was a reason, it quickly transpired, why everyone steered clear of the Solomons. They were the original Cannibal Islands. No one in his right mind would voluntarily seek to visit them unless he had an overwheening motive such as wanting to die quickly (on the point of a savage's spear) or die slowly (by arrangement with the mosquitos).

London, his wife Charmian, a navigator and two Japanese crew arrived in the Solomons toward the end of the *Snark*'s voyage. That was their first mistake. Their second was to accept an invitation to sail across from Guadalcanal to Malaita on board a recruiting vessel, the *Minota*. Recruiting was the polite name for slave trading. The impolite word was blackbirding. The object of the exercise was to supply the cheapest possible labour for plantations in Queensland and Fiji.

Whereas the savagery of the natives was controlled by tradition and custom, the savagery of the white interlopers was uncontrolled by greed. Not surprisingly there was the greatest imaginable resentment among native Solomon Islanders towards not just traders, but also, for a long while, planters, government officials and any other whites – missionaries included. But nothing was fairer game than a recruiting vessel. If one of these went aground – and sooner or later, because of the treacherous reefs, they all ran aground – it was each man for himself and heaven help the rest of you. And Malaita was a special case. Malaita was raided more persistently than any other island, because Malaitans, naturally stronger, could be made to work extremely hard indeed, once they had been 'civilized' or 'tamed'. Therefore, on Malaita, the level of resentment was twice what it was anywhere else.

Jack London sailed across to Malaita and promptly the *Minota* ran aground. There were some desperate hours before help arrived. London was lucky to escape with his life. But more to the point, the experience coloured everything he had to say about the Solomons. All the islanders were bushmen, all were armed with knives, bows and arrows, spears and the odd Snider rifle, and their only happiness was homicide. When they couldn't find a white man to murder they murdered each other, as witness the following paragraph that well typifies both the flavour and the content of London's narrative:

Another recent courageous killing I heard on Malaita was that of an old man. A bush chief had died a natural death. Now the bushmen don't believe in natural deaths. No one was ever known to die a natural death. The only way to die is by bullet, tomahawk or spear thrust. When a man dies in any other way, it is a clear case of having been charmed to death. When the bush chief died naturally, his tribe placed the guilt on a certain family. Since it did not matter which one of the family was killed, they selected this old man who lived by himself. This would make it easy. Furthermore, he possessed no Snider. Also, he was blind. The old fellow got an inkling of what was coming and laid in a large supply of arrows. Three brave warriors, each with a Snider, came down upon him in the night-time. All night they fought valiantly with him. Whenever they moved in the bush and made a noise or a rustle, he discharged an arrow in that direction. In the morning, when his last arrow was gone, the three heroes crept up to him and blew his brains out.

The *Minota* itself had been successfully attacked just six months before and her captain 'chopped to pieces with tomahawks'. Reprisals inevitably ensued. At Binu, where the atrocity had occurred, London sailed in just a few hours after a man-of-war, the *Cambrian* , had sailed out, leaving in her wake three burned villages, thirty dead pigs and a drowned baby.

But it was not these tales of Victorian violence that distressed me. After all, there must have been a few behavioural changes in the succeeding eighty years. Rather it was London's equally insistent catalogue of the diseases he and his crew encountered in the Solomons. Malaria, blackwater, dysentery, leprosy and yaws were everywhere he looked. In addition there were two local specialities, benefiting from the somewhat imprecise nature of their nomenclature; the Solomon Islands Fever, and the Solomon Islands Sore.

The latter particularly brought out London's descriptive talent: 'And the sores are not nice. They may be described as excessively active ulcers. A mosquito bite, a cut, or the slightest abrasion, serves for lodgement of the poison with which the air seems to be filled. Immediately the ulcer commences to eat. It eats in every direction, consuming skin and muscle with remarkable rapidity. The pin-point ulcer of the first day is the size of a dime by the second day, and by the end of the week a silver dollar will not cover it.'

It was while reading this passage that I began to have second thoughts about my upcoming tour. I had given malaria a passing reference in my outline, by way of whetting the publisher's appetite (publishers like the idea of authors risking life and limb on their behalf) and perhaps raising the ante (add on danger money); but at no point had I considered that there might be an actual hazard involved. Twenty-five pages of Jack London gave the matter a rather different complexion. Malaria might, with the help of modern prophylactics, be avoidable, but the Solomon Islands Sore presented an altogether more formidable opponent. And of course, it was well known that once sores set in other illnesses attach themselves like flies. My destination, I suddenly grasped, was no less that the Grim Reaper's secret lair, the place where he keeps his lethal laboratory and experiments with all the viruses and plagues known to man, along with a few that are not.

I pushed London aside and turned to the rest. There were several travelogues and memoirs by lesser writers. Yet each time I opened any one of them my eye fell on a roughly similar sentence, which took the form of: 'After those of us who were strong enough had buried Jones, we were faced with a second [or third, fourth or fifth] calamity . . .' The only constraint on death by disease it seemed was death by violence. And what the travellers reported the historians (such as there were) reiterated. The story of the Solomons was one of unmitigated moribundance. Philip Smiley had either been pulling my leg, or else the Reaper had instructed him to fetch me.

It was all too much. And what was also too much was the last section I looked at. The anthropology. Here, instead of a shelf lightly packed with faded reminiscences and thin pamphlets, was a wall of solid achievement. As far as the Solomons went the anthropologists had cornered the market with a vengeance. Evidently London had been allowed through the net *pour encourager les autres*. And now a small stern voice was telling me, Bad luck, mate, you've got to read the lot. Haven't you?

Well no, in fact, I hadn't. All I really had to do was call on the best of them: Sir Raymond Firth.

*

Sir Raymond was only slightly reluctant to be visited. 'Come and see me if you must,' he said on the telephone, 'but don't whatever you do bring a tape-recorder. Tape-recorders only catch ephemera. They are not to be trusted. They always take, and never give.'

'Very well,' I said, 'I won't bring a tape-recorder.' Which was just as well because at the time the one I had didn't work.

According to *Who's Who* Professor Firth was born eighty-six years ago, in 1901. This, however, is not strictly credible. When I arrived at his house, two-thirds the way up a steep lane in Highgate, the door was opened by a spritely individual obviously somewhere in his early-to-mid-sixties. Panting hard after the long climb from Highgate Underground, I asked to see his father.

'My father? He's been dead for years.'

'I mean . . . Professor Firth.'

'That's me. Come in.'

We went straight upstairs to a large and totally cluttered study in

22

which there was barely room for the two chairs: one behind Professor Firth's dining-table sized desk, the other by a gas fire in the fire-place. During our conversation Firth constantly leapt around, scavenging drawers, shelves and cupboards, digging out papers and photographs, making me giddy with a nonstop exhibition of energy. What was even more impressive was that his wife, Rosemary, also an academic, worked quietly away in the equally large but somewhat more orderly room next door. Although it was getting dark she did so without the means of artificial light. Both had beautifully clean eyes for their ages – their combined years came to over 160, 135 of which must have been devoted to scholarship. To behold them was, to risk an understatement, chastening.

At first Firth was suspicious of me – and why not? He wanted to know what *kind* of book I intended to write in the Solomons, to which of course I had no ready answer. I admitted as much. 'I haven't been there yet, so what can I say? Except of course that it won't be anthropological.'

'Then why have you come to see me?'

'Because, even though I'm not an anthropologist, I nevertheless accept the importance of anthropology.'

'Well, I suppose that says something for you. But if you're not an anthropologist, what are you?'

'A m-miscellaneous author, I suppose,' I said, stammering slightly. And the ice began to thaw.

There were of course certain rituals to be gone through. I presented the professor with a copy of *The Dragon's Almanac,* an anthology of oriental proverbs I'd published three years before. 'Keep it in the loo,' I said. 'That's where it usually winds up.' 'Oh I'll have more respect for it than that,' Firth replied. Then we talked about another professor we knew in common and I began to realize I wasn't about to have my head bitten off after all. Lady Firth popped her head round the door and asked for an aerogramme. Nimble as a gymnast Firth bent forward as though wanting to touch his toes and opened a bottom drawer. Then he sat upright and began answering questions about himself. The introduction ceremony was over. Yes it was true, he was one of Bronislaw Malinowski's first students at the London School of Economics; another was Sir Edward Evans-Pritchard. He had decided to do his early field work in the Solomons, among the Polynesians, from an early acquaintance with the Maori in New Zealand. In all he

23

had made four trips out there, the first in 1928, the last in 1973, spending most of his time on Tikopia, a smaller island. He laughed when I asked whether cannibalism was still practised in the 1920s.

'My dear man, oh no. In 1928 I asked some Tikopians whether their ancestors had ever eaten any men. They said No, did yours? When I replied in the negative they said: Why then did you ask if ours did?'

Firth laughed a second time.

'Oh no no. Not at all in Tikopia. In my time the only thing like that which survived was infanticide. If a man had a daughter to help his wife grow vegetables and a son to ride with him in his canoe he didn't need any more children. If one came along, as likely as not he'd turn its face down and let it smother.'

A little shocking at first, of course, but Firth's job hadn't been to judge or evaluate: it had been to work out why. Infanticide was perhaps their equivalent of birth control. A question of ecological balance. And that's what anthropology had taught him: to look at different cultures comparatively, not to rate them. Distinct social systems existing by themselves, almost in a vacuum. No use muddling them up with imported ideologies, although, for the purpose of analyzing them, and making models of them, certain aspects of those ideologies were useful. It was liable to work both ways, though. For instance, you might go along to a village looking for an equivalent of Marx's wage-labour in a culture that didn't possess money, or not as we'd recognize it, and find that it didn't really exist. So in the end you wound up revising Marx. But it comes full circle. First-and-second-world economic habits spread everywhere, so that the wage-labour equation, with all its attendant problems, is now a feature of Solomon Island culture. From the humanist point of view this was a great tragedy. The world described in Firth's books (for example *We, the Tikopia* or *The Work of the Gods in Tikopia*) has now almost completely vanished.

This gave men of Firth's generation something of an advantage over younger anthropologists, since it has become virtually impossible to verify work done forty or fifty years ago. Even in 1928 he found that half the Tikopians he encountered had converted to Christianity. Perhaps in New Guinea and certain parts of the Amazonian jungle there are still a few untouched tribes, but not in the Solomons. But to a large extent the where was irrelevant. Firth happened to do his field work on Tikopia, but there were scores of other places he might have gone, and the general result would have been the same. There would, he hoped, have been the same humanist enlightenment; the realization that moral values subsist within cultures, not outside and independent of them.

Then he told me how, among some Tikopians, it was the custom to bury their dead inside their homes. Sometimes he would enter a house and there would be a mat on the floor no one walked on. Underneath the mat was grandpa or grandma.

'Wasn't there a health risk?' I asked. 'Mightn't that be an absolute standard outside specific cultures?'

But Sir Raymond demurred. The sand in Tikopia was excellent for burying people in, he said. If not they probably wouldn't have done it.

'And tight corners? Did you ever find yourself in any tight corners?'

Not really, Sir Raymond replied, though there had been one occasion, early on, when he had to be careful to dissociate himself from the missionaries, but not so much that he lost the confidence of the converts, some of whom still practised traditional rituals on the quiet. It was difficult to know exactly where to draw the line. In general all Tikopians, but particularly the older ones, were very surprised at a white man's eagerness to listen to their ancestral stories. After all, most of the white men they knew, the missionaries, were the opposite of interested. But even so, you had to be careful. If a people were converted, and they knew you didn't hit it off with the priests, they might not be so keen to talk to you. Or it might be the other way round. If you got too close to the missionaries they might think you'd report them.

'At the time I was investigating a particular cycle of ritual. That was the thing, the wonderful thing, about it. Little by little you discovered that each individual ritual was connected to a larger system. The world that I have said has vanished was really a very large one ideed. At one point I was told that one ceremony I had been most anxious to witness would take place on the beach the following morning. At midnight, however, a man tapped on my door. The real ceremony was starting inland at dawn, he told me. So I got up early and presented myself. The head man was not at all pleased by this, but eventually he allowed me to stay.'

Sir Raymond paused, and smiled to himself.

'It's just as well I did answer my midnight caller, for without him I might not have been able to continue my research. I would not have been able to progress to the next stage of the ritual system.'

Otherwise . . . otherwise the worst thing that had happened to him was the threat of a typhoon. 'For three days the sky was leaden. It was completely dark. I was very frightened by that. At one point it looked as though I'd have to take all my research notes into the hills. You know, the tidal wave. The houses around me were all being battened down. But I knew if the typhoon broke, my research notes wouldn't stand a chance.'

He pointed to a narrow but heavy wooden chest sitting on the floor.

'I kept them in there,' he said.

And diseases?

'That's something that tends to be exaggerated by westerners. Skin ulcers were very common, but you learned to live with them. The real horror was blackwater – not on Tikopia, but in the adjacent New Hebrides [Vanuatu]. But imported diseases were a danger as well. Pneumonia for instance. I was very ill myself once. The Tikopians advised me to wait and die in my own country. But as you can see, I didn't. I stayed out there with the mosquitos. An awful lot of mosquitos, which is why ordinary writers, like Stevenson, stayed away. The place was too rough for them.'

'But now? What are conditions like now?'

'Much improved I think. If there's been one gain in the last fifty years I should have to say that it's in the provision of more and better medicines. That, and improvements in education. The chief loss has been economic disruption. The Solomons are now encouraged to give up subsistence agriculture in favour of cash crops like copra. That's okay in as far as it pays for the new medicine, but it's not okay when the crop fails or, as is more likely, the international market price falls. Then there can be havoc.'

'Gifts?'

'Money. It used to be tobacco-sticks, but there was a reason for that. If you were a European you could buy five tobacco-sticks for a shilling, but if you were Melanesian you'd only get three for the same amount. Discrimination pure and simple. Also, the white man could afford to buy in bulk. But now it's definitely money, though how much you should give in any particular circumstance is hard to judge. The Solomoners have a way of wheedling things out of you. In my time the standard ploy was *Friend, my knife doesn't work any more, my knife is blunt,* or *Friend, my brother has run out of fish hooks.* But you must also remember, the Solomoners owe you nothing. There's no reason they should donate their hospitality gratis.'

Professor Firth gave me one further piece of advice to take with me. I should not go to the Solomons, he said, without some idea of the islands' recent history. Two events in particular should command my attention. The first was the murder of William Bell, a District Officer, on Malaita in 1926. 'That may sound like a long time ago, but when you get there you'll discover it's not.' The second was Cyclone Namu, which had devastated the Solomons just a few months before.

'On no account should you go there and say you've never heard of Cyclone Namu. If you do, no one will take you seriously.'

*

I returned to the library and began reading Firth's accounts of the Tikopians. It was wondrous stuff, ten times richer, and twenty times more moving than Tolkien's *Lord of the Rings*. Compared to the Professor a man like Robert Louis Stevenson was indeed an 'ordinary writer'. But, for purely selfish reasons, I was not altogether unhappy that the world described by Firth had vanished. It absolved me from having to try it out for myself.

I suppose if I wanted to be polite about myself I would say that I am a typical *homme moyen sensuel*. If I were to be rude I would say I was a lily-livered hypochondriac. Either way the thought of camping out in a remote island village, beyond the host of amenities I am accustomed to, did not appeal. Travelling beyond the Orient would doubtless necessitate some deprivations, but I had no intention of allowing the occasional compromise to become a total surrender.

But what was I to write about?

On my last night in England I was taken, in a gesture of ironic appositeness, to the Travellers' Club in the Mall by two old friends, Peter Hopkins and Kaori O'Connor. Over dinner I expounded my view that where there is paradise there is also wickedness and intrigue.

'Oh well,' Peter jollied, 'don't get eaten. And mind that head of yours.'

'Don't worry,' I replied, concealing a dreadful jangling of the nerves at the mention of such things. 'They restrict themselves to thumbs these days. The trick is to avoid hitchhiking.'

Kaori, a sharp Hawaiian who had studied anthropology at Oxford, was less willing to let me off the hook.

'And this book of yours . . .?' she began.

'I've told you, I'll find something.' And then: 'If worse comes to worst I'll find Lord Lucan.'

'What? In the Solomons?'

'In the Solomons, or perhaps in the Sulu Sea. He must have gone to ground somewhere like that. And the great advantage of travelling alone is there won't be anyone to refute my discovery.'

'But what if Lord Lucan himself, always assuming he's alive of course, refutes you?'

'Then Lord Lucan will have come out of hiding and I'll take the credit for flushing him out.'

My friends looked at me earnestly. Then they glanced at each other and surreptitiously raised their eyebrows.

TWO

How to go to Thailand and not sleep with anyone

I began my journey in Thailand for several reasons, the most admissable of which is that I had been there before. In particular I knew the capital, Bangkok, almost as well as I knew London. To facilitate my new role as journalist I wanted to move from the known to the unknown, but slowly; and I had a potential trump card up my sleeve. Jonathan Meades, a feature editor at *Tatler*, had expressed interest in an interview with Queen Sirikit of Thailand. If I could pull that one off I'd be well on my way.

A second (less admissible) reason for going to Thailand was sex.

Thailand is justly held in esteem by travellers of all sorts. She is a kind of congees of all that is best about South-East Asia. Although her politics lack stability Thailand has nonetheless avoided the savage ideological warfare that has crippled her Indo-Chinese neighbours. Her people, her scenery and her food have won the hearts of thousands. Her temples, the costumes, the elephants and the merchandise constitute a feast of incomparable excellence.

Yet there is another side to Thailand that is equally famous, if not more so.

During the Vietnam War American GIs had an expression for Thailand. Bangkok especially they used to sum up in the words; 'more fuck per buck'. And for many visitors that remains the primary incentive. More fuck per buck.

One day (so the story goes) a Queen's Messenger arrived in Bangkok, all the way from Whitehall. He had an urgent communication for the British Ambassador. He went straight to his hotel and was shown to his suite. No sooner had the porter who brought up his luggage left the room than there was a knock on his door. It was the floor boy, anxious to help.

'You want girl, Sir?'

'Er . . . no thank you.'

'You want very nice young girl, Sir?'

'I don't think so.'

'You want two very nice young girl, Sir?'

'Certainly not!'

'What about a young boy, Sir?'

'Good heavens no.'

'Two very nice young boy, Sir?'

'I'm sorry. I don't think you understand. I've come to see the British Ambassador!'

'Oh, British Ambassador. Of course. Somchai understand. Sir want to see British Ambassador. Okay. No problem. Somchai go fetch British Ambassador. Only take time. Cost little bit more money.'

Everybody's at it. Every street is a help-yourself supermarket of uncanned goodies. The Thais understand that saying no only makes other people's lives unnecessarily miserable. Therefore they have developed the art of saying yes before being asked. And they have a very sophisticated attitude towards money. They realize that it's no fun being cleaned out. If you spend all your money on sex there won't be any left for the other good things in life, like Singha beer, fried prawns and more sex. Therefore they have developed the art of not asking too much; or, if you're completely skint, of not asking anything at all. Whatever happens, life must go on. A wasted erection is a blot on eternity. So every hour is happy hour.

Or in theory every hour is a happy hour. There are those who get left out for example, some of the wives of the Thai men, who are every inch as promiscuous as the plane-loads of tourists landing hourly at Dom Muang airport. For the wives life's not such a party, and some of them get pretty upset about it. Sometimes when their husbands persist in staying out until the wee small hours they become vengeful.

The standard form of revenge among Thai women is to lop the male's penis off with a sharp knife. There's even a special hospital set up to cope with such occurrences. Provided the male can get there in time the hospital undertakes to sew his peter back on again. Or, more recently, if he's very lucky he can have a transplant. Continued fighting on the Thai-Cambodian border ensures a regular supply of replacement members.

There are some men who have had their peters lopped off and stitched on again so often that the angles have been permanently readjusted. And of course, there are those who never made it the first time.

One such man had been particularly unfaithful. His wife had been at breaking point for months when out of the blue he telephoned her from his office and announced he was coming home. The wife was overjoyed. She rushed out to the market and purchased all the foodstuffs she knew he was fond of. She prepared him a meal fit for a rajah, then she dolled herself up. The husband, who'd almost forgotten what she looked like, was terrifically impressed. He offered her his sincere apologies and promised that, henceforward, he'd never make love to another woman again. 'I've been a fool,' he said, 'an idiot, a regular black monkey. I've scoured the country for beautiful girls and all the time the most beautiful of them was sitting here in my bungalow. Can you forgive me?'

'*Mai pen rai*, honey,' replied the wife. 'Have some more *mekong*, darling.'

The husband helped himself to more *mekong* and finished his dinner. Then he had a luxurious bath, which his wife had also prepared. When he got out of it she was ready and waiting for him in the bedroom. She had never looked so lovely before.

'Oh darling,' he whispered, removing his bath-gown.

'Oh honey,' she whispered, throwing off her robe.

As soon as he was on top of her the wife's hand reached for the sharp kris she had secreted under her pillow. For several weeks she had been practising on cassavas. One flick of the wrist and it was done. And before her husband had time to react she tossed it through the open window.

With a great yelp the husband rushed out into the garden. He knew he had only a few minutes to get to the hospital. Desperately he searched the ground for his member. But all to no avail. The neighbour's dog had got there first. It was squatting on its haunches and it was licking its lips . . .

But let me not exaggerate. Not every Thai is horny round the clock. The Thais are legendarily proud people (alone of S.E. Asian peoples they were never colonized), and one or two of them are actually quite circumspect. For instance, the story of Police Sergeant Nitipong Kaewsonthaya was reported in the *Bangkok Post* as follows, under the headline 'Policeman shot in call girl row at hotel':

A POLICE sergeant claims he was shot twice in the back by his superior officer after a row over a girl in a Bangkok hotel room on Wednesday.

Speaking from his bed at the Police Hospital after he had the bullets removed, Pol Sgt Nitipong Kaewsonthaya of the Special Branch alleged he was shot by Pol Cpt Thongpoon Wongmart.

The sergeant claimed the attack took place when Capt Thongpoon ordered him to bring him a girl while he was supposed to be providing security for a group of Chinese diplomats.

Sgt Nitipong said he was bitter after being told by some officers to say the shooting was accidental and that he was not shot by his superior.

He and Capt Thongpoon were assigned to escort the diplomats, who are currently visiting Thailand.

During the reception for the envoys at a first-class hotel on Wednesday night, Capt Thongpoon told him to bring a girl to a room in a hotel where they were protecting the diplomats.

He said he had not eaten at the time and was told to eat outside the hotel.

'At the time, I thought police should have dignity and to fetch a call girl is inappropriate,' said Sgt Nitipong, who said he told the captain he did not know where to find the girl.

'But *phukong* (captain) was persistent,' he said, and ordered him to find a girl who is young, with fair skin, long hair and the price should not exceed 1,500 baht.

'I took a *samlor* and went hunting for girls, but couldn't find one,' said Sgt Nitipong, who eventually telephoned an escort service at an apartment and asked for a girl with those specifications to be sent to hotel room 711.

The escort service manager was non-committal, but asked Sgt Nitipong to phone again at 10 pm. Apparently desperate, the sergeant said he returned to his hotel room and soon received a phone call from his *phukong*, who demanded to know whether he was successful in fetching the girl he wanted.

He said he was verbally abused after he told the *phukong* the truth. 'A second call came afterwards and I was again reprimanded,' he added.

Sgt Nitipong further disclosed that while he was waiting in the room there was a knock at the door at about 10 pm. Opening the door he found a girl sent from the escort service, and he invited her in.

'Then I went downstairs to inform *phukong*. But the moment he saw me he reprimanded me,' said Sgt Nitipong, who admitted that he then answered back with a four-lettered word and went upstairs 'hoping to give the girl a taxi fare and telling her to go home.'

He said his superior followed him closely to the room. 'Obviously angry, he drew out his gun and started beating and kicking me. Then I heard gunshots,' he said.

'I didn't think he would shoot me. I felt I could raise my hands. Then I felt *phukong* touch my leg and profusely apologise,' said Sgt Nitipong.

The former Border Patrol policeman said he demanded his superior take him to the hospital. He radioed his chief inspector, codenamed Sayam 101, and gave his valuables to a Foreign Ministry official to keep for him.

Pol Cpt Thongpoon was not available for comment last night.

(Bangkok Post, Friday 28th Nov.)

And small wonder, Pol Cpt Thongpoon was probably out on the razzle again.

In Thailand it is both easy and common to become obsessed with it; and I would be a liar if I tried to pretend that I have never succumbed to temptations which have reduced men with far stronger moral constitutions than mine to sybaritic giggles. Indeed my first novel, *Paradise For Hire*, is something of a homage to Bangkok's legendary stunt-cunts. Most readers thought it erred too much on the side of fantasy, whereas in reality it was little more than a transposed diary I kept on my first visit to Thailand in 1977. No piece of fiction was ever so well or so lovingly researched.

At the age of 37 it is conceivable I wanted another run at the bar-girls. Needless to say I told my wife I didn't, but then what man doesn't? I belong to a generation, a subculture, that regards infidelity as an option, not a sin. The only stipulation is: keep it covert. But, this time round, whatever clandestine pleasures I may or may not have been anticipating were ruled firmly out of court, and it was all down to the man who sat next to me on the Thai Inter jumbo.

When I took my seat the man was already fast asleep. And he stayed asleep until the pilot announced that the plane would shortly be passing over Moscow.

The man woke up.

'Excuse me,' he said, looking out of the window. 'It's time to go to the khasi.'

'Did it!' he exclaimed when, fifteen minutes later, he came back. 'Hope I've given Gorbachev another.'

'Another what?' I asked.

'Another funny mark on his greasy Soviet bonce,' he replied, and went back to sleep.

The plane motored on through the Asian night. As it landed at Delhi I thought I saw five people falling off a single bicycle in a backstreet, but wasn't sure. The plane refuelled and took off. It was toward the end of Burma that the man woke up again.

'Had all your injections?' he asked. 'Your cholera, your typhoid, your tetanus?'

I nodded.

'Ah, but did you have anything for hepatitis?'

'Yes,' I said, 'my doctor gave me a shot of gamma globulin. He always does.'

'Then he shouldn't have.'

'What do you mean?'

'Gamma globulin. Blood product. Very risky.'

'I don't see . . .' And then the penny dropped. Aids. 'I'm sure it was heat treated,' I countered.

'Oh that's what they all say, doctors. Heat treat this, heat treat that, heat treat everything. Bloody pack of lies. Anyway, probably no point. Look at Africa. Hottest place in the world, and most of them have got

34

it. That's heat treatment for you! And Bangkok can't be any better. I'll be surprised if there's anyone left alive by the time we get in. But not to worry. If you've got it you've got it and there's no harm in getting it again I suppose. That's my philosophy. Either you have or you haven't, but either way you're going to. Know what I mean?'

'Yes,' I replied, 'I think I know what you mean.'

Aids. Up to that moment I hadn't thought about it. But now, to make up for my oversight, I never stopped thinking about it. My hypochondria, the healthiest thing about me, henceforth was on overtime, and any lascivious intentions went to the wall.

It probably was as well that someone reminded me that things ain't what they used to be. And if chastity was to be the order of the day, why not write about it? I could turn in a nice article about Aids in Bangkok. As a would-be foreign correspondent I couldn't have wished for a better subject to cut my teeth on. What I didn't appreciate, though, was that the two topics, Aids and Mom Rajawongse Sirikit, would be mutually exclusive.

Thus I arrived, essentially none the worse for wear, but all shook up. Bangkok, I discovered, hadn't changed an iota. The sidewalks were brim full of white male tourists arm in arm with gorgeous golden Thaigirls, or gorgeous golden Thaiboys. It may have been lunchtime on Sunday but the bars were nevertheless bursting with business. The only discernible difference was that the streets themselves were under two feet of water. The Sukhumvit Road had become, since my last visit, the Sukhumvit River. But even the explanation for this was thoroughly in keeping with the country as I remembered it. The day before had been Loy Krathong, one of the big festivals in the Thai calendar. By tradition the evening is taken up with much candle-floating on the *klongs*, or city canals. But there had also been a storm brewing in the Gulf. For the municipal authorities this posed a quandary. Should they, as they did every year, open the *klong* sluices, to let as many people as possible float as many candles? Or should they exercise prudential restraint and keep the sluices closed? In the end caution gave way to happiness. The sluices were opened, the storm pounced and the city was flooded.

There's a moral in there somewhere, I thought, as I sat stranded in a taxi on the wrong side of the mighty Sukhumvit. I could see my hotel, barely 200 metres away, and there was nothing I could do about it. Around me Thais were wading through the water, pulling their trousers and skirts up to their waists, or just getting soaked, but with my various bags I hardly felt like joining them.

One or two of them, however, were quite willing to join me. As I looked out of the car one way the door on the other side opened and a girl slipped onto the adjoining seat.

'Hey mister, you want go swim?'

'Er . . . no thank you.'

'You want go swim my place.'

'Not today.'

'What your name?'

I told her.

'My name Oi.'

Oi extended her hand. As soon as I shook it she burst into peals of laughter.

'Hey mister, you go hotel?'

'I hope so.'

'You want Oi come with you? Or you want Oi do it now, in taxi?'

'I'm sorry,' I began, 'but you don't understand. I've come to see the Queen.'

'Queen? What you mean Queen?'

'Queen Sirikit.'

'Oh,' Oi was terribly disappointed. 'I think mister mean he want to meet lady-boy. If mister want lady-boy Oi have brother. Very nice lady-boy.'

'It's very sweet of you, really, but not today.'

'You want Oi go now?'

'I think you should.'

'Have cigarette?'

'Sure.'

I opened my duty-frees and gave Oi a pack. With all the grace of a court dancer she made a *wai* with her hands and slipped back into the water. I watched her splash her way up the line of cars ahead, peering into the windows to find a customer. She was probably 19, and her hips moved like a miniature see-saw. Ecstasy was there for the asking. But so perhaps was something else. The worst part of it was that she was delightfully slim. But of course, weight-loss was one of the symptoms . . . Abruptly a formidable cognitive dissonance took hold. Slim. That's what the plague was known as in Africa. But slim girls, especially slim Thai girls, turned me on something dreadful. And now

36

they were out of bounds. Thanks to my neighbour on the Thai Inter jumbo they were all impounded within an exclusion zone I dared not penetrate. Slim girls *verboten*, for the next hundred years at least. But the memories of them, the memories of them . . . Bangkok, this time, was going to be hell.

I closed my eyes and silently chanted my marriage vows like a sutra. When I opened them again another girl had materialized by my side. Mechanically I reached for my duty-frees and gave her some.

'Chokdee,' I said. 'See you.'

'Chokdee mister. Khob khun kaah.'

And it wasn't much better when, ninety minutes and six packs of cigarettes later, the taxi finally limped home into the forecourt of the Nana. The hotel was islanded. Having dumped my bags, brushed up and seen off the floorboy (*You don't understand, I've come to see the British Ambassador*), I made my way downstairs. What I wanted was lunch followed by a sleeping pill.

Lunch was no problem. None of the hotel shops sold sleepies, however, and I was told to go across the road to a chemist's in Nana Plaza.

'Nana Plaza?'

'Nana Plaza new entertainment complex. Have many nightclubs. Good for making friend. Bring friend back hotel no charge extra for room. Bring ten friend back still we charge you single. What you want sleeping pill for?'

No. Bangkok hadn't changed at all. It was the same as ever, only more so. The Nana Plaza, bang across the *soi* from the hotel, was a deep courtyard with three tiers of go-go bars stacked one on top of each other. And it had two druggists.

To get there, to cross the still-swollen tributary that flowed into the Sukhumvit, I flagged down a motorcyclist and gave him five baht to ferry me across. In the chemist's the sales assistant took one look at me and covered the glass counter with a selection of powerful antibiotics.

'Ampecilin very good, mister. Take ampecilin today, feel very well tomorrow. Same thing happen come back next week give you more ampecilin. Feel very good again. No problem.'

'What I'd like,' I said, 'is some sleeping pills.'

The assistant looked at me with blank incomprehension.

'Sleeping pills,' I repeated, miming what I wanted by making a *wai* and then resting my cheek against my hands.

'I know what mister mean. I not stupid. But what you want sleeping pill for mister?'

'To make me sleep.'

'You crazy, mister.'

Reluctantly she fished among the shelves behind her until she found a large box of Dormicum.

'These ones, four hours. Take two, six hours. How many you want?'

'Give me thirty.'

'Thirty? You really crazy, mister.'

One by one she counted them out.

'You really crazy man mister. What wrong with you? You want kill yourself? Take thirty pills go straight to heaven. Maybe you come back cat. Cat sleep all day. But mister, one thing. You kill yourself then you no tell anyone where you get so many. You make promise.'

'I make promise.'

I slipped the pills into my pocket and looked for another motorcycle to take me across the *soi*. There weren't any. On the other hand there was an outdoor bar at the entrance of the the Plaza. On the counter I could see several tall beakers. Iced tea! And being outside there was relatively little danger of my being set upon. There were one or two girls sitting on the stools, but they were all fully dressed and taken care of. I decided to join them.

No sooner had I sat down than the stool next to me was obliterated by 200 pounds of prime American beef.

'Gimme a beer. No. Make it two. Being alive is thirsty work.'

The American turned to see whether I was enjoying his humour.

'Hi,' he said. 'I'm Jim. I come from Alaska.'

It didn't take much to get him going. Within five minutes I knew virtually everything there was to know about Jim. He was 47, unmarried and owned a jewellery store in Anchorage. He preferred whores. Whores saved time, and probably money as well. In the long run. As far as he knew he'd had every whore in Alaska. Show me one I haven't had and I'll give you a hundred bucks. He'd also had a good percentage of the whores in Bangkok. He'd been coming to Bangkok twice a year for twelve years. He couldn't recommend it enough. If you can't mix business with pleasure then you're in the wrong business. Thailand was *the* place for precious stones, and *the* place for fancy pussy, and generally speaking he was used to buying the two commodities in equal measures.

38

'How interesting,' I said. 'How often do you get dosed?'

'I never get dosed. At any rate not here I don't. Maybe in Alaska a couple of times, but never in Bangkok. The people here, they wash themselves. That's what I like about them. Also, I'm careful. I go for the plain-looking ones, the ones with hidden treasures. So long as she's got a nice pussy who cares about the face? If they're really ugly I put a paper bag over their heads.'

But what about now? What about Aids? Wasn't Alaskan Jim just a little scared of that?

Alaskan Jim refused to be fazed.

'Don't bother me none,' he insisted and downed another Singha. He repeated what he'd already said about his clean bill of health. 'Don't think I'm bragging or anything, though I s'pose you could say I've reason to be proud of my record. It don't bother me because why should it? I'm not interested in either young men or shooting needles. Anyone who is has got it coming to them I guess. And maybe they deserve it.'

'In Africa though . . .'

'Don't give me that Africa crap. I know about Africa. But Africa is a special case, and for four good reasons. Number one their immune systems are already highly depressed due to years of disease and malnutrition. Number two they're covered in anal sores. Number three they're all into sodomy. Number four they're all bisexual.'

'I've heard bisexuality's not unknown here . . .'

'Sure. Down in Patpong there's plenty of it. But not around here. I'm smart. I stay away from the danger zones.'

'I admire your confidence.'

'So do I.'

'Incidentally, what's the going rate these days? I've only just got in.'

'Five hundred baht. Not a cent more, and not a cent less.'

I looked down into my iced tea and did some simple arithmetic. My thirty sleeping pills had cost me 180 baht, or six baht each. If I took one every time I felt tempted by a woman I'd be saving myself 494 baht, or £13 a go. And who knows, I might also live to be as old as Jim.

'Hey!'

The Alaskan was pumping my arm.

'You know what you are, don't you? You're a jerk.'

'Thank you,' I answered. 'Let me get you another.'

And I had reason to buy Jim a drink. He had given me a good hook for my article. In a word, Jimism.

*

Someone else who was equally unruffled by what in Thailand is called *roke aids*, or, among the cognoscenti, more simply the roke, was Dr Seree Wongmata, Dean of the School of Journalism at Thammasatt University, and a self-professed homosexual.

'But I'm not what in your country, or in America, would be called a gay leader,' Dr Seree admonished within moments of my entering his office. 'In Thailand there is no shame attached to the homosexual act, and therefore there is no need to campaign for special rights. It is quite usual for a young man, if he finds himself the object of an older man's attentions, to give in, even if himself he feels no sexual attraction. It is simply a custom with us. It's a personal matter between two individuals and of no concern to the public, the same as the relations between a man and a girl. And this is helpful. If a man who is used to going with girls suddenly finds himself wanting to go with a boy then he need not feel bad about it. Similarly, men like myself, who find themselves only wanting to go with boys, can do so without being ostracized. If I am well-known as a homosexual that is because I am also well-known as a teacher. There are advantages in defining a homosexual community in my country, but these are all practical. For instance, it is nice to know that there are gay bars and gay restaurants and gay massage parlours, because then we can meet others of our kind more easily. But there is nothing political about it. Politically we have the same rights as everyone else, therefore gay leaders are unnecessary.'

Having got that off his chest he addressed himself to the question at hand.

'Aids is not a problem here,' he began. 'To date there have been only six confirmed cases. Those are the official statistics. And one way or another they were imported. Thai people who had been working abroad, or foreigners visiting our country. Two of the six were foreigners. Now you must admit, compared with the United States or France or Britain, the figures here are very low. There is no epidemic, and very little panic. When the first cases were reported yes, we did experience a phobia of sorts, within the gay community. But that's over now. It was an over-reaction. What you have to understand is it's not in the Thai character to be worried by such things. We enjoy life, we don't want to be prevented from enjoying it. You know our expression: *mai pen rai*: it doesn't matter, life must go on. We're very

40

lucky, I think. We're also very clean. In the West, when people make love, they unzip their jeans, any place, any time. Then they zip them up again. But we do things differently here. We have a shower first and we have a shower afterwards. So Aids is not a problem. But don't just take my word for it. Go and see for yourself. Go to some of the gay bars in Patpong. *My Way* perhaps, or *Lolly Boy*.'

To this I listened in horror, or would have done had not virtually everything Dr Seree had to say been a repeat of what I had already been told by Mr Thawee, the Press Officer at the Department of Public Relations.

'Aids is not a problem,' Mr Thawee had said. 'We have had only six confirmed cases. Now they have all died. Here are the statistics. See for yourself. I'll put what pressure I can on the Palace to secure your interview with Her Majesty, though I'm a little doubtful as to the outcome. She has not been well lately. On the other hand, if you would like to see the Princess instead, that's easily arranged.'

I looked at the piece of paper Mr Thawee had put in front of me. It was a memorandum from the Department of Communicable Diseases at the Ministry of Health. It said there had been only six confirmed cases of Aids. It was dated June.

'Can you give me an update on these?'

'I'm sorry, but they are the latest figures.'

'Then when will there be an update?'

Mr Thawee smiled and shrugged. He was a small thin man in his mid-fifties who was doing his best to run a chaotic office. He had a staff of twelve, though, by the look of things, he needed a staff of fifty. Huge files tumbled off rickety shelves and spewed across the floor. A pool of typists clattered away making mistakes on every line. Antique fans spun irregularly on the ceiling. Sometimes galvanized by a sudden rush of electricity they would devastate the piles of paper underneath, raising short-lived white sculptures on the desk-tops. But there was no flap. The office itself was in an old building of the sort most Thai civil servants have to make do with. Not for them the incredible air-conditioned modernist concoctions built and monopolized by the city's banks and corporations. And the salaries were correspondingly miserable. But *mai pen rai*, it was all in a good cause, and someone had to do it. It was one of the happier places I had been in, and Mr Thawee one of the most obliging individuals. He gave me the impression that he really did want to help. He wanted my stay in Bangkok to be as fruitful and as pleasant as it possibly could be. If it was up to him I'd have been on my way to the Palace there and then. Unfortunately, however . . . unfortunately there were small matters of bureaucracy and protocol.

I felt sorry for Mr Thawee. It was most unfair on him, I thought, that he should be put to so much trouble when he had so much else to do by yet another importuning *farang* journalist. But there was no helping it. This was my first Monday, and how many more Mondays there would be probably depended upon what sort of momentum I could generate today.

'Let me ask you, then, what kind of screening programmes is the government running?'

Again Mr Thawee smiled considerately.

'I'm afraid screening is very expensive. Our government doesn't have the money. Even so, we've issued as many homosexual prostitutes as possible with blue cards. But one thing. Probably you know many Thai people go to work in Saudi, and the Saudi government insists on screening. So every time a Thai worker goes to Saudi he has his blood tested. To date 50,000 workers have been screened.'

'And?'

'No one has Aids.'

'But what about the prostitutes? And the tourists? Shouldn't they be the ones to be screened?'

'Probably, Mister Wintle. But we don't have the money.'

Then Mr Thawee launched into a critique of the Thai character identical to Dr Seree's. Aids was not a problem in Thailand because no one wanted it to be.

'But I will try to arrange a meeting for you with Dr Vinij Asswasena. He is Director of the Department of Communicable Diseases. And the other thing, I will try to do that for you as well. I will speak to Her Majesty's private secretary this afternoon.'

Armed with these pledges I checked out my next port of call, the British Embassy, a huge glass and concrete fortress near the Sukhumvit where security locks clicked endlessly and the air-conditioning had obviously been purloined from the refrigeration compartment of a deep-sea trawler. It had been agreed that a middle-ranking diplomat would answer questions on an off-the-record basis. The Embassy had no medical officer as such, but of course the Embassy was 'keeping an eye on the situation'. It was all extremely cordial.

42

'Sorry it's so chilly in here,' Mr A----- began, 'but there's not much we can do about it. No one knows where the on/off switch is.'

'Chilly, or chilling?' I asked archly. 'What exactly is going on here?'

'Of course, you want to talk to me about Aids. You've been to the Ministry of Information? Then probably you know as much as we do. Officially there have been just six cases. That's the latest statistic.'

'Released in June . . .'

'June, was it? You're right. Time flies, doesn't it?'

'And you believe that?'

'I suppose I have to. There's a screening programme run for emigrants going to work in Saudi Arabia, and so far the results confirm what the government is saying. I admit it seems a little odd. One problem is the general standard of health care. People can get most of the drugs they need over the counter at a chemist's. A lot of Thais are too poor to make regular visits to a doctor. The prostitutes particularly don't like going. They're frightened the doctor will find something wrong with them which would mean going to a hospital and losing their earnings. And if a person dies they don't always bother to establish the cause. If a man's dead he's dead. Why waste your baht finding out why? That is disturbing. It's a hot country and there are a lot of fever-related diseases, particularly pneumonia, which of course comes into the Aids picture. Who knows? Except, if there were an epidemic you'd expect to see a lot more visible signs of it. So far that appears not to be happening. It's difficult to get the Thais to talk about it. Some of them think that Thai people have a natural immunity. That can't be right. On the other hand there is some very silly scare-mongering. Not so long ago there was talk of the Aids virus being carried by mosquitos. That probably originated south of the border in Malaysia, where there is something like a public panic. Fortunately the mosquito just isn't built for the job, otherwise we'd be looking forward to death by the millions. Technically it's just about possible, but the mosquito would have to jump so nimbly from the infected to the non-infected individual that the only circumstance in which that seems likely to happen is when both individuals are hard at it in bed.'

'But doesn't it seem unlikely to you? After all, Bangkok must be the world's biggest, most cosmopolitan sex fair.'

'It seems very unlikely. People should be dropping like flies but they're not. Needless to say the Foreign Office deluges us with admonitions to be on our guard – I've got a whole drawer-full of them.

But they're for our personal information. They go out to all our embassies. We're advised to think twice before visiting any third-world hospital. Have a blood transfusion in the Congo and you're asking for it.'

'Is the Embassy taking any steps to issue warnings to incoming British tourists here?'

'What? About blood transfusions?'

'Yes. And prostitution.'

'The short answer is no. As I said, there's no evidence to suggest an epidemic. We can only go on the evidence we have. But in any case, as regards the second part of your question, we take the view that it's not our duty to interfere in matters of private conduct. That, after all, is why we are here. To protect the individual liberty of UK citizens.'

'Then let me put another question to you. Supposing there were an outbreak of cholera. Would you be advising British subjects against drinking unboiled water?'

'Of course.'

'But if you thought there was an Aids epidemic . . .?'

The diplomat's face turned a subtle shade of scarlet.

'Yes,' he said. 'I see what you mean. It's a tricky one, isn't it?'

I waited for Mr Thawee to set up my interviews. Nothing could be done to expedite the bureaucratic process, but that didn't mean I was idle. I stopped by all the old haunts and confirmed the impression that nothing had altered, that the Thais and their foreign friends were as hard at it as ever. From the perspective I had locked into it was incredible. I even called in at one of the two gay bars recommended by Dr Seree, the *Lolly Boy*. It was indistinguishable from the sixty or seventy girlie bars surrounding it in Patpong. The lighting was a little dimmer perhaps, but the place was full of . . . girls. They were up on a stage dancing, wiggling their behinds for all they were worth. They were lounging in their clients' laps, whispering sweet nothings. They were in the toilets, putting on their make-up. Only they weren't girls. They were boys. As soon as I appeared through the street-door half a dozen hands began crawling over my body. It wasn't nice. I took one good look around me and fled. It wasn't the homosexuality, it was the fear that if I stayed any longer one of them would stick a needle in me as a gesture of heightened hospitality. I could explain my status, I could tell them I had come as an observer, but what was the point?

Probably that's what every man said when he tried his first gay bar in Bangkok. It would simply double the boys' efforts to make me feel at home. I'd get the needle twice as fast, twice as deep. And so, at the very threshold of my new career, the intrepid journalist cringed and bolted.

Estimates of the number of prostitutes (male as well as female) working the bars, the hotels, the massage parlours and the streets in Bangkok vary dramatically. Some put it as low as 80,000, some as high as 250,000. One unpublished research thesis I picked up many years ago put the figure at 750,000. Much depends on the season, and on how well the rice crop has fared. A bad crop and from all over the country the farmers send in their daughters. But it also depends on how you do your counting, whether you restrict yourself to the catshops, or whether, for example, you broaden your criteria to include the city's many thousands of restaurants. In my own experience the majority of waitresses, if given the smallest encouragement, were as available as the official hookers. And the same went for many bank clerks and shop assistants. In the end it was a question of whether you paid them or not. In the past it seemed unfair not to. Their natural earnings were miniscule, so why shouldn't they, too, be enabled to treat themselves to a new dress or new pair of shoes? If you struck lucky with a waitress and took her shopping and bought her a handbag was that paying for it? Perhaps the only way to find out was to strike it lucky with a waitress and not go shopping with her. Only that was nasty, that was the unfriendly way of exploring the Thais. Or, come to that, of exploring the Orient. In the Orient it is the man's duty to show an open hand. It is the continental custom. Do it any other way and you make yourself unpopular.

I set about making myself unpopular, but not by closing my hand. I wanted to find out the ground temperature. In the evenings I talked to the girls, hundreds of them. Had they heard about the roke? Were they worried? Had they started taking precautions? Did they have any idea what safe sex was?

There were indeed very few indications of panic. About thirty per cent of the girls claimed never to have heard of roke aids. Twenty per cent of the girls admitted they had heard of it, and were concerned. The rest dismissed it. *Mai pen rai.* I go with you? Only one girl, who'd had a caring American amongst her lovers, insisted her men wear condoms. And she was in a sorry state. None of her customers would come back to her, so she had to keep finding new ones.

45

'No have boyfriend. Boyfriend no like use rubber one, so Wana have to look look look, all the time! Have many boyfriends, but no have boyfriend.'

Safe sex was as palatable to Bangkokians as a Christian burial would be to the Ayatollah.

Boyfriending was one of the ploys used by the girls, a leftover from the days when GIs flew in by the sackload from Saigon for a spot of R and R. Being a clean animal the average GI was paranoid about contracting gonorrhea or syphilis, so he used to settle for a regular whore for the week or ten days or fortnight he was in town. 'Be your boyfriend honey, no go butterfly.' And the practise still continues, at least in theory. Many of the girls pretend they don't butterfly, but in reality they all do. They have to. Even if they can find a client (businessman, holidaymaker or professional hedonist) willing to act out the fidelity fantasy the relationship seldom lasts more than fourteen days. The customer packs his bag, flies off again, back to America or Australia or Britain or France or Germany, and a replacement has to be found.

Meanwhile there is a sizeable tranche of prostitutes whose interest in banknotes is more honed. These are the short-time artistes. At 500 baht a thrash they expect to earn anything up to seven times that amount a day.

Among these last I made myself particularly unpopular. They tended to be the ones who did know about the roke, and they had the greatest vested interest in keeping any scare at bay. Normally, when I began asking them what they knew, they flashed little pieces of paper at me.

'Me clean. Me have no disease. Look, me go doctor, have test. No have veedee. I go with you?'

They quite understood a client's anxiety about gonorrhea and syphilis. They even appreciated it. If a client was anxious there was a reasonable chance he was uninfected. But the roke was another matter altogether.

'Me clean, me no have disease, me have card from doctor.'

Oh yes. Most of them had cards all right. Some of them were even stamped with last week's date. But how did they know, how could they know?

As soon as it became apparent that I hadn't dropped in for a pick-up the atmosphere changed. None of the bargirls wanted a killjoy in their midst. Nor, come to that, did any of the punters.

'Hey fella, clam up or scram, will ya? You're disturbing the peace.'

All of which tore me apart. In principle I am fond of Bangkok girls. Collectively I have a love for them. As a community they are wonderfully lacking in snobbery, and four times out of five their hearts are as warm as any other part of their anatomies. They are not at all bourgeois. Possessions are meaningful to them, but their horizons don't stop there. In 1978 a bunch of them had picked me off the floor. Their sustained friendliness transformed a low point in my life into a high point. But now it was working the other way. Their company induced a kind of nausea. However pretty, they were no longer beautiful to look at. On the contrary, the more pretty they were the more harrowing they seemed, if only because these were the ones I looked at the hardest. In every sleepless eye, in every slender limb, in every skin-rash I thought I could detect news of the plague. And still I adored them.

*

Ever since my first visit to Bangkok I have had a recurring dream about the Grace Hotel. The Grace Hotel is, or used to be, the hottest spot in town. It was the biggest cathouse in the world. Downstairs was a coffee-shop-cum-nightclub where, every night, literally hundreds of girls assembled in a non-stop riot of provocation. Those men lucky enough to have got themselves a room upstairs could just wander in and out whenever they pleased and obtain whoever they pleased. Its nickname was the Human Stock Exchange, and I had once stayed there a full month. After a week I lost count of the fun I was having. It just went on and on until my visa expired and my ticket fell due. Then I flew back to England and wrote the first draft of *Paradise For Hire*. The centrepiece was a hotel called *The Glory*.

The dream, which is a species of nightmare, goes like this. I find myself back in Bangkok, at the Grace. The Coffee Shop, however, has been renovated. Gone is the exhilarating shabbiness I knew and prized. In its place is an appallingly dehumanized designer solution. Very nice to look at but dead. Sometimes there are perhaps a couple of girls, tucked away at a table behind a freshly plastered pillar, and sometimes there is no one at all. Either way, there is no joy. I know I could stay in the Coffee Shop of the Grace for the rest of time and no one would disturb me. Even on the good nights, when there were girls

47

behind the pillar, they adamantly refused to look at me. They were no longer interested in men.

In this dream, the coffee shop is a symbol for all of Bangkok, and its emptiness the perception that no one, not even me, lives their life twice. In a curious way the dream had now come true. Emptying Bangkok of its mother load was only one way of putting it. Not emptying Bangkok, but placing the motherload out of bounds, was another. The message was the same in either case, and the message hurt.

Naturally I called in on the Grace – my curiosity wouldn't let me do otherwise. To my astonishment one part of my dream had been fulfilled non-symbolically. The Coffee Shop had indeed been modernized, sterilized. It was still big, and there were certainly plenty of men-interested girls in it. But the girls were different. They were no longer the sleek, cheeky playmates I remembered so well. Rather they inclined to corpulence.

The mystery of this was soon solved. The Grace had been turned over to the Arabs. On the second floor there was a hall in which chairs and settees had been replaced by rugs and mats. Upon these Arabs drank coffee, surrounded by bevies of fat silent girls, not daring to look at each other, not willing to concede that life and prostitution might have something in common.

A nightmare!

The Grace was somewhere else I hurried away from. More and more I hurried away from everywhere. One afternoon my wanderings led me into a complex of temples near the Royal Palace. It wasn't one of the big tourist showpieces, like Wat Po or Wat Phra Keo, but a working temple full of monks going about their business. Nonetheless, its buildings were impressive. They had the usual ornate gables, white walls and red pillars. Gilt dragons frowned incuriously upon the passer-by. It was the sort of compound, in other words, where, even in the hey-day of my womanizing, I had liked to rest and could feel tranquil in. But even this haven of repose now seemed oppressive. The air was too thick, the dragons too close to each other, the gables too heavy. At any moment they would keel over on my head.

In the whole of Bangkok there was soon only one place where I could bear to be. Not my hotel room – that, too, was claustrophobic – but the open-air bar at the entrance of the Nana Plaza, where nobody gave any hassle, where the world could be viewed from the safety of an iced tea, and where even women tourists, taking in Thailand as part of a larger Eastern tour, could sit without feeling at once shamed and reduced by their energetic oriental counterparts. Here people sometimes talked sense, before yielding to the senseless blandishments of the night. Here, too, those who worked in the city, who had a legitimate pretext for being there, dropped by for an hour's unwinding.

Only at Lucky Luke's was speculation on the chosen theme sometimes allowed free rein, unchecked by ignorance, indifference or pride. Among the enlightened few two scenarios especially were entertained. First there was talk of a 'massive' cover-up, geared to protecting what was probably the strongest feature of the Thai economy. Though not as well-organized as the American Mafia or the Chinese Triads, the 300-odd families who owned the bars, the massage houses and the hotels certainly had the power. The biggest of them had placemen in both the cabinet and the civil service. More to the point, they also controlled the media. If the majority of Thais knew little or nothing about the roke one had only to pick up the newspapers to understand why. Only the English-language *Bangkok Post, World* and *Nation* seemed cognizant of its existence. Clearly there was a concert of interests, acting to suppress a truth whose hour could only be postponed, not cancelled.

The second conspiracy theory, in essence equally anti-establishment, targeted not the Thai but western governments. Western authorities had deliberately exaggerated the reach of Aids, to induce improvements in the moral climate. In this case the Thais were simply keeping their heads. They were refusing to be panicked, and would go on refusing until the evidence was incontrovertible. The triumph of eastern sagacity over occidental linear (i.e. exponential) logic.

Allied to these positions were all manner of fantasies. In the wildest of them (but no more wild than the assertion that Aids marks the frontier of Jehovah's compassion) the political geography of South-East Asia was about to be redrawn. Aids would spread catastrophically, Bangkok become a no-go area for tourists and the economy collapse. Enter, or re-enter, the Communist insurgents, backed now by China, where extra-marital sex continues to be a punishable offence, and the plague is therefore checked. Bangkok falls, followed by Manila, Jakarta, Hong Kong, Singapore, Taipei, Seoul . . . One by one the bastions of capitalism (sexual decadence) crumble. Even Japan falters. The Middle Kingdom, sheathed in a cadmium red flag, is gloriously restored. Leading to: the end of the world. The USA and Russia hastily patch up their differences and combine against the common foe. But too late, China has already mass-produced the bomb . . .

Everything about this was far-fetched. It ignored the liberalizing efforts of Deng Xiao Ping, it ignored existing international alignments, and it ignored the very deep-seated antipathy toward communism in Thailand. In essence it was no more than a re-hash of the 'yellow peril'. Yet for all that it was unimaginable that something wouldn't give. The no-change order simply couldn't last indefinitely.

A more realistic consequence of the roke's progress was as follows. Once Aids had got a grip on Bangkok there would almost certainly be a successful bid for power by the extreme right. Ever since the 1976 *coup* there has been a hard core of 'moral reformists', both in and out of government, agitating for a clean-up. It was their time, not the communists', that was probably imminent . . .

And so, on successive nights, the talk proliferated. I didn't set very much store by the conspiracy theories. It was difficult to see how the 300 families, each pursuing its own narrow interests, could succeed where the Mafia had failed, and in any case Thai pride by itself provided a sufficient explanation for the city's nonchalance. *We are Thai people, we are clean and good and loving, therefore we cannot suffer your contagion.* Every time I left Lucky Luke's the message was the same. And as for the charge levelled at western governments, that didn't wash either. I had just come from the West. People were dying there. Some of my acquaintances had been hit. Alas, what was actually happening was that those Thais in a position to learn anything, the English-reading élite, had been affected by western reporting of the disease. Like the rest of us they perceived Aids as something more than a slow-spreading viral illness.

*

But it was one thing to discuss issues and outcomes over iced tea in the forecourt of the Nana Plaza. It was another to contemplate the possible consequences of Aids in human terms. On my rounds I made myself unpopular, but not in every quarter. Sometimes I relaxed my vigil. The bargirls' bodies might be forbidden, but their friendship was not. Bargirls, whatever we may think of them, are made of the same clay as ourselves, and like ourselves they are full of dreams. They, too, want out. Born under a different star, they share the same aspirations. They, too, would like to live forever.

There were three types especially who attracted my attention: three different types not of bargirl but of woman. Ga, Pranee and Kanda.

Ga, the least lascivious of the three, was 22, half-Chinese and full of stories. What she really wanted to be was a writer, which is why, perhaps, she was ready to give me some of her time when there was no money in it. Conceivably she was taking heroin. When I took her out for dinner – I might be abstaining from the main course but that was no reason to dine alone – she remained somewhat sullen until after she had spent twenty minutes in the ladies' room. When she returned to the table all her dials were spinning. She came from a good home, she said, but the trouble in her life began at school. The art master. The art master was a very nice man who had a way of making things clear to her. For instance, the necessity of art. He asked the class what they would do if they wanted to put their hair up. The class answered that they would buy combs of course. But what sort of combs? Cheap ones, or nice-looking ones? Nice-looking ones, answered the class. Well, said the art master, the same with art. Art is a way of keeping the hair from falling over the face, of keeping the sight-lines open. And the great secret is beauty. Buy beautiful combs and life will be twice as promising.

But the art master also had a way with real combs. One day he asked Ga to stay behind after school had finished. He combed her hair for her, then he peeled off her panties. She was still only twelve.

After a while Ga began to feel very ashamed at what had happened. She confided in her friends, but her friends got straight on the bamboo telephone and told everyone. Very soon her family found out. Her step-father was terribly angry. He accused her of the most terrible things and kicked her out of the house. Everybody bent over backwards to defend the art master. The little girl had provoked him into behaviour that might have cost him his job. But because it was well known how little girls behave he kept his job, and Ga was expelled from the school. Nor did her mother have any pity to spare. The step-father was her second husband and a rich man. She couldn't afford to lose him. Also she had her other children to think about. So when the step-father said that her daughter was no longer welcome in his house she had no choice but to agree. Either Ga went on the streets by herself, or they both went together.

Ga went alone. For a few weeks her school-friends helped out, giving her food and hiding her in their rooms at night. Then *their* parents found out, and the game was up. Ga sought refuge in the only place that offered it: a massage parlour.

At least there she was clothed and sheltered and fed. The proprietor told her that he would keep the money she earned in a deposit account at the bank. She couldn't have it now, he said, because she was under-age. So for four years she worked hard, looking forward to the day when she would have enough in her account to send herself to college. But when she was 16 the proprietor sold the massage parlour to another man and disappeared. On that day she learned which way the dice were loaded.

But still she was hoping. She no longer worked in a massage parlour. These days she managed herself. She lived in a small bungalow with four other girls, and in the evenings went with them to the hotels. One day soon she would have a bank account, one day soon . . .

And then Ga started on her stories, the stories she would write after she'd been to college. There were seven or eight of them and she told them all. Or at least, I assume she did. For Ga's stories had a tendency to run into each other, and a tendency to make sudden connections with her autobiography, which she expanded to accommodate them. For example, there was a long convoluted saga about a girl confined to bed in a mental hospital. Nothing much happened to this girl until one night her favourite disc-jockey jumped out of her bedside radio and spirited her away to his radio station. At this point Ga let slip that since she had been in a mental hospital she was perfectly capable of telling the story as it should be told. In the end the handsome, white-suited, record-spinning altruist returned her to her ward, but now the girl could face being mad, because she knew that 'out there somebody care for me'.

Or the story about big brother. Big brother was the hopeless sort who fancied his little sister rotten. 'And I know that one too, because Ga have a brother just like him . . .' Followed by a northern tale in which a family of Thais falls out with a family of Chinese. Only the two families weren't human families, they were dogs. 'When my family young we live north, we live Lampang. Have many many dog . . .'

She was no longer talking to me. Her plate of vermicelli (or, according to the menu, Tran's Parents' Noodles) remained untouched. Ga was merely imagining out aloud. Her eyes had become red and glazed. Inside her head her brain was heating up to incredible temperatures. At any moment she was going to explode. But before she could do that – clunk! Her head dropped onto the table. Ga had fallen asleep in mid-sentence.

I took her back to the club where I had found her, deftly parried the thrusts of her colleagues and made my way back to the Nana Plaza. There I was buttonholed by Pranee.

Pranee was dazzling. Her eyes, her teeth and her fingernails all glistened like diamonds. The rest of her, too, had been sprayed with a high-class sheen: her skin, her hair, her lips. She was seduction incarnate, and unlike Ga she seemed aware of everything that went on around her. She sparkled with intelligence.

First she offered to buy me a drink. This I had difficulty in refusing. I knew where alcohol led. Even the guys who shared my apprehensions forgot them after a couple of beers, and generally what tempted them wasn't a tenth as hyperbolic as Pranee.

'I'm not looking for a girl,' I said.

'And I not looking for a man!'

Briefly Pranee pouted. Then she was off.

'I ask you you want drink, that's all. Look. Have money. Have money enough buy you drink. After that money finish, Pranee go to prison. *Mai pen rai*. But first Pranee buy you drink, okay?'

She was a real sweetheart, and on the understanding that we both kept our clothes on I let her order me an iced tea. For herself she ordered a double vodka orange, which she polished off in one gulp. Then she looked slowly and critically at the faces around the counter. Most of them wore moustaches and most of them were gazing at her.

'You like this place?'

'I've seen worse.'

'We go your room?'

'I'm sorry, but . . .'

'Not for kissing. For talking.'

I shifted uneasily on my stool.

'I know what you think. You think I come your room, do kissing, take all your money. But I not like that. I only want you listen me. I listen what people say here. People all say you good man, people say you work newspaper. But nobody listen to Pranee. So Pranee in big big trouble.'

It was quite useless. As soon as Pranee put her hand on my arm my resistance popped. It was her face that did it. From somewhere under the glitz she shot me such a look of earnest desperation that it would have been caddish not to accede. Muttering silent oaths I took her to my room.

But Pranee meant what she said, even if, as a conscientious communicator, she insisted on using the bed as her medium. Mercifully she gave no indication of wanting to take her clothes off. As soon as the door was closed she emptied her handbag on the coverpane. Then she put everything back save three items; two photographs, and a telegram. These she arranged neatly in a row. Looking at them she began to cry.

'Tomorrow,' she began, 'maybe Pranee go to prison.'

She touched the first photograph, a picture of a small boy astride a toy tricycle. This was her son. Like many Thai prostitutes she had married young, and then been deserted. In Pranee's case, however, her husband had been taken away from her, to serve a life sentence for killing another man. Not that it made any difference. She wanted her child to have whatever it was in her power to give him, so, like thousands of other girls, she began frequenting the bars, first in Hat Yai in the south, where she'd grown up, then in Bangkok.

Being, even by Thai standards, remarkably attractive Pranee had no difficulty in making the money she needed. Indeed, she made more than she needed. Many of her customers, wanting to monopolize her favours, volunteered handsome tips. Soon she was able to afford luxuries. She took out a mortgage on a small apartment near the Sukhumvit, and she bought herself a car, a second-hand BMW. (Here Pranee pointed at the second photograph.) But these goods had become liabilities. One by one her family showed up at her flat and stayed. Her mother, two sisters, her out-of-work brother – they were all living with her, eating her food, demanding pocket money. She'd even bought her brother a motorcycle, so he could find casual work as a messenger.

From time to time she had to get out of Bangkok. That's why she had purchased the BMW, so she could bomb down to Hat Yai, where her son was living with his grandmother, and where she still had old friends. But she never really planned these trips. She made them on impulse, sometimes in the middle of the night, or after a few drinks. And why not? That was a large part of her charm. An enchanting Lolita who owned a BMW and did things impulsively.

She'd already had four accidents, and her licence had been revoked. Now she'd had the big one. Pranee herself wasn't hurt, but the driver of the other vehicle was. Being a reasonable man he agreed not to press charges. But Pranee must pay his not inconsiderable hospital fees. She must either raise the money or face prosecution.

The obvious solution was to sell the BMW, her biggest asset. The only alternative was to get rid of the apartment and make her family homeless. But that was easier said than done. The BMW had been taken to a garage in Hat Yai for repairs, and the garage-owner, aware of Pranee's legal difficulties, had turned nasty. He refused to release the car until the mechanic's bill was paid. More, he had persuaded her to sign a document in which she agreed to give up her BMW if her account hadn't been settled by a certain date. Now the deadline was up. She was sure, under Thai law, the document carried little weight, but a lawyer had advised her to steer well clear of the courts for the present.

What she needed was an immediate 30,000 baht to pay off the garage, and another 60,000 baht to settle the hospital. What she had in her purse was less than 1,000. Understandably she had decided that earning the differential in one night was beyond even her capabilities. And she had other debts as well. The mortgage was unpaid, her brother had also had an accident, one of her sisters was ill. And so on.

Pranee picked up her third exhibit and pushed it into my hands.

'Listen to me,' she said, 'Read it.'

It was a telegram. All it said was: *Coming soon love Johnny.*

'Who's Johnny?'

Johnny was Pranee's special friend, an American living in India. She had known him for six years, and he always came when Pranee got herself into a particular scrape. As a last resort she had sent him a wire. But would he come in time?

Pranee gathered up the two photographs and telegram and put them in her bag. Then she swung the bag over her shoulder and stood up.

'Listen to me,' she said. 'What can I do?'

I stared back, powerless to help. I was undecided whether to believe more than two words of what she had told me. But even if she were telling me the truth, what was I supposed to do? Give her 30,000 baht?

Or 60,000? Or 90,000? It was unthinkable. If I was ever to get to the Solomons I must husband every penny I had.

'Either Johnny come, or tomorrow Pranee go prison.'

It looked like prison. There was no date on the telegram, but it was so crumpled it could have been sent any time in the last six months. And who in their right mind would hang their all on a man called Johnny?

Probably it was all an elaborate hoax, a blue-chip honey-trap. For instance, the car. Anybody could lay their hands on a photograph of a BMW and claim it was theirs.

'I'm sorry,' I began, 'really . . .'

'You no be sorry. I say thank you to you. You listen my talk, you only man do that. So Pranee say thank you.'

She turned to go.

'Hang on!' I took out my own wallet and looked to see how much I had. 'Here's a thousand. I'm sorry it can't be more but it's as much as I can give you. Perhaps it'll help you send Johnny another telegram . . .'

The consummate actress, Pranee made a brief attempt to refuse my gift. Then, advancing back towards the centre of the room, she let her bag slide off her shoulder.

'You good man,' she said, 'have good heart. You want I stay tonight. You give me money and I no stay then Pranee feel bad.'

I was tempted. Oh God, I was tempted.

'No,' I said. 'I have work to do. Newspaper man, always busy.'

'Newpaper man, always busy,' Pranee repeated, as though committing the phrase to memory for future use. 'Newspaper man, always busy.'

She smiled, a flake of heaven fluttering down to earth, and left.

Afterwards I was not inclined to believe her. The odds were I'd been had. But at least I was able to console myself: in the circumstances it probably was better to have been had than to have done the having.

However, I was wrong. The following night, Thursday, I went to sleep early, mainly to avoid the likes of Ga and Pranee. Their differing accounts of themselves were altogether too close to the bone. Many more like that and I'd be sure to fall from the straight and narrow. So I downed a Dormicum and slept.

Four hours later, at 3am, I was awake again. In the room next door was a mighty commotion. From the sound of things my neighbour was sawing through the floorboards. Any minute I expected arms, legs, bottoms and breasts to come popping through the wall. What was I to do? Take another pill? Or take a walk first?

I dressed and went down into the street. Along the *soi*, as there always are at night, several foodstalls were selling congees and grilled meats and fruit. Batter-fried cicada were the speciality of the month. At tables set up on the pavement were a few groups of late-night revellers. Men who had lost their women, women who hadn't found a man. But only a few. For Bangkok the place was almost deserted. Why, at the top of the *soi* the traffic was moving quite freely along the Sukhumvit.

Much to my surprise someone called out my name. Among the half-lit faces I spotted Pranee. She was not alone. With her sat a well-postured man whose head was either bald or shaven, who wore gold-rimmed spectacles and who radiated what's generally called an inner calm. Until he opened his mouth I assumed he was a monk, and that Pranee was taking some last-minute spiritual guidance.

'Hello,' I said accusingly. 'I thought you'd be in the slammer by now.'

Pranee looked up and smiled.

'Johnny come,' she said. 'This is Johnny.'

'Hi!'

The introductions effected, I joined the table. Johnny was the most un-Johnny-like individual imaginable. By profession he traded in antiques, sending artefacts from Calcutta to California. Just recently he had expanded his business: he had started shipping small buildings across the Pacific – old temples and the like. But his profession was incidental, a means to an end only. He preferred living outside America.

'The peculiar thing is I'm making money. That's not how I intended it. It's just ... happening. Automatically. I find myself having conversations with people who want nothing more than to sell some useless family heirloom. I buy it, then fall into another conversation and someone else buys it from me. I never mention prices. I leave that to them. Yet somehow, at the end of the day, there's always a profit. Maybe one day soon the tide will change and I'll begin transacting at a loss. People will begin giving me the wrong prices. My conversations will bankrupt me. But it doesn't matter. You've got to stick with the tide. That may be bad news for Pranee here, and one or two others, but there's nothing I can do to stop it. If you break with the tide you might as well break your own neck.'

As Johnny talked Pranee eagerly nodded her head at all the right moments. She was oddly anxious that Johnny and myself become friends. After a while she got up and said she was off to fetch something from Johnny's hotel, further up the *soi*. Clearly she thought, left to ourselves, our comradeship would develop more quickly.

'Oh well,' I said, 'looks like you've come at the right time.'

Johnny's gaze followed Pranee until she was out of sight.

'How much did she tell you?' he asked.

'Not a lot. She seems to be in a fix, though.'

'Yes, Pranee *is* in a fix. I'll tell you about it.'

Johnny proceeded to retell Pranee's story, not word for word but certainly item for item. His testimony had the added advantage that Johnny was acquainted with the girl's family. They were spongers every one of them. They took everything from her, but when it came to giving they told her that because she was a prostitute, because she went with *farang*, she didn't deserve anything. Yet because they were her family she couldn't turn her back. In Bangkok it was not an unfamiliar tale.

'And you are helping her?'

Yes he was going to help Pranee. He was going to see off the garage-owner in Hat Yai. Then he was going to set up a new bank account for her. He'd put some money in, and he hoped in due course she would add to it. But she wouldn't be able to make any withdrawals without his signature as well. What he wanted was for her to start up a business. That was the goal. She couldn't go on being a bargirl forever, no one could. In any case, she was too smart for that. She should use her talent for getting on with people in another channel.

'But I don't know what will happen. When I say business I don't mean open another bar, which is what most of the lucky ones do when they find a sponsor. I mean something like selling fruit. But selling fruit is hard work. It means going up country, bargaining, and then bringing the stuff back to the city. It's another world from the Nana Plaza. Perhaps the tide will take her there, perhaps it won't. It's not up to me. It's not even up to her.'

'Why not just take her back to India with you?'

'Wouldn't suit her. In any case,' – Johnny paused, smiled reflectively – 'she's not my girlfriend. She's not even a girlfriend.'

Then why was he giving her so much help? I wanted to ask, but didn't. The answer was obvious: the Tide.

58

Shortly Pranee returned. Hardly had she sat down when a phantom clothed in black leatherettes ripped past on a large motorcycle. Three minutes later it ripped by again in the other direction, a broom of black hair streaming in the slip.

'That's Kanda,' said Pranee. 'Kanda just come back Bangkok. Kanda going to kill herself. Kanda very very happy.'

Feeeooooowwwww!

When the motorcycle passed by again Pranee stood up and waved at it. Momentarily Kanda's head turned to look at her, giving me a glimpse of improbably large lips and teeth the size of postage stamps. Otherwise Kanda was all skin and bone.

'Praneeeeeeeee . . .!'

The motorcycle went on down the road, then screeched to a halt. Back it came again. Kanda parked it in the gutter and strode manfully toward the table.

The first word she said was *shit*!, and most of what followed came from the same menu. Her command of English, or rather American-English, was excellent. In addition her voice had a husky rasp that would have left most Sicilian peasant women gawping. From beginning to end she was pure Fellini; and irascible *donna mobile* addressing the backstreet night in full cry.

She didn't sit down. Instead she lifted a bare leg and thumped her boot beside a plate of squid. Then she looked at her leg, which seemed to disconcert her. It was as if it had never occurred to her before that she had a leg.

'Shit,' she said. 'Fucking fucking shit.'

Pranee was more or less right. Kanda had flown into Dom Muang the day before after two bad years in London. She'd married a Scotsman and regretted it immediately. He'd started playing around as soon as the wedding ceremony was finished. She'd taken as much as she was going to take. Now she'd come back home. She had one aim in life. She was going to copulate with every man that looked twice at her. And she'd made a good start. She'd already slept with a German in the afternoon, and a Swede after dinner.

'Fucking listen to me. Even on the plane a fucking man offer me fucking money to fucking fuck him. But I have fucking money. I have nine thousand fucking baht. I don't need fucking money. So I tell this bastard next to me on the fucking plane, if you want to screw someone go screw your father.'

Kanda was unstoppable. In this mode she went on and on and on, as splendid as she was rotten worthless, like a dipsomaniac with a trumpet, carving jagged trenches in the night. Only when dawn came did she pause for breath.

'You should make a record,' said Johnny approvingly. 'We should give you a microphone.'

At the word microphone her cellophane-bright face puckered.

'What you say? What that fucking word?'

'Microphone,' said Pranee.

Incredibly microphone was foreign to her vocabulary. For a few seconds it was as though the whole universe was about to fall on her head. But when Pranee laughed at her Kanda came out fighting again.

'I know what fucking microphone mean! Microphone can mean anything!'

There was nothing that could daunt her. That being so I decided it was high time to retire. I said goodbye to Pranee and Johnny, attempted to say goodbye to Kanda, and headed for the entrance of the Nana.

Halfway across the forecourt I heard Kanda's voice roaring up behind.

'Hey mister! Fucking mister! I'm coming with you!'

She was running toward me, and the others were urging her on.

I started sprinting. I still had thirty yards on Kanda, and there were another thirty yards to the door. She was coming on me like an express train, and my legs were turning to jelly.

'Open that door,' I yelled at the night porter, 'and fucking close it behind me.'

Kanda hit the glass.

THREE

Moon River

On Friday morning Mr Thawee rang. He'd spoken to Her Majesty's private secretary, and to Dr Winij. Dr Winij would not be available for the next six days. He had to journey outside Bangkok over the weekend, and early the following week he was expected to present his department's budget to parliament. Queen Sirikit, meanwhile, would be making up her mind. The private secretary had put my request to her and now she was thinking about it.

Another week in Bangkok! Once upon a time nothing could have been more welcome. Now I shuddered.

'Oh well then, I'll go to Ubon,' I said. 'I'll try to be back next Friday.'

In fact Ubon Ratchathani, the easternmost provincial capital in Thailand's I-San or North-East district (roughly a third of the country's land area), was already on my itinerary. I had told the London *Times* I'd file a travel feature on the town, though quite what aspect of it I'd be writing about I wouldn't know until I got there. From what I'd been able to discover Ubon had just two things going for it: it had once been a United States Air Force base, and it was situated on the banks of Moon River.

The aerodrome was certainly big enough. Two runways stretched from one horizon to the other, and it was flat terrain; a vast, unbroken, semi-arid plateau very gently tilted towards the great Mekong, the river that marks a natural boundary between Thailand and the Democratic People's Republic of Laos. To the south was Cambodia. From the air it was immediately obvious why this was the least visited part of Thailand. It looked dry, it looked hot and it looked empty. The only other *farang* on the small six-o'clock jet from Bangkok was an imposing Canadian evangelist minister, a missionary of sorts. His jaw stuck out by a metre, but even he wore a worried look.

Cadging a lift into town on the airline crew minibus I checked in at the Phatumrat Hotel, allegedly the best there was. At reception I encountered the first obstacle. The receptionist refused point blank to cash a traveller's cheque. In Ubon the banks didn't open on Saturdays, as they did in Bangkok. I must wait for Monday morning. Until then I could sign for everything, although, the receptionist pointed out, the restaurant was closed all day. The hotel had been booked by a wedding party, and there was no one to prepare me so much as a sandwich. On the other hand, I could always go and have a coffee at the Long Beach, when it opened at two . . .

The Long Beach, needless to say, was the hotel's in-house massage parlour. There were also, I noticed, a couple of nightclubs. Evidently the Phatumrat was the centre of civilization in those parts – an impression that was confirmed when I ventured outside.

Having been assured by Mr Thawee that Ubon Ratchathani was a thriving commercial hub, I had just enough cash on me to buy a plate of fried rice and twenty cigarettes. There was not a single money-changer to be seen. The main street might been another American runway. It was very straight, very broad and very long, and it was lined with rusting concrete shop-stores. Apart from groceries (plenty of sticky rice, for which the region is famous) these sold pumps, small generators and weighing machines. Clearly Ubon was no more, and no less, than a place where farmers purchased their necessities. Any spare baht probably went on the Long Beach or the few cocktail bars in the vicinity of the hotel. Virtually there was no sign of life. Virtually. Once every five minutes a soap-board truck sped by, advertising a local cinema. On its side were cut-outs of a soldier brandishing his weapons. On its top a clumsy loudspeaker hailed non-existent pedestrians with simulated machine-gun fire. Or perhaps it wasn't simulated, which is why the runway-street was empty.

Then six lorryloads of real soldiers crawled past in a compact dust-storm. Of course! The beginning of the dry season. All over I-san the

Thai military would be winding up for its annual tête-a-tête with the Vietnamese.

I walked on and found a restaurant that was open. Over my rice I studied my Ubon Ratchathani information pack. Ubon had been founded two centuries before by two deserters called Thao Thitphrom and Thao Kham who decided that living in the middle of nowhere was better than having their livers ripped out by the bellicose King of Ventiane. As soon as they had constructed a system of moats they petitioned the then king of Thailand, Taksin Maharaj, to incorporate their settlement within his dominion. King Taksin graciously consented. Then he installed a governor. For four generations the governor's family ruled Ubon Ratchathani, after which the position was regularized and Ubon was swallowed up in the normal pattern of provincial administration. Among the usual hoard of local customs and festivals two only stood out. The first was Boon Bang Fai, in May at the end of the dry season, when home-made rockets (lengths of bamboo filled with saltpetre and charcoal) are fired into the air to irritate the rain god. (The rain-god, in his anger, unleashes himself, and the harvest is saved.) The second was 'Merit-making at the End of Buddhist Lent'. On this occasion the populace present the monks with Prasart Phung, or miniature pavilions, made from woven bamboo strips and banana-plant leaves. The pavilions are stuffed with sweets, fruit, sugar-cane and all manner of other goodies. They are decorated with boiled bees, standing in for flowers.

I fancied the boiled bees. They were just the thing to make readers of the *Times* sit up. Unfortunately, though Merit-making at the End of Buddhist Lent took place in October, which meant I'd have to wait another eleven months, I wasn't that desperate. Yet what else was there? The list of alternative attractions was slender indeed. Haad Wat Tai, a sand-bank in the middle of the Moon; Kaeng Saprue, another river isle; Hu Toi – you've guessed it (only this time in the Mekong itself); Haad Hin, a rock bank overlooking the Mekong; or Pha Taem, a 200-metre cliff not overlooking anywhere, inscribed with prehistoric drawings dating back 5000 years (interesting – until I turned the page and saw a photograph of said cliff-drawings, which had been all but obliterated by the weather). Otherwise it was all waterfalls and temples, with the odd whirlpool thrown in. Wat Supattanaramvara-viharn, described as a 'third-class royal monastery'; Wat Pa Nana Chat, boasting an Australian Abbot: Wat Buruparam, which used to be 'the place where several reputed mediator-monks stayed, who left behind only their images made from stones collected from fivers'. Rivers? The trouble with temples and monasteries was that, in Thailand, they come ten to a cent.

And that was it. Except for the nightspots. But was I really to furnish the Thunderer with 1500 words on the Sabai Thong massage parlour in Phichit Rangsan Road, or even the nearby 'Sicky Pub'?

Avoiding the attentions of two waitresses hovering dangerously close to my elbows I reviewed the options. The more I thought about it the more it looked like the Australian Abbot. Cresting a beaut, sport? *You've got it.* Unless of course something truly unexpected showed up. Which, in Thailand, was always possible.

But my immediate concern was money. The Phatumrat was not Ubon Ratchathani's only hostelry. There was, for example, the Krung Thong, or Golden City. With a name like that they should certainly be more obliging. At least it was worth a try.

Finishing my rice I set off. Further along the Chayangkul Road (Runway Street) I came to the first food market. Here the sight of a scrawny dog urinating over a cut of beef made me turn quickly away. Nobody else had seen it, or if they had, they weren't bothered. I continued, and little by little Ubon became less inhospitable. Chayangkul Road finally ran out of tarmac and I found myself on the edge of a large square park. There was a moderately attractive temple shrine in its middle, and people of all ages were out flying kites. And beyond were more temples, the gold of their stupas shining through generously leafed trees; a lot of wooden houses; and eventually Moon River. Of course! I should have known. Old Ubon, the real Ubon Ratchathani, was bound to be down by the water. Where else could it have been?

I stopped for an iced tea at another restaurant. Without warning the glass exploded in my hand. Was that a good omen, or a bad one?

Without very much difficulty I located the Krungthong and happily struck a deal with the manager. In return for changing a traveller's cheque I agreed to stay at his hotel from Sunday onwards. Indeed I would have moved there immediately, except that I considered it unlikely the Phatumrat would forgo its pound of flesh. The rooms at the Golden City were not as good, though invitingly cheap. I might as well have at least one night of the best that Ubon could offer . . .

*

'Here I am, sitting at a table in the foyer of the Krung Thong,' goes my journal entry for Sunday 22nd November. 'My room's too dark to write in, too hot, too pokey. It's nice to be here though. Anywhere but the Phatumrat! I'm looking side-on at the grandfather-clock. Or rather, the grandfather-clock is looking side-on at me. Ubon is full of the things. The clocks themselves are made in Germany, the cases carpentered locally. They're not the most beautiful artefacts I've ever seen, but they are reassuring. It's good to think that there are some Thais who don't spend all their money on Singha beer and girls. Also, the regular rhythm of the clock soothes. It helps me work. As I write, the hotel staff look on approvingly. They too must think it good that not all *farang* spend all their money on wine and women. I can see they are smiling at me. If I look up however their smiles broaden. At the very least they want to talk. I'm aware too that the Krung Thong also has a massage parlour, through the swing doors next to the lift. But so far there has been no attempt to inveigle me inside. It's already four o'clock. But I'm keeping my head down. It's easiest to keep on working. The lazy way out maybe, but . . . *mai pen rai.*'

As planned I had checked out of the Phatumrat on Sunday morning. Instead of 350 baht a night I was now paying only 200. Life was a whole lot easier. Even taking into account that there was no hot water at the Krung Thong, no radio and no proper air-conditioning, life was a whole lot easier. I could even take the sticky chicken served at the Krung Thong's food counter. The rice was not so sticky, but the chicken came in stringy slithers like half-dried glue. These stuck to the lips and hung down like stalactites of saliva. But I was happy to be where I was. I wouldn't have gone back to the Phatumrat for all the gold in Wat Po.

A confession. The day before, Saturday, after I got back to the Phatumrat, I went to my room, did a little writing and lay down. I'd been up since four in the morning. At four in the afternoon I woke up and went downstairs. The restaurant (in reality another coffee shop) still wasn't open. Nor, because of the wedding, was it going to be open until after six. I needed some coffee to wake me up. So I went to the Long Beach. Of course I could have gone to one of the places outside, but I didn't. It had to be the Long Beach. Why? Simple curiosity. It wasn't even a question of wanting to continue my Bangkok research. It was curiosity. Nothing else.

Inside the Long Beach was exactly like the dozen-odd massage parlours I visited ten years ago up country in Chiang Mai, Chiang Rai, Chiang Saen. A big over-air-conditioned bar area with a glass wall behind which a lot of under-dressed girls wearing plastic discs with numbers on sat watching television. The television had its back to the punters, which meant of course the punters could look at the girls' eyes without having to look into them. The girls themselves were seated on brightly lit golden tiers. They looked like sweets on offer in a Paris sweetshop, and about the whole place there was a sort of film-set luxury: it looked good even if one knew it wasn't. Money had been spent on fantasy, on the wrappings – money that needn't have been spent. Men will always go to brothels whatever the décor, so why gild the lily?

The customers were all Thais. They were mainly middle-aged men, and poorly dressed. It wasn't a spivs' rendezvous. Some of them – farmers, and one or two mechanics – still had the soil clinging to their trousers. And they sat there, getting immediately drunk on their beers, ogling the girls and discussing numbers. The girls whispered among themselves. Although the glass in these establishments is supposed to be one-way, here it patently wasn't. From time to time the manager would speak into a microphone and call out a number. *Yessip song. Sipeat.* Twenty-two. Eleven. And the girls wearing these numbers on their plastic discs would look to see who had chosen them. Sometimes they registered pleasure, sometimes they registered surprise, sometimes they just grimaced.

Every three or four minutes the manager would stop by my table. *Number six*, he'd say, *good*. Or, *number twenty-six, very good.* Or: *Forty-one, very very good.* Patently if I waited long enough I'd discover which one was best. But I had no intention of waiting, and soon it became embarrassing . In the end I told the manager I wanted number nineteen. Number nineteen had just been called by another man. 'Oh,' I said aping disappointment, 'that's a pity. Number nineteen's the one I really want. *Mai pen rai.* I'll come back.'

Thus I made my escape. A devilish piece of diplomacy, though it almost caught up with me later.

When the roke does come, I thought to myself, it'll find the going made easy in Thailand. Because it's not just the big towns that have their Long Beaches, it's every little town as well. The Thames Water Authority itself could hardly have organized a better feed system.

But that was only the beginning of the Phatumrat horrors. As soon

66

as the coffee shop was open I slipped in for an early dinner. Again I was confronted by a typically Thai institution. Inside the coffee shop were about fifty tables and a small rostrum. The tables were mainly occupied by dressed-up youngsters. In East Asia the generation gap is twice as big as it is in the West. In the West the old folk have their own places, but in Thailand the old folk stay at home. A lot of them have to babysit their children's mistakes. Where the children get their happy money from I don't know. Yet get it they do. Come Friday, Saturday, Sunday evening, they've all got a few hundred baht in their pocket. And that's the great strength of oriental money systems. Circulation takes the heat off supply.

Simply the Thais love their food, their drink, their sex and their music. And they love having them all at once. On the rostrum was an electric keyboard and a set of drums. A third musician held a guitar, while in more or less strict rotation five or six girls stood up, one after the other, and sang songs. Thai songs, and western songs. Any songs. And sang them well, considering. All over Thailand there are literally thousands of girls standing up and singing professionally on Friday, Saturday and Sunday nights. Usually they do it for ten baht a song, which works out at around 50 cents. Though of course, while they're singing they're also parading themselves. When the evening finishes they hope at least one customer has stayed behind to see them home. Then the real money begins.

Which isn't bad, if you think about it. I mean, how many girls in Kings Cross or hookers on Third Avenue would have the balls to stand up in front of a crowd of 200 and sing like they had been doing the cabaret since they were three years old?

I ate and I listened. There was one girl who was particularly pretty and sang particularly melodiously. (Those whom luck favours, luck favours.) Each time she finished she walked by me and dropped a little smile on my plate. She was at a table at the back of the room. Not to be churlish I got into the habit of returning the smile. After all, she'd be singing at least until midnight, and by then I'd be chastely tucked up in Room 507. What harm could there be?

The harm started with a tap on my shoulder.

'Hello mister, where you from?'

I looked up and saw that I was being addressed by a young man.

'England,' I replied. 'Why do you ask?'

'*Angrit*. Very good. Meow say she want to meet you.'

'Meow?'

He pointed to the table at the far end. The pretty singer, Meow, was with a group of Thai men. One of them had his arm pugnaciously around her neck.

'Well, I'm here.'

'But you alone. Why not you come our table, drink beer. We all students. My friend, he been America. He been university America.'

My first inclination was to decline graciously. But that was stupid. If I was going to lay my hands on anything interesting in Ubon Ratchathani these might be just the people to lead me to it.

'Okay,' I said, 'I'll come over.'

From that point it was all downhill. To begin with, the students (there were three of them) came from far away. Quite what they were doing in Ubon they wouldn't say, unless it was for the sole purpose of sampling northeastern girls, whose dark features have given them a certain notoriety (much as fairness has given Chiang Mai lasses their reputation). At any rate, after twenty minutes they announced that they were going off to *atami*. Was I going to join them? Knowing what *atami* meant – a massage parlour – I said I wasn't.

So off they went, which left just the three of us: myself, Meow, and Meow's boyfriend, whose name was Dran.

Then Meow went off to sing, and we were two.

Dran wasn't a student, nor was it likely he ever would be. To do him credit he did speak a little English. The three phrases at his beck and call were (1) What your name? (2) You CIA man? and (3) Hate the CIA.

The poor fellow had obviously been reading too many comics. To make up for his education he was strappingly built. He was three-quarters Chinese, and like all three-quarter Chinese he knew how to throw himself about. It has something, I believe, to do with the impurity in their blood.

'What your name?'

'James.'(One can never be too careful.)

'You CIA man?'

'Not at all. I'm English. *Angrit*.'

'Hate the CIA.'

This went on a long time, during which Meow returned and left us twice. I, too, tried to leave, but at each attempt Dran pulled me down again.

'What your name?'
'You CIA man?'
'Hate the CIA!'
And then, as a complete surprise, he threw in:
'You my brother!'
At last I thought, he's understood. But his next question was:
'You CIA man?'
Eventually even Dran got tired of saying the same lines over and over and expressed a desire to go somewhere different.
'Hate Coffee Shop,' he said. 'Go nightclub.'
'I'm with you all the way,' I concurred.
My plan of course was to make a bolt for it once we were on our feet. But Dran made that impossible. He grabbed my arm and refused to let go. 'You my brother,' he drooled, 'you my wery wery brother.'
The nightclub was like the coffee shop only several degrees cooler and several degrees darker. Another three-man band occupied a small stage. They even played the same songs, which were sung by the same girls. Exactly the same girls. They came upstairs from the Coffee Shop, did their thing, and disappeared again. Soon Meow materialized at our table and sat down with us.
Dran said:
'Love you wery much. Love you wery wery wery much.'
Then Meow left us and Dran said:
'Love you wery wery much.'
This went on a wery wery long time. Dran by now had me in an affectionate half-nelson, and it was no use telling him that yes actually I was a CIA man. But I was not without hope. Dran kept ordering himself more beer, and gradually he was losing his grip. After a while it was like being stuck in a lift with a soggy bull.
The band stopped playing and evaporated. The music, however, continued. Now it was disco time. Madonna. Dran suggested we dance. I suggested we didn't
'You my brother. Hate CIA.'
Meow came back. She had half an hour's break. As soon as she was seated, another man, of Indian appearance, and wearing an ostentatious white suit, glided into the empty seat beside her. Meow let him hold her hand.
Dran was not as discomposed as he should have been. On the contrary, he momentarily scaled the heights of lucidity.

'This my wery good friend,' he said, pointing to the fellow in white. 'Him doctor, best doctor in Ubon. Speak wery good English.'

But if this was true, the doctor wasn't about to admit it. He exhibited a marked disinclination to converse with myself, and an even greater disinclination to converse with his good friend Dran. The only person who interested him was Meow. He pulled out his wallet and showed her its contents. Meow was suitably impressed and shortly they left together. Tonight her singing was finished.

When Dran grasped what had happened he vented his spleen not on his wery good friend the doctor, but on Meow.

'Every time she do that me,' he moaned. 'Every time come Ubon Meow butterfly. You CIA man?'

The least I could do was help Dran drown his sorrows. I ordered two more beers and set them both in front of him. The waitress must have switched labels, however. Instead of softening him up further the new beer revived him. His free hand now commenced an excavation of my thigh. His face also was getting closer and closer to my own. I had the uneasy feeling that at any moment he would assay a kiss.

'You my wery good friend,' he said, 'you my brother.'

As I said, Dran was a well-built oaf, and I've been in enough Thai watering holes to know how suddenly a mood can change. In Nathorn once I was next to a bunch of Thais who were being almost as friendly towards each other as Dran was being towards me. Then a gun appeared, and it was everybody hands up backing slowly towards the exit. As far as I could tell Dran wasn't armed, though of course any attempt at a discreet body-search would only have complicated matters. Nonetheless I was apprehensive. What would Dran do once he realized I wasn't too keen to substitute for Meow?

Happily it was Dran himself who came to my rescue. He had a bright idea. Why didn't we go to the john together?

'You go,' I said. 'I don't need it.'

Dran was slow to accept this modification to his proposal, but when I promised I wouldn't run away he acceded.

Needless to say, when Dran got back I was gone.

My first thought was to ring London. I badly needed to speak to my wife. But this could not be done. To make an international call, the night manager told me, I must wait till tomorrow. So the next best thing, I decided, was fruit. Instead of going to my room I wandered outside to a night market down the road and stocked up with bananas and guava. Then I returned to the Phatumrat. To my dismay Dran was leaning heavily on the reception desk. Before I could retreat he turned and saw me, and lunged in my direction.

'I'm wery, wery hurt,' he said. 'Wery wery hurt.'

The man was crying.

'And I'm very very sorry,' I said, 'but you can't come with me.'

'Wery wery hurt. Everybody try to hurt me.'

Thank God the night manager understood, and sympathized with, my predicament. He came out from behind the desk and gently disentangled me from Dran's intense embrace.

I didn't stay to express my gratitude. Nor did I take the lift for fear Dran discover what floor I was on. I used the stairs, gaining the fifth floor in approximately four bounds.

An hour later the telephone rang.

'Room 507?'

Oh Lord, I thought, it's Dran. But it wasn't. It was the manager of the Long Beach.

'Number 19, she ready for you now.'

'Is she?' I said. 'It'll have to be tomorrow. I'm busy now.'

'Mister busy now?'

'Yes, Mister busy now. *Mai pen rai.*'

And I was busy. I was busy thinking: What if, instead of being a foreigner, I had been a Thai girl, working in the Long Beach or any other massage parlour? And what if, in that case, Dran had come along and called my number? Then I'd have no choice in the matter.

Suddenly I saw the Thai sex scene for what it really is. A question of putting myself in their shoes, and not in their pants.

*

On the subject of Thai mores the Abbot of Wat Pa Nana Chat's mother was less strident. 'Thailand,' she said, 'is a country where everything is allowed to go to its natural extreme.'

Getting to see the Abbot was easy. Getting to Wat Pa Nana Chat, a forest monastery twenty miles outside Ubon, was decidedly wracksome. It was not until I went to a branch of the Thai Farmers' Bank on Monday morning, to cash a second traveller's cheque, that I found anyone able to tell me the way. Smiling broken crystals the submanager explained that I must first take a pink bus to Warin, then go to the terminal and find a green-and-yellow bus. But so long as I kept on repeating the magic formula, Wat Pa Nana Chat, sooner or later I'd get there.

The pink bus came and carried me across Moon River – a flat expanse of unmoving water that, at 10.00 am, did not deserve its name. I was dropped off in a back street of Warin, a suburb of Ubon that was twice the size and three times as busy. Eventually, with no help from anyone, I stumbled on what appeared to be a bus terminal. I looked in vain for a green-and-yellow coach. 'Wat Pa Nana Chat' I kept saying to anyone within earshot. But I'd got the wrong terminal. Redirected I found the right terminal. Still no green-and-yellow buses. Only red ones and blue ones. 'Wat Pa Nana Chat?' *Take a red bus, mister.*

I climbed into a red coach. Up front it had a television, a video player and a cassette recorder. 'Wat Pa Nana Chat' I said to the driver. The driver nodded vigorously. I then conveyed that I wasn't just saying Wat Pa Nana Chat for the hell of it, but wanted to go there. Again the driver nodded vigorously. 'Wat Pa Nana Chat,' he said. 'No problem.'

But the other passengers were more doubtful. The general consensus was that if I wanted to go to Wat Pa Nana Chat I should take a blue coach.

The driver of the blue coach also nodded vigorously. Wat Pa Nana Chat, no problem. This time the passengers agreed with him.

I found myself a seat near the front. Immediately I was joined by an old woman carrying two baskets of chickens. They poked their beaks through the wickered interstices and pecked repeatedly at my arm. It wouldn't have been so bad if it hadn't also been unbearably hot. None of the fans on the ceiling worked, and even when the bus moved off the air that came in through the windows was suffocating. For the first time since coming to Thailand I began to sweat profusely.

'Wat Pa Nana Chat', I said to the ticket boy. 'Don't forget!'

'Don't worry, mister. I never forget.'

Forty minutes later the coach screeched to a halt in the middle of the highway. The driver had overshot the mark, and the ticket boy had fallen asleep. Everyone was shouting Wat Pa Nana Chat and pointing back down the road.

There was nothing for it but to walk. The sun was directly overhead and there was no kind of shelter. Flat fields stretched out on either side of the highway, and such trees as there were had all been taken by

72

peasants. They smiled heartily at the stranger passing by but kept their water bottles to themselves.

Two miles further and I came to a dust-track leading off towards a wood on the horizon, and a signpost that read 'Wat Pa Nana Chat – Ban Wai Forestry Monastery'. Another mile at least. Now, in water-logged ditches, I observed lethargic buffalo, one of which delivered a very creditable rendering of the river song: 'Mooo-ooon rif----errr.'

The next sign-post and I was almost there. I could see the plain wooden arch, and the notice board: Wat Pa Nana Chat.

Just a few more paces . . .

Once inside the wood, everything changed. The air of the 'forest' was a fragrant *eau-de-nil* and astonishingly cool. It was also wondrously quiet. The occasional twittering of a bird resounded like rockfall in a canyon.

Astonishingly cool, and astonishingly empty. Following the path I came to a circular wooden building that resembled nothing so much as an open-air canteen without the tables. Parked beside it was an abandoned car, its doors left wide open.

'They've seen me coming,' I thought, 'and they've hidden in the trees. They don't want to meet me.'

All around the clearing paths radiated spoke-like into the wood. I chose one and before long encountered a saffron-robed bikkhu. In my halting Thai I attempted to explain myself. The monk looked at me with zero curiosity.

'That's okay,' he said, 'I'm from Lincoln.'

'Really?' I stared at the fellow, and asked stupidly: 'Are you happy here?'

Without hesitation Lincoln told me that Wat Pa Nana Chat was perfectly okay unless something better came along.

'And do you think something better will come along?'

'Who knows? In a forest monastery nothing comes along.'

Somehow I didn't think Lincoln and I were destined for a very long or productive intercourse. Rather than waste any more of his time or mine I came straight to the point. Would it be possible for me to see the Abbot?

The monk nodded like one used to the request. 'This way,' he mumbled. 'The Ajahn is having a rest or meditating, but either way he will talk to you.'

We criss-crossed through the wood. Between some of the paths were small wooden huts raised on stilts, each in its own clearing. When pressed Lincoln explained that these were the other monks' quarters. Otherwise he kept silent. Remarkably he didn't have a single question to put to his compatriot. But Lincoln's mind apparently didn't run to interrogatives. He already had all the answers he needed.

A second monk appeared ahead, coming, as it were, very fast dead into camera. We almost had to jump out of his way. The monk shot straight past, oblivious of anyone else's existence.

'What was that?'

'The walking meditation,' Lincoln answered drearily.

At last we came to a larger, two-storey hut, made of glass and concrete as well as wood, in the middle of a bigger clearing. The Abbot's house.

Lincoln whistled softly.

'Ajahn,' he called. 'Ajahn Pasanno?'

A head, wearing gold-rimmed spectacles, appeared through a window. For a moment I thought it was Johnny, Pranee's friend. The likeness was startling.

Ajahn Pasanno came downstairs and invited me inside. Lincoln, without further ado, vanished.

The Abbot said 'Have a seat' and pointed to the floor. Then he beseated himself, in the semi-lotus-position, on a low, stoutly built table.

'What can I do for you?'

'You are the Abbot? The Australian Abbot?'

Ajahn Pasanno smiled.

'I'm the Abbot yes, but I'm not Australian. I come from Canada. My predecessor left a while ago. My name, as you might have gathered, is Ajahn Pasanno. Ajahn means teacher. It used to be Reed Perry. When I was a student in Winnipeg.'

I gave the Ajahn my card, and we exchanged further particulars. Soon I had a working picture of Wat Pa Nana Chat. Forest monasteries were a distinct phenomenon in Thai Buddhism, and not to be confused with the ubiquitous temples. Temple monks by and large had a much closer relationship with the people who supported them. Sometimes they were expected to act as social workers. But in a forest monastery the primary duty of the monks is meditation. Wat Pa Nana Chat was open to anyone who wanted to pay a visit, but the onus was on the visitor to make the effort. Such teaching as the Abbot and his senior colleagues offered was more by way of example than by way of exegesis, although much of the Ajahn's time was taken up training novices. In this respect Wat Pa Nana Chat was different. While it belonged to an order of thirty or forty other forest monasteries scattered round the country, and was presided over by a Chief Abbot, the Venerable Ajahn Char ('a holy man'), it alone catered for foreigners wishing to become monks. Foreigners could enter other monasteries and other temples, but to do so gainfully they had to learn Thai. Here that wasn't necessary. At Wat Pa Nana Chat there were several Thais, but most of the monks came from Europe, America and Australia.

I listened patiently, taking in as much as I could of what the Ajahn, in his understatements, related. But something about the Ajahn bothered me, made it hard to concentrate. The more I looked at him the less Johnny-like he became. Indeed, if he truly resembled anyone it was me. The Abbot was the same size and shape as me, and . . . the penny dropped . . . roughly the same age.

I asked him about this. 'How old are you?' I said. It transpired that the Abbot was exactly two months my junior. Sitting at his feet suddenly became an elaborate joke.

The Ajahn thought so, too. 'Yes,' he said, relaxing his lotus position, 'it is funny, isn't it?'

Now we talked to each other as equals. When he meditated, I wanted to know, what did he meditate *upon*? 'The present,' replied Ajahn Pasanno, 'the here, the now.' And I thought, oh yes, you monks, you ascetics, you're all the same, you're all greedy for time.

As though he had read my thoughts the Ajahn said, laying great stress on his words, 'We make a good contribution to the planet, I think. We're not obligated to save anyone. That may sound contradictory, but I hope it isn't. For example, take Thailand. The point about Thailand was very beautifully expressed by my mother when she came here to visit me. Thailand is a country where everything is allowed to go to its natural extreme she said. By everything she meant perhaps desires. It's important, therefore, that some people in Thailand live, as nearly as they can, without desires.'

'When you say "save", what do you mean? Are we talking personal fulfilment, or are we talking eternal salvation?'

'You want to ask me about heaven. There's not much I can tell you about that. In Buddhist teaching it's a grey area. Some sects put a very marked emphasis on the idea of a hereafter, others dismiss it completely. There are important concepts of karma, transmigration and reincarnation, and these are much fought over. If you achieve nirvana in one life you have achieved it forever. But this I admit is difficult to explain, and doesn't give immediate satisfaction to the question. Let me tell you what my own teacher, Ajahn Char, says. When his students ask him if there is an afterlife, a heaven, he doesn't answer directly. What he does say is, "If I said yes, would you believe me? And if I said no, would you believe me?" '

Good. But it wasn't eschatology I wanted to discuss so much as massage parlours. I had a very precise question to put to the Abbot, but the hard part was finding an opening.

I settled for the long way round. I told Ajahn Pasonno that, for want of a better word, I would describe myself as a Darwinist. Yet, as a Darwinist, I could see a compatibility of sorts between Darwin and the Buddha. The Buddha had shown his followers that life is all hardship, pain, disease, and growing old. And Darwin had described, or at least delineated, much the same qualities in nature, of which of course man is a part.

The Abbot nodded. There was no reason, he said, why he shouldn't agree to that. Indeed, between Buddhism and science there was more compatibility than incompatibility.

'It's the relativity of things I'm after,' I said, gearing up. 'The same phenomenon, seen from different but related points of view. Which brings me on to my next question. Please don't take offence, but if one looks at those town temples we were talking about, those fruit salad confections of white and red and gold and green, and then one looks at, say, the equally gaudy massage parlours, for example, isn't there something of a similarity? Aren't the two types of seemingly very different buildings perhaps rather intimately connected? Don't they have this in common, that they both promise some sort of release from day-to-day frustrations?'

In vain I scanned the Abbot's face for any hint of a disturbance.

'No, there's no offence,' he replied quite calmly. 'No offence at all. If you talked to some of the younger monks at Wat Pa Nana Chat you might find out they think more or less the same. But come, I'll show you over.'

The Abbot took me on a guided tour of the monastery. There were several interesting features. A crude crematorium for instance, no more than an open-topped brick oven; the twenty or so huts where the monks slept and meditated; a workshop where, among other pursuits, the dye for colouring their saffron robes was made – by crushing the wood of jack-fruit trees. But the object that most seized my imagination was the skeleton. The skeleton was standing upright in a glass case in the main *viharn*, or prayer-hall.

'She died two years ago,' the Abbot explained, 'in a motor accident. She lived in a nearby village. The husband brought us the bones. Now everybody can look at them.'

I was reminded how Buddhist monks are instructed, whenever they find themselves aroused by a woman, to visualize her intestines. Beside the glass case was the main altar, stacked three or four deep with Buddha-images.

'Originally we didn't want any images,' the Abbot commented. 'Images distract. But people kept on bringing them, and it's hard to say no.'

Without the images, but not without the skeleton, the *viharn* might have been designed for the worship, or at least the contemplation, of almost anything, Darwin included. It was a very quiet, very beautiful room, with large unglassed windows opening so directly onto the surrounding flora that several brilliant flowers had invited themselves inside.

'You know what you are?' I said suddenly. 'You're spoiled silly.'

The Abbot laughed.

'Go on.'

'I mean it must be very nice to be a forest monk. Okay, you have to be up at half-past three every morning, and you mustn't swallow anything except water after your large breakfast. There are plenty of jobs to be done as well. Making the dye for your clothes, for example, which you showed me. Pumping water from the well. But for the rest of the time you're as free as a dicky bird to sit around and think. What could be nicer?'

The Abbot laughed again.

'Well,' he said, 'if you want to make a contribution, give it to the alms-keeper. I'm not allowed to touch money. Then I'll take you to the gate.'

I dug into my pocket and left 200 baht on the sill of the alms-keeper's office. Then, with the Abbot, I set off for the gate. On the way we passed a group of peasant women, coming to present alms perhaps.

As soon as they saw the Abbot they fell on their knees. Nor did they stand again until he had taken several paces beyond them. But if Ajahn Pasanno was remotely embarrassed by such a display of feudal humility he didn't show it.

'Spoiled silly!' I repeated as I took my leave. 'Perhaps I'll come again one day.'

'Do,' said the Abbot. 'Though I must point out, we don't proselytize at Wat Pa Nana Chat. As I said, we're under no obligation to save anyone.'

I started on the long walk back to the high road. At a hundred yards a Warin-bound bus roared by. It would be a good half-hour before the next one came. To amuse myself I began earnestly taking photographs of the earth-bound, mud-caked water buffalo.

That night was the first bad night. Walking several miles under a midday tropical sun had done me no good whatsoever. In the small hours I awoke scarcely able to move. Further, my brain was playing evil tricks. I was no longer a traveller in 1986, but an exile in 1886. Nor was I in the Golden City Hotel, but in some species of wooden dwelling close by the sea. I was also at least twenty years older, and I was dying, of an obscure tropical disease. At some point in my past I had worked for the government, either my own, perhaps in a diplomatic capacity, or for that of a foreign power. But some Conradian tragedy had overtaken me. A small negligence of some kind, or simple misjudgement, had wrought my downfall. And now I was dying. I knew it. And the experience of dying was more alarming than anyone who has not died could conceive. The only consolation was that I was alone. There was nobody to see me die. In a day or two my rigid body would be discovered face up on the bed, eyes open, one hand dropping to the floor. The ultimate epitome of a wasted, an unnecessary, life. But also: the ultimate counter-statement. The denial of everything – Conrad included. The whole of life, the whole of culture, the whole civilization – pointless!

I died. The brain just guttered out. Not one thought left to observe the occurrence of death. And then the nightmares began. Scores of them, like sightless birds in a too-small aviary, all screeching and flapping their wings and digging their talons into each other. The grand discordant babble of life, perceived perfectly.

I stayed in my room all morning. I had to. As soon as I finally surfaced from my nightmares my stomach attacked. I lay on my back staring at the fan that revolved lugubriously on the ceiling immediately above me. From time to time I staggered to the writing table and scribbled something in a notebook. Then it was time for the toilet. I dived for the bathroom, returned to the bed and waited for the next onslaught.

There was nothing else to do. In the afternoon, though, my bowels eased up. I was vouchsafed enough breathing space to visit the airline office and bring forward my flight to Bangkok by two days. Then it was post haste back to my room.

By Thursday I was in the capital again, and feeling better for it. 'Delhi belly,' I noted in my diary: 'Bound to happen sooner or later, and maybe good to get it out of the way.' I rang Mr Thawee. What news? Mr Thawee was still waiting. Her Majesty's private secretary so far had not had the opportunity to elicit an answer from Her Majesty. Ask me again next week. And Dr Winij? Ah yes. Dr Winij. Dr Winij was in his office. Mr Thawee would definitely ring Dr Winij on my behalf.

In more senses than one I felt I was treading water. I telephoned the Ministry of Health direct, but Dr Winij was unavailable. Then I read the newspapers. In Ubon I'd been unable to buy either the *Bangkok Post* or the *Bangkok World*. Now I made up for lost print. To my surprise I found three Aids-related articles.

The first was a regular doom warning. A longish piece, set in a black-boarded box, headlined *A Plague On Everyone*. But nothing in it referred specifically to Bangkok. It had a syndicated feel about it, and my guess was it originated from a desk at *The Christian Science Monitor*. However another much shorter article, on the previous page, was germane. In this 'brief' Dr Winij (who else?) denied reports that further cases of Aids had been found in the city. Interestingly he quoted the mandatory screening of all Thai nationals on their way to Saudi Arabia. Yet in the third article, in the *World*, published the previous evening, it was reported that three more victims had been identified at Chulalongkorn University Hospital. Chulalongkorn University Hospital was one of only four officially authorized to carry out the Saudi tests.

I rang the Department of Communicable Diseases on a different number, and got through to Dr Winij's secretary. After some insisting I got through to Dr Winij himself. Yes, he had heard from Mr Thawee that I wanted to talk to him about Aids. How could he help?

Dr Winij took me over all the old ground. So far there had been only six cases in Thailand, and these were all 'imported'. His department was keeping a close eye on the situation. As soon as the government felt it necessary to update the June statistic it would do so. But now that was unnecessary. In Thailand Aids was not a problem.

'But I see from the *World* that three further cases have been identified at Chulalongkorn University. Can you comment?'

Dr Winij admitted he was not unaware of the report. 'But you must understand, we are awaiting the results of further tests before issuing any confirmation.'

'These three unconfirmed cases, though, are they the result of the mandatory screening requested by the Saudi government?'

'That is not important. When we have the final results, then we can discuss the mandatory screening. But as of now, nothing has changed. The official statistic is that there have been only six confirmed cases.'

'All of whom, I'm told, have died. Is the government carrying out any programme of its own to identify anyone who might be carrying the virus? Are you testing for antibodies?'

And then came the show-stopper.

Dr Winij told me that twelve sero-positives had been identified. But because none of them had any of the symptoms of the disease they were being regarded as immune to the disease.

*

If before, Bangkok had been oppressive, I now found it demented – a reflection perhaps of my own disintegrating state of mind. On my first sortie to Lucky Luke's I ran into Kanda. While I had been in Ubon she had been visiting her family in Ayutthya. All the sparkle, all the gaiety had deserted her. Her face had gone into permanent collapse. At first she was loath to say anything. But then, in a sudden flurry of anguished vehemence, it came out. 'Kanda good girl,' she cried, 'Kanda go home Ayutthya, see mother, give mother money. Then Kanda find out. Kanda fucking find out that her fucking brother is fucking her sister. She is just eleven year old. Now Kanda never go Ayutthya again.'

Behind her back the other girls were calling Kanda names. They were calling her Local Suzy Wong. And even the few good things I found in the city rang false notes. The Ambassador Hotel, for instance. I remembered it well from previous visits. When it opened it had been just another spacious luxury establishment. But now it had grown into a monster. It had swallowed up all the land around it. New wings had been added in every direction. Among its endless facilities it boasted no less than seventy restaurants and foodbars. What was the point of it? Or the Helabis. Faisal and Pitim Helabi were a couple whose name I had been given in London by a mutual friend. Pitim was a Moslem Thai, from the south, Faisal a partner in a company called Arabian-Thai Intertrade. The other partners were his brothers, and their main business was the manufacture of a rare Arabian oil. To make this liquid, more precious than gold, required an equally rare species of sandalwood, which grew only in Cambodia. Obtaining the trees was hazardous and costly. Faisal hinted that those who brought the trees to the border had suffered casualties. But the supply never quite dried up. The business prospered.

Visiting Faisal and Pitim (who was starting up a clothing concern in the same building) became something of a daily ritual, a necessary escape from the sweltering chaos outside. It was also an education. Faisal, a sleek, well-groomed modern Saudi, bewildered me with his hospitality. I was never allowed to leave without a meal, no matter what hour of the day it was; and no matter how urgent his business, Faisal was always master of his time. If this was the Arabic way of conducting relationships then I unexpectedly found myself heartily approving Arabs.

I was also struck by the apparent lack of tension between the brothers. I could not imagine two, let alone three, English brothers being able to run a vegetable stall for more than five minutes, whereas the Helabis had been at if for years. But the greatest pleasure was Faisal's Arabian coffee, as unlike the coffee I am used to as his Arabian oil was unlike western perfumes. (One drop, rubbed behind the ears, or elsewhere on the body, lasts six or seven months. Its seemingly prohibitive price therefore represents a saving. And its scent! Neither sweet nor cloying, but a reasoned argument directed at the mind as much as the nose.) After I had eaten, a servant would appear, carrying a long-spouted pot. Placing a tiny cup in front of me, she poured the coffee from a considerable height, slowly raising the pot to the level of her shoulder, directing the needle-thin jet of amber beverage to its target with pinpoint accuracy, never spilling so much as a drop. The cups filled, she withdrew. Were there any other duties she performed? If there were, I never witnessed them. But such was the satisfaction she gave, in that one small task, that her employer would have been justified in demanding nothing further of her.

Arabian coffee, Faisal, Pitim. They didn't belong in Bangkok. In Singapore, or Tokyo, or Hong Kong, maybe: their presence in those places would have been consistent. But not in Bangkok. But then I had turned against Bangkok. Nothing good could come out of it, therefore something was awry when I found anything good. The Helabis just didn't make sense to me.

Yet what did make sense? Day by day less and less. Aids consciousness was taking hold, distorting my perceptions of a city that had many other things to do apart from sell its body. But because Bangkok did sell its body, more regularly, more visibly and more persistently than any other city, its other functions were lost in a fog of unseasonable concupiscence.

I wanted to leave. Instead, hoping to uncover some fresh evidence that might give coherence to the material I already had, I lingered on. I also hoped Mr Thawee might have good tidings. But even before we spoke again I knew what the outcome of my royal petition must be. On the Sunday evening, writing up my diary, I received a highly irregular call. The voice was that of a young, educated male, who refused to give his name.

'Mr Win-tel?'

'Speaking.'

'You wish to interview Her Majesty?'

'Yes.'

'Then why you researching other thing?'

'What other thing?'

'Roke aids.'

'I'm a journalist. May I ask who I am speaking to?'

'You want to interview Her Majesty then you stop asking about other thing, okay?'

'Which department are you calling from?'

'No department. I just telephone you. And I tell you, it not good you try see Queen and write about other thing. Her Majesty very good lady. It no good what you trying to do.'

'Are you calling from the palace? If you can't tell me who you are, or what your authority is . . .'

The caller hung up.

My immediate reaction was to construe this call as an offer of a trade-off. Provided I dropped Aids I would be allowed to interview Queen Sirikit. That seemed to be the gist of it. In which case of course I had no option but to hold my present course. But the more I thought about it the less certain this interpretation was. It was just as possible that the young man was acting on his own initiative. Thai pride again, motivated by an excessive respect for the royal family. And if that were the case, there was no knowing the caller's provenance. He might be one of Mr Thawee's assistants in the Public Relations Department. Less probably, he worked for the Palace or for the Ministry of Health, and had learnt of my activities on the grapevine.

The thing was a mystery; but just because of that I felt threatened. Of course, if there was any truth in the cover-up theories, I should have expected it. In a way the call was just the sort of fresh evidence I had been looking for. But it was also soft evidence. Unless I went to great lengths to ascertain the caller's identity its data-value was precisely nil.

On the other hand, if I did make a fuss, if I did stick my nose in, the most likely outcome was I'd rapidly make myself twice as unwelcome as, apparently, I already was. And if push came to shove, I was vulnerable. I was not an accredited journalist, and there was no large organization I could call on for support.

An unwarranted individual initiative, or a concerted attempt by a third-world government to gag a foreign freelancer? Between these two positions I lost a fair bit of sleep that night, until I realized that until I spoke to Mr Thawee again there was no way I could begin to unravel the conundrum. But when, next morning, I rang Mr Thawee I was none the wiser. Mr Thawee told me there could be no question of my seeing Queen Sirikit immediately. She was still unwell, and also her timetable was habitually booked up several months in advance. However, when I returned to Bangkok in April, I should give Mr Thawee another call. It was not impossible that the Queen would agree to see me at the later date.

'Oh well. Thank you for that. I spoke to Dr Winij by the way.'

'I heard. I rang him, too, to fix your appointment. I hope he gave you some useful information.'

'Yes. To an extent.'

Nothing that Mr Thawee said indicated that he was aware of the previous evening's telephone call. Conversely nothing he said ruled out collusion either. Postponing the royal interview until April could be interpreted both ways. The coded message could have been: if between now and then you publish your Aids report, you certainly won't get to see Her Majesty.

I was completely at sea. I was in it over my head. Memories of unrealistically heroic movies (viz, *The Year of Living Dangerously*, or *Defence of the Realm*) suggested to me I should stick with the story, whatever the cost. But unrealistic was the word. I was not a hard newsman, nor had I ever been. I had no business getting sidetracked into work that properly belonged to older hands. And it was unimaginable that if the *Washington Post* or *Time* wasn't already investigating Aids in Bangkok, one of them wouldn't be doing so shortly.

With little reluctance I decided the time had come to leave. If I stayed any longer I would only add to my sense of failure. I hadn't secured the interview I wanted, and the research I had done on Aids was inconclusive. There was no article in it, no scoop.

And having made up my mind I immediately felt relieved. Deep down inside I had never wanted to interview the Queen anyway. I had a certain picture of what might happen. Thai protocol demands that those approaching the King or the Queen in audience comprehensively prostrate themselves. I saw myself entering the throne room, Her Majesty standing at the far end, an object in her hand. Beside her, a guard leaning on his long-handled axe. As I approach I see what it is Her Majesty is holding. It is a copy of my novel, *Paradise For Hire*. Half in deference, half in shame (such a disgusting book!) I bow my head. As I do so the Queen opens her hand. The long-handled axe swishes through the air. The book, and its author's head, hit the deck simultaneously.

The Queen And I? No thank you.

*

I left Bangkok and went, by train, to Hua Hin, a coastal resort 170 kilometres south of the city on the Gulf of Siam. I wanted to clear my head for a few days before plunging into Malaya. A little rest, a little holiday, was needed. And where better than old-fashioned Hua Hin? Five years earlier I'd spent an almost idyllic ten days at the Railway Hotel, a traditional establishment run with the utmost propriety by the government. It had much fine topiary and a botanical garden, where, not before time, I had read, from cover to cover, *The*

Origin of Species. Further, it backed onto the sea where three or four quiet bars provided most life-support services at exceedingly reasonable prices. Best of all, when the waiters served you breakfast or lunch they didn't invite you to take photographs of their sister.

There was much truth in the saying that Hua Hin is the Aberystwyth of the Orient without the castle and without the funicular. It was on my way, so why not avail myself of some peace and quiet?

I arrived after dark. Pausing only for a vitamin drink at the station kiosk I made straight for the Railway Hotel, a mile away down a perfectly straight road that runs across the main Bangkok-Had Yai highway. With each step my constitution revived. I had escaped Bangkok, my head was still on my shoulders, and now the going had to be smoother.

The first intimation that everything was not as it had been occurred when I reached the hotel gate. Instead of the small sign saying 'Railway Hotel' there was a large sign saying 'Central Hua Hin Resort'. Below these words the management offered its sincere regrets for any inconvenience caused to guests during reconstruction.

The management?

A smart young woman at reception filled me in. The hotel and its grounds had been sold off to a private consortium composed of, *inter alia*, the Hyatt Group and Bangkok's Central Department Store. The only room available was an annexe, and that would cost 600 baht.

'600 baht! But the last time I came an annexe cost 200.'

'Sorry. New Management. No can make cheaper.'

There was nothing for it but to stay one night at least. I chewed a while on a particularly ferous spaghetti bolognese in the restaurant, then, when a waitress began smiling at me, made tracks.

Just down the highway was another new hotel, only this time it really was new. To my dismay the Royal Garden Resort, as it called itself, was a full-scale Pattaya Beach-type pleasure place. When I inquired about room-rates I was told that, even with a fifty per cent discount, I'd still need 1000 baht a night.

The second receptionist of the night smiled sadly when I told her I'd move on.

'But you come Night Club,' she urged. 'Have best girl Hua Hin.'

I made my way back to the Railway. The main street was still safe, but foolishly I decided to try a short-cut along one of the minor alleyways. Immediately she appeared from nowhere.

'What your name?'

'Cuthbert. What's yours?'

'Me Pasanu. How old you?'

'107.'

'Me thirteen.'

She wore a lot of eye-shadow and several kilos of orchid-mauve lipstick. I asked her where she lived. Pasanu pointed to a wooden shack and I took her there at once. Her mother appeared neither surprised nor aggrieved that her daughter seemed to be enjoying the company of a foreigner three times her age. Rather, she invited me to buy them both some beer.

Unsure whether this matron wasn't eyeing me for herself, I beat an inelegant retreat. Once back at the Railway I thought about going to my room, but in the end strolled down to the beach. As well as the quiet bars I remembered the local kids coming onto the sands at night and sitting round fires to sing songs beneath the Southern Cross. It would be nice if they were still there.

But they weren't. The beach was thoroughly deserted. Worse, the bar huts had vanished without trace. Instead what I saw was the timber-frame skeletons of some new holiday bungalows going up in a space formerly occupied by rare botanical specimens.

In despair I turned and saw another notice. This one read:

As there are now vendors or some other sellers building up their temporary shops on the public beach which belongs to the country, this conduct is somehow against the Cleanness and Tidiness Regulation Act of Thailand.

With immediate commencement, the municipality forbids all outsiders not to proceed any activity in the public as it is now underdeveloping and adjustable plan in order to maintain its beautiful nature for future tourist destination.

Out of the darkness a voice whispered, 'Hey mister, what your name?'

Part Two

FREE FALL

FOUR

Rock of ages

Mister was not out of the woods yet. I stayed four days in Hua Hin, and for two of them I was very sick indeed. I had caught the common cold. In Thailand the common cold is a good deal more virulent than it is for instance in Stoke Poges. It is like pneumonia in a minor key, and you can die if you don't take something for it. But the real problem was I didn't know it was the common cold. I thought it was the other thing.

Aids. There was just no getting away from it. At first it was a mere buzz on the horizon, travelling in an opposite direction. But the odd thing was it kept getting louder, until the word rang permanently between my ears. I couldn't switch on without hearing it. And then I went down with the common cold, only I didn't know it was the common cold, all I knew was the symptoms. Night-sweats, diarrhoea, general flu-iness, leg cramps, sore throat and aching lungs. Of course, the gamma globulin! In my case the virus hadn't waited, it had struck with the utmost celerity. This time I really was dying.

I couldn't hear myself think properly any more. Only the odd memory made any sense. For instance, a fling I'd had with a woman from Ghana, a year before my marriage. I could almost smell the caramel of her body on the sheet beside me. But Ghana of course was close to Zaire, and Zaire was the epicentre . . . And what was it I read yesterday in *Newsweek*? In New York people who hadn't had sex for eight years were queuing up for the test.

89

I had changed to the more modest Supamitra Hotel in the centre of town. Before finally committing myself to my deathbed I staggered out to a chemist's and loaded up with ampecilin. What I should have done is find a doctor, but doctors, in their white uniforms, now represented the enemy. Their pockets were full of unsterilized syringes. Or perhaps I was afraid they would take one look at my wasting body and think ah-ha, our seventh case, another *farang*. I had a vision of my life being needlessly prolonged, so that I could be exhibited at Chulalongkorn. The ampecilin would either cure me, if it wasn't Aids, or send my immune system into such a spin that I'd die at once.

One thing, though; now that I really was dying, being alone was no consolation at all.

I slipped four capsules into my mouth and swallowed hard. Then, for good measure, I took a couple of paracetamol, chased by three Dormicum. Within five minutes I was out cold. Twelve hours later, much to my surprise, I regained consciousness. I ordered up bread and a bowl of soup from the kitchen, and took three more ampecilin. I had no temperature whatsoever. A trick, of course. The medicines weren't curing me, they were simply repressing some of the symptoms.

To while away the time until my demise I read a book. But that didn't do any good either. All I had was Peter Fleming's *News From Tartary*, one of the classics of long-distance travel. In it Ian Fleming's brother describes crossing forbidden China in the mid-1930s, nearly 4,000 miles on horseback, ponyback and foot, putting up with virtually every discomfort known to man. But not one day lost to sickness! In comparison I was the complete wimp. The only point where our two journeys began to resemble each other was when Fleming wrote: 'He who starts on a ride of two or three thousand miles may experience, at the moment of departure, a variety of emotions. He may feel excited, sentimental, anxious, carefree, heroic, roistering, picaresque, introspective, or practically anything else; but above all he must and will feel a fool.' I could not recall feeling excited, roistering or introspective when I left England, but I certainly felt a fool. In fact I felt more of a fool as each day passed. But never so much as now. To find oneself dying of an undiagnosed disease in a third-class hotel at a beach resort that cared not for its better name was probably the most foolish thing there was.

'But I know how swiftly the beanstalk of procrastination grows in the soil of Asia,' Fleming had also written.

Beans' talk? Or Bean's talk?

My mind was flaking again. I looked at my watch. It was past four in the morning. I was sweating all over. High time for another Dormicum. Anything to silence that evil word.

One paradox of the tropics is that an illness often absconds as swiftly as it strikes. Next day I was horribly well again. At ten o'clock I grinned at myself in the shaving mirror. 'You haven't got it,' I gloated, 'and you're going to make it to Malaysia.'

I put on fresh clothes and scuttled off in search of amusement. In the market a crack-cheeked pedlar offered me an amulet – an old clay tablet with a relief of the Buddha on both sides encased protectively in plastic.

'Have two faces,' he urged, 'bring you many wives. Very lucky.'

So I bought it, not because I wanted many wives, nor because I wanted to think of myself as a Buddhist, but simply because it was a nice object, and it pleased me. It reminded me of Wat Pa Nana Chat and the structured existence some people are lucky enough to lead, so I decided to take it with me, and perhaps it would see me through. I was in that kind of mood. Merely finding myself alive on my two feet was sufficient grounds for a surge of frivolity.

As well as the talisman I purchased a silver chain and a large tin of St Luke's Prickly Heat powder. Next I stopped for a plate of rice at a restaurant on the road leading down to the beach. There I had an almost free haircut. The waiters and waitresses admired my new pendant, and pretended to be surprised at how little I had paid for it. 'You very clever, mister, you no let anybody cheat you.' Then one of the women approached to request a favour. She wanted me to take down a letter to her boyfriend in England. On condition that she afterwards show me a good barber, I agreed. But that was unnecessary. The woman had worked in a salon. She would cut my hair for me. For half an hour I sat semi-naked on a chair in the middle of the restaurant while the various waitresses took it in turns to give my head a new shape. Then I wrote the letter, following the chief hairdresser's dictation.

'Dear Simon,' it went (Simon incidentally lives in Bethnal Green), 'Thank you very very much for your sexy letter. I never forget you. In fact I think I really never forget you because now I am having a baby. You like me have your baby? I like it have your baby. Please come back

Thailand, come back Hua Hin, very very soon. Love you very very much, Simon. Love from Nit. Kiss kiss kiss.'

Nit was extremely pleased. In fact she was so pleased she asked me to write another, this time to Manfred (who lives in Mannheim).

'Dear Manfred,' I transcribed, 'I never forget the time you come Hua Hin and make me very very happy. In fact you really make me very very happy because now I am having a baby. You like me have your baby? I like it have your baby. Nit love only you, so Nit hope you come back Hua Hin very very soon. Love you very very much, Manfred. Love from Nit. Kiss kiss kiss.'

The second time round Nit was slightly less pleased. She looked at the two letters I had written for her and pulled a face.

'Same same,' she said, 'this letter, that letter, same same.'

'Yes, I'm sorry about that,' I replied. 'Same same. I see what you mean. It's really no good at all, is it?'

I swam, then I walked up to the station to book myself a seat on the Bangkok-Butterworth/Penang express. On the platform I fell in with a Californian Iranian whose name was Sean. Sean was pointing an extraordinarily long camera lens at the station bell just three feet in front of him.

'What are you doing?' I asked.

'Uh? I'm waiting for my Thai friend. Hey, would you do something for me? Would you tell me what you think of my video?'

'I think I'd have to see it first'

'No problem. We'll take you to the house. Len's got the car, and he'll be right here. We can have some food as well.'

A few minutes later Len showed up with his girlfriend, and I spent the early afternoon watching videos in a very private villa in a settlement of very private villas three miles down the coast. The house belonged to Len's father, who was a big shot in Bangkok – a general or a cabinet minister or the president of a company, or all three.

Sean's video was packed with good intentions. It was also stunningly iffy. Its subject matter was Wat Tham Krabok, an up-country temple whose Abbot had devised a new method for treating heroin addicts. The addict first swallows a secret mixture of rare herbs. Then he drinks four or five gallons of water. The herbs and the water interact to make the addict vomit the contents of his stomach in a sudden jet of yellow liquid that has the diameter and force of a fireman's hose. As this is going on the addict clutches his sides in an avowal of horror.

The thrust of the cure was twofold; it purified the addict's corrupted insides, and it imprinted an unpleasant association in his mind between taking heroin and the water torture.

'Don't you think you should try this in London?' Sean asked. 'Don't you think it's what's needed to clean up our cities?'

'Oh yes, try it in London,' Len put in. 'Drive over Buckingham Palace. Tell your Queen.'

What made Sean's video different from any other video about Thai temples and Thai monasteries was its narrator. The narrator was one of the monks, a black American from Harlem who delivered a selection of Buddhist precepts with hot-gospelling ardour. It was as if the soundtrack had been hijacked from another documentary and tacked on to fill a vacuum.

'Trouble is,' said Sean perspicaciously, 'he's still a Christian.'

'Yes,' said Len. 'Him Christian, him plant, him CIA agent. Want some?'

As we watched Sean's masterpiece Len had puffed away at marijuana cheroots. Now he was experimenting with a plastic detergent bottle. Smoking gancha through a plastic detergent bottle was his discovery, Len insisted, *his* copyright. But I was welcome to try it. Or if I didn't want to try it through a plastic detergent bottle I could stick to a coke can like everybody else.

'Thank you, but I'd rather not.'

'Body hurt,' Len went on, inhaling hard. 'This morning go swim, take gancha. Yesterday see man ride by horse smoking. So I want to try go swim smoke gancha. Must be number one turn-on. But now body hurt, chest hurt. Maybe go to sleep soon. You want to see other video, American video?'

As something started bubbling in one of his detergent bottles Len sprang to his feet and slotted in a fresh tape. Instead of the anticipated pornography I found myself viewing the title sequence of *Citizen Kane*.

'That why come here,' Len explained. 'No one my family like Orson Well, so no can show Bangkok. Come Hua Hin, watch Orson Well, smoke gancha, make happy time with girlfriend.'

'Oh yes?'

'Every week come Hua Hin. Every day.'

I looked pointedly at my watch.

'I think perhaps it's time for me to be going.'

'You want to walk beach fly kite? Smoke gancha fly kite number one fantastic turn-on.'

'No. You stay here. You look very comfortable.'

'You want to ride horse. Ride horse all the way back Hua Hin, look like John Wayne. Why don't you do that?'

'Because I'm not John Wayne?'

Len laughed. The fact that I wasn't John Wayne was clearly the number one fantastic turn-on to end all number one fantastic turn-ons. He laughed and laughed and laughed. Then he began to guffaw. Guffawing is not an activity one readily associates with Thais, but even so Len guffawed. He guffawed so hard that soon his face began breaking up. This, though, was no great feat. The peculiar thing about Len was that, age-wise, he was indeterminate. He could have been twenty or he could have been forty. Just as easily he could have been fifty. There was simply no way of telling. His face was not lined so much as seamed. It was a face that had been put together in a hurry. His ears were different colours and different sizes. Ditto his eyes. Even his teeth looked borrowed. And when he guffawed all the components of his face began to separate, as though anxious to return to their original homes.

After a while Len stopped guffawing and started choking. Sean said, 'I don't want to watch this,' and went to another room. At once Len's girlfriend appeared and began massaging his shoulders. Len meanwhile continued choking.

I left. I walked a hundred yards up the beach in the direction of Hua Hin, stopped, removed all my clothes and plunged into the sea. I swam out a long way, found my feet still touched the sand, and swam out further. Normally I would have been afraid of jellyfish and sharks, but not today. Today was okay, today was all right. As soon as I was out of my depth I began floating on my back. The current spun me round in slow circles. The distant palm-fringed beach came and went, came and went. On the seventh gyration I observed a figure running to and fro along the beach under a fish-shaped kite that bobbed seventy feet up in the sky. It was Len. Either he had made a startling recovery, or his spirit had liberated.

But how old was he, I still vexed: twenty, forty or fifty?

Then it came to me. A poor man's California. That's what Thailand was. Bangkok, Ubon Ratchathani, Hua Hin. Everywhere, same same. Poor man's California.

*

'If you go by train when you might have gone by air,' Peter Fleming wrote in his book, 'you are certainly old-fashioned, hard-up or a fool.' What applied in 1936 applied twice as much fifty years on. On the other hand I did have a legitimate excuse for doing it the hard way. My visit to Hong Kong the year before had not been altogether fruitless. Among the people I had met on Lantau Island was Derek Davies, the editor of the Cathay Pacific flight magazine. When I dropped him a note outlining my Solomon Islands journey and asking whether I could be of service *en route* Derek responded enthusiastically. He was lining up a special issue on railways and he needed someone to log either the Bangkok–Singapore run, or the Jakarta–Surabaya run. Blithely I undertook to log both. The money would pay my core expenses, and I would be able to stop off wherever I liked.

For instance: from Singapore I could nip across to northern Borneo, where I had another, more private, commission to fulfill.

On the map it all looked so easy. The 2000-odd miles of railway track telescoped into less than five inches, and by the end I would still be on course. Once in Surabaya I could go along to the docks and find a cargo bound either for Port Moresby or for Honiara itself. No sweat. Simple as parrot pie.

And so, to begin with, it was. To be sure, the train that took me from Bangkok to Hua Hin was not the quickest thing on sixty wheels, but at least it was safe. In the open-plan second-class carriage all the female passengers between the ages of 15 and 50 wanted to know where I came from, and what my name was, but there was not very much they could do with this information once they had elicited it. Conceivably there was a massage parlour in another carriage ahead or behind me, but so long as I kept to my seat by the window no great harm could befall me. Indeed, sitting quietly by the window was a pleasure in itself. The vastly appealing tropical landscape slipped by at just the right speed. Generally there were blue mountains in the distance, rice paddies or jungle in the middle ground and wooden shacks along the side of the track. It could have grown monotonous, but in fact it was therapeutic. The rhythm of the scenery and the rhythm of the train blended in thought-provoking harmonies. And from time to time there were memorable vignettes. For instance, somewhere between Phet Buri and Cha-an I espied a young woman washing her hair in paddi water, a bottle of shampoo on the ground beside her. She was bent right over, examining the reflection of her face between the rice stalks. Then the sun rolled down and soon I saw a mountain temple silhouetted against the western sky. I could have been in Italy; for once the God I didn't believe in was smiling.

Periodically the on-board police removed their holsters and swept the carriage floor. The only threat came from the man on the other side of the gangway. From the moment the train left Bangkok Central he glared at me. He was built and dressed like a member of Dran's clan, i.e. he was very large and probably a farmer. He was also something of a saliva factory. Once a minute he gobbed a cartonful of the stuff out of his window. Between gobs he produced a flow of hideous noises from the depths of his craw. But he never once took his suspicious and unfriendly eyes off me. Even when he gobbed, with unnerving accuracy, his stare remained fixed. Yet all he really wanted was one of my biros. As soon as he was given it he stared at that instead, and then there was nothing in the world left to disturb my peace.

Even the bowl of *tom yum* soup, served in a cracked and grimy blue plastic saucer, did me more good than harm.

Prior to the Bangkok–Hua Hin train-ride my experience of *tom yum*, or Everything Soup as it might be called, had taught me to avoid it whenever possible. *If you take Tom Yum and within five minutes don't find yourself rushing for the john the chances are you'll live*, I once wrote in a notebook. *If you can hold out fifteen minutes then it is possible you won't have to go to hospital. And if you can make it to twenty-five minutes, you may avoid a fever.* This time I held out all the way to Hua Hin. To my amazement, when I stepped off the train, keenly followed by the avalanche of my bags, I actually felt *better*.

Not that that state of affairs lasted very long of course. The common cold was ready and waiting. Chronic vicissitude became the pattern of my travel. One day I was up, the next two I was down. After a while I even grew wary of feeling good because I knew whenever I felt good I would shortly be feeling awful. Nor was there much consolation to be drawn in reverse. Bad days were not necessarily followed by good days. Usually they were followed by very bad days.

Take for example the next leg of my train journey. No sooner had I recovered from the common cold than I was again beset by fears and anxieties. On paper nothing looked easier than crossing the Malay border on steel tracks. All I had to do was sit quietly by the window and the rest would see to itself. But this would never have satisfied my paranoia. There had to be something untoward. This time the theme was suggested by Sean's companion Len. The Bangkok-Butterworth express? Of course! Drugs!

Clearly the disaster about to overtake me went as follows. Somewhere between Hua Hin and Padang Besar, where the train enters mainland Malaysia, I was going to fall asleep. This was certain to be because all the Bangkok-Butterworth trains travel through the night. Whilst I was asleep a professional drugs-runner was going to secrete a few kilos of white death somewhere in my luggage – since it had no lock, my typewriter was the obvious candidate. I'd wake up to find a bevy of armed and uniformed customs-men applying the cuffs. There'd be no breakfast until I was securely under lock and key, and then it would be a cup of hangman's tea or a slice of executioner's toast.

Or try this scenario. I get to the border. No one has planted anything on me. Even so the customs officials are decidedly interested. The lone male travelling south after several weeks in Thailand, etc. One of them finds the counterfoil of my plane ticket to Ubon Ratchathani. 'So, mister, you've been up country? Now please, don't give us that routine about visiting a Canadian abbot. Look. Even your own tourist literature makes it clear. In I-San there are only Australian abbots!' Next up my little red canister of Linus Vitamin C Powder. 'Perhaps you'd care to open this for us?' I do so. The contents are taken away for forensic analysis. The results are not what they should be. The lab technician is a malicious incompetent. Clink, clunk, clonk!

Or, instead of the vitamin powder, it's my malaria pills that are confiscated. In due course they are returned. 'Sorry sir, our mistake.' But meanwhile, as I lie languishing in a bamboo prison for a week, the mosquitos have gone to work. Now I am too weak even to say, *That's all right chaps, keep on with the good work*. For the irony is I'm not altogether sure drug-runners shouldn't have their heads chopped off. These days they were distributing a double mortality.

Of course, I'd been listening to too many back-packers. Every day hundreds of passengers crossed the frontier at Padang Besar untouched by either drug-dealers or corrupt/incompetent customs officials. But back-packers don't like safe travel, so they exaggerate and invent wildly.

'It's diabolical what some of these people will get up to,' a semi-bearded Australian said on my last night in Hua Hin. 'Take last

month. Last month a man and woman flew down from Bangkok to
K.L.. Flew down, mark. In her arms the woman carried a baby. It was
dead, naturally. It had had its insides taken out and replaced with pure
opium. Can you imagine? Beats swallowing condoms any day of the
week.'

'And were they caught?'

'How should I know, sport?'

So here was a new challenge: how to get in and out of Malaysia
without being misapprehended for a drugs smuggler and strung up on
the gallows?

It did not bear thinking about, which is why, in my room at the
Supramitra, I thought about it a great deal. The best thing, I decided,
was to book a first-class couchette to myself. I returned to the station
and changed my ticket. At first the station-master was loath to help.
Booking a first-class cabin was a complicated business. He had to ring
Bangkok on a bad line, and there was no guarantee his instructions
would be either comprehended or carried out. But for once I was in no
mood to take no for an answer. I began shouting at the man and
continued shouting until I got what I wanted. Sometimes you have to
shout at people until they understand you are serious. It's a crude and
undignified procedure, but it always works.

Afterwards, though, I wondered whether it had been appropriate to
shout. I could imagine the station-master at Hua Hin making another
call, to his close chum the Chief of Police at Padang Besar. 'Sorry to
bother you old man, but I thought I should let you know. I had a
hysterical *farang* in here this afternoon. Yes, that's right, an Englishman. Insisted on a first-class berth all to himself for tomorrow's train.
Obviously up to something. Name of Wintle. Will you pick him up or
shall we?'

When I boarded the train my card was, I felt certain, already
marked. The first thing that happened was a man calling himself the
purser confiscated my passport.

'What for?' I demanded nervously.

'Give immigration office Had Yai. When train reach Had Yai mister
asleep. No want to wake up. I take care everything for you.'

'But really I'd rather keep my passport. If anyone wants to see it I'll
show it to them. I don't mind being woken up at Had Yai. In fact I'd
like to be woken up at Had Yai.'

I snatched the passport back, but the purser snatched it away again.

'Mister don't worry. Mister not need passport again.'

When it came to locking me up in my expensive cabin, however, the purser was a good deal more obliging. He did it with alacrity and he did it with grace.

The cabin itself was a plausible simulacrum of the prison cell I'd been dreaming about. It had a small barred window, a bench bed and an evil washbasin that folded into the wall beneath a deeply patina-ed mirror. The only thing I probably wouldn't find in jail was the air-conditioning. Or perhaps I would. Like its counterpart in the British Embassy it could not be switched off. By the time the train pulled into Padang Besar at eight o'clock the following morning I was reduced to a slab of frozen mutton. All that was needed now was the butcher's saw. When I heard the long-awaited tap on my door it was with some difficulty that I drew back the inside bolt. But it was not just the ice-cold that made my fingers shake uncontrollably. It was also apprehension. The hour had come. In fact I shook so badly that the customs official had to ask twice if I was feeling myself.

'Yes yes, I'm perfectly all right. Honestly. Which one would you like to look at first?'

The man ran his eye over my belongings and pointed to my army kit-bag.

'What's in that one?'

'That one?' I practically jumped out of my skin. 'Oh, that one. Clothes I'm afraid. That is, ninety per cent clothes. A few papers as well, perhaps. And the odd roll of film. I'll show you.'

'It's not necessary.'

'Not necessary? What do you mean it's not necessary?'

The customs official smiled. Every day he had to quell the anxieties of frightened passengers like me. Every day there was at least one who had incarcerated himself in a first-class couchette. It was the most demanding, the most tedious part of the job.

'You've got nothing to fear,' he said. 'We work on tip-offs. We know who's carrying drugs. And you're not one of them.'

'Really?'

'Yes really. If you go outside on the platform you can collect your passport.'

'And my baggage . . .?'

'Your baggage will be perfectly safe where it is.'

Welcome to Malaysia!

Outside was a row of booths like stalls at a fairground. A hundred other passengers had formed into seven or eight queues. They all looked tired but happy, having ridden in the second-and third-class compartments without concerning themselves. And they had the blessing of their new hosts. The tannoy system blared out vintage Rod Stewart. Only one man seemed remotely to share my anxiety. He was tall and of rugged appearance. For no particular reason I adjudged him a Swede. His distinguishing feature was a glass eye. At least, I assumed it was a glass eye. The fellow's jowl also twitched tremendously. How much heroin had he packed in his socket?

Several uniforms were also taking an interest in the Swede. Then I saw they were looking at me, too, and my jowl started twitching.

It was wholly irrational, but nothing I could do kept my face still. I saw what would happen. First they would arrest the glass-eyed hippy, then they would arrest me, as his putative accomplice.

Desperately I wanted to remove both my eyes and hand them over. To show that they were real. That I had nothing to hide.

*

Malaysia offered a sober contrast to the country I had just left. The TV (tropical vegetation) was darker than in Thailand and, instead of endless patchwork paddis, I now saw, through the tiny window of my cell, endless plantations. Rubber, palm oil, banana. S.E. Asia as redesigned by the British Empire. Orderliness on the imperial scale. Fewer people, too. Possessing approximately the same land area as its neighbour, Malaysia has less than a third of the population: 13,000,000 on the mainland, another 2,000,000 across the water in Sarawak and Sabah, the two provinces of Borneo not under Indonesian rule.

Stepping off the train at Butterworth the first thing I noticed was crash-helmets. Sikhs apart, all Malaysian motorcyclists are obliged to wear crash-helmets. In Thailand I couldn't recollect having seen a single crash-helmet, on or off a cyclist's head. A small thing, but indicative of a fundamentally differing attitude towards life.

Or again, this statistic, culled from a copy of *The New Straits Times* purchased at Padang Besar: sixty per cent of home buyers in Malaysia belong to the civil service.

For remaining loyal to the Crown during the Emergency of 1948–55, when the peninsula was infested with Chinese communist bandits, the Malay people had been rewarded with independence. In 1964 there was a smooth transition to self-rule. The old colonial administration, already staffed with Malay nationals (Malays, Tamil Indians and a few Chinese), survived almost unchanged, a ready-made bureaucracy for the fledgling polity. In S.E. Asia the new Federation of Malay States was the first corporatist state.

The trouble started in 1965 when Singapore, predominantly Chinese, pulled out of the Federation. This helped refuel an abiding rivalry between the Malays and the Chinese, culminating in bloody riots in the capital, Kuala Lumpur, in 1969. The central problem was, and is, crude British-style democracy. The Malays, who understandably look upon Malaysia as belonging exclusively to themselves, comprise less than sixty per cent of the people. The Chinese make up roughly thirty per cent, and Indian immigrants ten per cent. In addition, in Borneo, there are various ethnic minorities (the Dayaks, the Iban) whom nobody wants very much to be associated with. Nonetheless, because of the first-past-the-post electoral system, the Malays are firmly in control. Only in one of the Federation's thirteen states, Penang, is the regional government dominated by anyone else, the Chinese. But because Penang is also subject to federal rule, it is inhibited from developing as quickly as it would like. With striking yellow ferries toing and froing across a narrow strait from Butterworth, Penang looks like another Hong Kong. It is the country's most prosperous city. But the government doesn't want Penang to become too prosperous. It is afraid that Penang will follow Singapore down Independence Avenue. Better the goose that lays half a golden egg than a goose that lays claim to its whole produce.

But why should hard-working, business-minded Chinese burghers want to secede?

In theory they shouldn't. In theory they should be free to pursue their traditional diasporic philosophy: it doesn't matter who holds the head of the cow so long as we are allowed to milk it. This they were able to do under British rule. Pax Britannica and all that. The point of course is that the Chinese were good at milking, which the Malays weren't. The Malays, as it happens, have proved themselves good at running the sort of large bureaucratic structures bequeathed them by their colonial masters. But they do not excel as businessmen. They lack entrepreneurial *esprit*.

So why not just give the Chinese free access to the udder and levy reasonable taxes thereafter, for the benefit of those Malays unlucky enough not to have joined the Civil Service?

But Islam's not like that. And it is because of Islam that, little by little, Malaysia is sinking in the mire.

It didn't take long to smell what was happening. It was evident on the front page of every copy of *The New Straits Times* I read. Under the stewardship of Prime Minister Datuk Seri Mahathir Mohammed the all-Moslem cabinet was introducing a series of reforms designed to turn Malaysia into a more stridently Moslem state than it already was. Yet the curious aspect of this policy was that its motivation appeared to be economic as much as cultural or religious. The 'Chinese Question' had faded during the 1970s, largely because the Malay economy, based on tin and rubber, had flourished. The 1980s, however, told a different story. By 1985 the Malay economy was in sharp recess, principally, but not solely, because of a collapse in tin prices. In 1986 there was little sign of recovery, albeit other ASEAN economies (Thailand, Indonesia, even the Philippines) were picking up again. The reason Malaysia lagged behind, Moslem commentators suggested, was that Malaysia was not like Japan or Korea. If the country was to gain its rightful place in the world market what it needed was a one-people, one-language, one-culture system. Minorities were bad news. Minorities should be brought to heel.

The Cabinet, if it wanted a model for international success, would have been better advised to look at America. Odd though it may seem, Malaysia has more in common with the United States than it does with Japan. Both are multi-cultural societies, both have plentiful stocks of natural resources. But pluralism is anathema to Islam. Therefore the cabinet had irrationally opted for the Japanese model, thus breaking the first principle of any politics: work with what you've got, not with what you'd like to have.

In Malaysia everything is slowly being forced to its unnatural extreme. Thanks to the bigotry of a small ruling élite, reinforced by an antiquated aristocracy that furnishes eleven of the thirteen states with costly sultanates, the outlook is bleak. Not so long ago it was a nation that saw itself on the brink of the future. Now its future was on the brink of ruin. The dire fortunes of other Indo-Chinese colonies (Vietnam, Cambodia, Laos) had been avoided. But as tomorrow comes this is scant consolation. Thanks to a new cultural chauvinism, veiling an old racism, Malaysia is a nation losing its heart while yet in its infancy.

Even the Chinese are going round in circles:

Yeap's mum treated his wives alike court told
By Alan Neoh

PENANG; Tues. – The two women married to millionaire Datuk Yeap Hock Hoe during a double wedding in 1951 were treated equally by their mother-in-law, a High Court was told today.

Madam Lee Cheng Lee, 61, said that Madam Lee Cheng Kin, her cousin sister [sic] and wife of the late Datuk Yeap Chor Ee, had treated the two women – Mdm Hooi Sooi Wan and Mdm Yam Kim Lean – equally.

'She told me that herself,' Mdm Lee Cheng Nee replied when defence counsel Gurdial Singh Nijar suggested that Mdm Lee Cheng Kim was closer to Mdm Yam.

Mdm Lee Cheng Nee was testifying in a suit by Mdm Hooi Sooi Wan, 53, who is claiming that she is the principal wife of Datuk Yeep Hock Hoe, the son of the founder of Ban Hin Lee Bank, Datuk Yeap Chor Ee.

Mdm Hooi is seeking a declaration that her sons – engineer Leong Soon, 33, and businessman Leong Gwan, 32 – are Datuk Yeap Hock Hoe's lawful sons so that they would be entitled to certain benefits under Datuk Yeap Chor Ee's will.

Datuk Yeap Chor Ee died on May 26, 1952, leaving behind an estate worth $9.5 million [Malay dollars].

Mdm Hooi named Mdm Yam's three sons – Yeap Leong Theam, Leong How and Leong Chin – as defendants.

Also named as defendants are Jimmy Yeap, Leong Aun (who was shot during a kidnap attempt last year) and trustees Yeap Teik Leong and Stephen Yeap Leong Huat.

Leong Theam, the late Jimmy Yeap, Leong How and Leong Chin have been named as beneficiaries.

Mdm Lee Cheng Nee said after the wedding, Mdm Yam moved into a house which was two houses away from the Yeap's residence on Jalan Sultan Ahmad Shah – Homestead – while Mdm Hooi lived with Datuk Yeap Hock at Homestead.

She said that the house was built and financed by Mdm Lee Cheng Kin, specially for Mdm Yam.

'After 1951, Kim Lean and her family came regularly to Homestead for visits,' she said.

Earlier Mdm Lee Cheng Nee said she stayed at Homestead from 1946 at the invitation of Mdm Lee Cheng Kin, and lived there until 1971.

103

When she first moved into Homestead, she said, Datuk Yeap Hock Hoe was married to Mdm Hooi Kum Chee, the elder sister of Mdm Hooi Sooi Wan.

She said she first heard of Mdm Yam from Mdm Hooi Kum Chee who said that her husband had a mistress living in Lorong Selamat.

However, Mdm Lee Cheng Nee said she did not believe it until after Mdm Hooi Kum Chee's death. Mdm Lee Cheng Kin told her that her son was going out with his late wife's fourth sister.

But the relationship did not work out and sometime after, Datuk Yeap Hock Hoe began going out with his wife's fifth sister (Hooi Sooi Wan), Mdm Lee added.

Later, Mdm Lee Cheng Nee said she moved out of Homestead after Datuk Yeap Hock Hoe accused her of being a 'kay-po' (busy-body).

Hearing continues tomorrow.

New Straits Times

Anyone with the patience to unravel a quarter of the above is, I suggest, already batting for the close of play*.

After Bangkok, I had no wish to concern myself with the state of the nation. I wanted only to be the ordinary traveller, coming from one place and going to another. Yet even on the most cursory visit the mood, which was one of disenchantment, got through to me. It was there, in the air, all around. Slouched in their sarongs the Malay men stared dolefully from behind their scrawny Charles Bronson moustaches. The Malay women in their traditional Moslem dresses, like sleek, faintly voluptuous nuns, fastened their eyes demurely on the ground. Everywhere there was a lack of excitement, a lack of fizz. Even in Penang, among the modern Chinese, the people seemed to move around a gear lower than in other oriental cities. There was something mechanical about the way they packed soberly into the fast food restaurants at the end of the day. Probably they were making money, but they weren't getting rich. Their relatively comfortable existence was no more than a habit, a duty. Outside, caught tangentially by the setting sun, the green-stuccoed neo-classical buildings along the old harbour front somehow failed to take advantage of the last light. Georgetown was already asleep. It had been asleep for twenty years.

Sad. Or was I simply failing to respond? Against the odds I began

*Six months after writing this section two prominent opposition leaders, Lim Kit Siang and Karpal Singh, were jailed for two years apiece, for 'encouraging racial unrest'.

missing Thailand, for all her faults. I missed the monkey business, I missed the restless friendliness, I missed – yes, why not? – constant temptation. Being constantly tempted against my better judgment was bad enough, but not being tempted was worse. The Malays were perfectly civil, but none of them were out to share their humanity. On my way back to the ferry-point I walked straight through a market without anyone trying to sell me anything. The only joy was a notice tacked to a shuttered shop: *Jellyfish Manufacturer*, it said.

At the Kuala Lumpur Hotel in Butterworth, where I stayed two nights, there was an attempt to get me to visit the Happy Health Club on the second floor, but even this was half-hearted.

'You want to have a massage?' the Chinese receptionist (female) yawned. And again, as I lay on my bed watching *My Fair Lady* on telly, a man telephoned and asked the same question.

'I'm fine as I am,' I answered. 'But thank you for asking.'

'That's okay, sir. Happy Health Club very empty tonight. Come down any time.'

And, with another yawn, the line went dead.

It was strange, though, the Happy Health Club at the Kuala Lumpur Hotel in Butterworth. As far as I could tell, checking through the list of hotels given me by the Malaysian Tourist Board, the Kuala Lumpur was one of only three establishments in the whole country that boasted such a facility. Not of course that that was why I chose it. I chose it because the rooms were relatively cheap, and because it was within walking distance of the station.

It was not until I was in Perak and met Norbert Dass that the matter was properly explained to me.

'The Kuala Lumpur Hotel in Butterworth is well known,' Dass said. 'Just because it is cheap and near the station it's the sort of place first-time drug smugglers stay when they get off the train from Bangkok. Naturally they want to have a massage. Usually the Happy Health Club sends a girl straight up to their room. After she has done her thing the girl asks casually whether her client would like a smoke. If he says yes she provides him with some Thai-stick perhaps. Then she asks him if he wants something stronger. So the talk turns to narcotics. If it turns out he already has his own supply they report him to the police. So he gets properly fleeced. And perhaps he gets properly hanged as well.'

Sylvester Norbert Dass, a civil servant who ran the employment office in the small town of Sitiawan in the state of Perak, was the best thing about mainland Malaysia. A man of considerable charm and intelligence, he had managed, by dint of hard work and virtue, to achieve a middling to high grade. But further promotion was unlikely – Norbert was a Tamil and a Christian. Within the last two years his prospects had been dashed. He wouldn't say why they had been dashed, only that they had been.

'I can sing Rock Of Ages until I'm seventy,' he said, 'but I'll still be where I am today – if I'm lucky!'

Singing Rock Of Ages was Norbert's favourite expression. He used it forty-seven times a day. But then in Sitiawan hardly a minute went by when he couldn't use it. Even driving around the backstreets the excuse might be right in front of him, or right behind him.

If Norbert found himself stuck behind a slow-moving truck he'd honk the horn and say:

'What does the blighter want me to do? Sing Rock Of Ages?'

Or if Norbert found himself in front, carefully observing the speed-limit, with another vehicle hooting impatiently in his rear, he'd grin sideways and say:

'Oh let the blighter sing Rock Of Ages! I'm not putting *my* foot down to break the law!'

Norbert and his Chinese Christian wife Lucy lived, with their two children, in a smart *kampong* on the town's outskirts. Lucy contributed to the household economy by working as a nurse at the hospital in nearby Lumut. I had been given their address by a relative, then living in the Belgravia house where Lord Lucan's nanny had been murdered – the event that presaged Lord Lucan's disappearance. I had never met the Dasses before, but that didn't prevent them, when I rang from Butterworth, from insisting I stay a few days at least. This promise of Asian hospitality, which of all hospitalities is the most readily proffered, was greatly welcome. Since arriving in Bangkok I had lived in hotels, and hotels, however accommodating, tend, over a period of weeks, to discombobulate the personality. A spell of law-abiding domesticity was exactly what was needed.

To get to Sitiawan I continued my journey down the west coast as far as Batu Gajah. The local train trundled like a wheelbarrow on a cinder track through places whose names sounded to me like items from the menu of a vegetarian restaurant on Mars: Bukit Mertajam, Nibong Tebal, Parit Buntar, Alor Pongsu, Salak Utara. At Batu Gajah I hired, for a mere £7, a dented Mercedes Benz and its driver to take me the remaining 40 kilometres. The Dasses, when I arrived, had already vacated their main bedroom in favour of their unknown guest. The turkey gobbling in the front garden, bought the week before for the Dasses' Christmas dinner, looked as though it had just been shampooed.

They did not treat me like royalty, however. They treated me as a person should be treated – with warmth, sincerity and a growing affection. Nor, like some orientals, did they attempt to present themselves in a better light than they normally inhabited. They talked openly about the difficulty of making ends meet, and in the car they criticized each other's driving. 'This car is going straight to blazes!' Norbert cried when Lucy very deftly avoided crushing a teenage cyclist against the side of a truck overtaking on the inside. 'Norbert is singing Rock Of Ages again,' said Lucy when Norbert didn't accelerate from the lights quite as fast as Nigel Mansell. 'If you can buy the milk,' her husband returned, 'why buy the cow?'

'We're awful, aren't we?' Lucy apologized.

'Not at all,' I replied. 'Any wife who deprecates her husband's driving is giving vent, in sublimated form, to a concern for the integrity of his skin. It's a well-established psycho-sociological fact.'

'Oh yes,' said Norbert. 'I don't know what you mean but it's as true as Galileo's telescope.'

What could be nicer, what could be more delightful than a few idle days *chez* Dass? Norbert was a twenty-four-hour encyclopaedia. He taught me the rudiments of tropical vegetation, how for example to distinguish between the date palm, the oil palm and the coconut palm. Indeed, once Norbert the naturalist got started there was not a lot I didn't learn. Every path we walked along he transformed into an Indian apothecary. This plant was good for curing pneumonia, that plant contained an antidote to hepatitis. Eat the leaves of that one over there and your ulcer will go to blazes. A whole new Culpeper. But Norbert was equally at home with anything mechanical. He knew the strengths and weaknesses of all the other citizenry. 'You see that fellow going into the Post Office,' he might volunteer, 'he's heading for a smash. He used to be a policeman, now he's trying to sell his wife's apron.' Or: 'That man's an oily man. You know what an oily man is? A thief. He goes naked at night, covered in oil, so nobody can catch the rotten blighter.'

The scenery was equally hospitable. The land around Sitiawan was all highly cultivated, which gave me my first close-up view of a rubber plantation. Indeed I stumbled onto a plantation unwittingly. On the morning after my arrival I crossed the narrow road in front of the Dass residence accompanied by the Dass Xmas dinner. At first I thought it was just a bit of uncleared forest. Then I saw something peculiar. Somebody had tied an old tin cup to one of the trunks, about three feet above the ground. Why should anyone want to do that? Then I noticed all the trees had cups tied to them and the penny dropped. 'I've been inspecting the quality of the *kampong*'s latex,' I announced triumphantly when asked what I had been doing.

Better still was the local coast, and the sea eagles of Pangkur. Lumut itself, despite its proximity to a newly built naval arsenal, had a certain charm. Formerly it was a small colonial port and sea-spa. It had a sanatorium on the water front, overlooking the estuary of the Dingding River. Now all that remained were a dozen wooden posts protruding from the water – the protected bathing area. The old buildings had gone, replaced by a new government rest-house. At dusk the mile-long promenade, lined with heavy iron lamps and primitive Dutch cannon, swarmed with sightseers. The sight they had come to see was a Lumut sunset. On a good day a Lumut sunset deserved to hang in a gallery.

Or perhaps they were returning from Pangkur. Pangkur is a resort island approximately seven miles from Lumut and approximately seven miles long. Anybody who knows Phuket will know what I mean if I say that Pangkur is like Phuket before the Thai Tourist Board recognized Phuket's potential as yet another venue for foreign visitors to sample Thai women. As yet the facilities were basic. Tiny A-shaped bungalows for sleeping in, and noodle-stalls up and down the beaches. Thither I was taken, to dip myself in the periphery of the Malacca Strait.

The water was warm, but soiled. The sea-eagles, however, spotted from the boat going home, made up for that. There were two of them, pirouetting high in the empyrean, crisp white against the polychromatic pastels of the early evening. And then, closer to land, a third, describing the same slow circles before a curtain of jungle creeper that overhung a high sheer cliff. Around and around and around, a chain of linked rings designed perhaps to mesmerize its prey. For suddenly the bird was gone, and suddenly the bird was there again, something small, live and thrashing in its beak.

*

After Lumut, Pangkur, sea-eagles and an Indian restaurant where
dhosi was served on fresh banana leaves – obliged to use my fingers, I
had the uncanny sensation that I was no longer in Malaya, but had
been mystically transported to a suburb of Calcutta – there was one
supreme treat to come.

Late on Saturday night the Dasses asked whether I wanted to
accompany them to church in the morning. I declined politely. I had
letters to write, I said. When I awoke I went downstairs to find the
house deserted. Setting my typewriter on the dining table I clacked
away for twenty minutes. Then I fell into a reverie.

For some years I have made a habit of listening to anyone who
participated, in whatever capacity, in the Malay Emergency. My
interest in the Emergency is diffuse. To begin with it was the last
colonial war fought by the British in S.E. Asia. Secondly, there was a
connection with the Vietnam War which has never been properly
brought out, for the tactics used by Gerald Templer to defeat the
Chinese communists were copied, disastrously, by some Americans.
What seems to have happened is that a few of the Chinese 'bandits'
sought refuge in Hanoi, where they were later able to advise the
Vietcong of the nature of the measures adopted against them. It was
not just their experience of British counter-insurgency techniques that
enabled them to do this: they had also compromised British intelligence. Thirdly, like any war, the Emergency threw up all manner of
weird/entertaining/ghoulish stories. Fourthly, my informal researches
brought me into contact with Britons who belonged not just to
another generation, but almost to another culture. There were many
good reasons why one might wish to take off for the jungles of Indo-
China, but killing Chinese, whether or not they were communists,
should not have been one of them.

The Emergency can be summarized as follows. Before the Second
World War there was a small communist element in British Malaya,
but not a significant one. Mainly it was restricted to certain of the
Chinese-led trade unions. During the war, however, the communists
in Malaya gained some respectability by pitching in against the
common foe. They were given rifles and told to go and kill some Japs in
the jungle. After the war they hung on to their rifles and started killing
white imperialists. Their motives were somewhat suspect since, being
Chinese, any claim they made for themselves by way of being a

liberation army was at best tendentious. The Malay population wanted nothing to do with them, so the only inference that made sense was to behold in their activities the long arm of an international communist plot. (Interestingly, although they did receive support from communists outside Malaya, there is also evidence that they received financial encouragement from the Japanese, whose interests clearly did not coincide with the restitution of European dominance in post-war Asia.) Beginning in 1948 the insurgents began attacking select targets from their jungle hide-outs. The white planters, living in isolated houses on their plantations, were particularly vulnerable, and there were any number of unpleasant episodes. But the Malays were also terrorized. The standard tactic of the bandits was to visit a village and tell the villagers to have food and other provisions ready by the following day. If the food wasn't ready, they said, they'd rape some of the women and kill anybody who tried to get in their way.

The terrorists did well. In fact they did very well. Eventually 250,000 imperial troops were dispatched to deal with them, and still they weren't beaten. It was not until the bandits ambushed and murdered the Governor General, Sir John Gurney, in 1952, that the tide was turned. Field Marshal Templer, the British Army's most formidable disciplinarian, was posted to take charge. He worked (a) to bolster the troops' morale (b) to improve the network of police spies, and (c) to protect the villages, or *kampongs*. The way he did this last was, in essence, to surround the *kampongs* with tripwire so that any unwelcome intruders were immediately identified. As a result the guerrillas soon started running short of supplies, and their own jungle discipline deteriorated. Flushing them out became easier, and Britain won the war. (In Vietnam the Vietcong dug tunnels under the tripwires, and the Americans lost the war.)

My favourite Emergency stories concerned the Gurkhas, brought in because their Asian physiques ideally suited them to Asian warfare. The Gurkha regiments were staffed by British officers. One of these was Major G, also known as the Major With Black Privates. Major G's contribution to war tactics was to disguise his soldiers as harvest women and post them in the fields. Along came the bandits and threatened to rape them unless, tomorrow, they gave them food. Tomorrow came, but no food with it. *We're afraid in that case we'll have to rape you*, said the bandits, unbuckling themselves. The harvest women lifted their skirts, the kukris flashed, and the bandits discovered their mistake. The trouble was, Major G began taking an unhealthy interest in the details of his Gurkhas' make-up. With each sortie they became more and more alluring, until one day Major G decided his Ghurkhas weren't men any more. They really were beautiful young girls, and he began responding to them accordingly. But it was all right in the end. Major G finished his campaign in a nice white mental hospital where he was looked after by nice white nurses. Patently these nurses were Scots Guards in drag, but by sticking to both illusions the Major recovered his balance.

Another good story was the tale of Sergeant Y. Sergeant Y was a hard-working, hard-killing Gurkha whose refusal to wash made him unpopular with his fellows. Soon he stank to high heaven, and his commanding officer decided to take action. He warned Sergeant Y that unless he took a shower he'd have him court-martialled. Sergeant Y refused. Rather than carry out his threat, the officer ordered a squad of other Gurkhas to march the man to the bath-house. At first Sergeant Y wanted to stand under the shower with all his clothes on, but the officer told him that unless he took them off he really would be court-martialled. So, with the utmost reluctance, Sergeant Y removed his battle dress. Tied around his waist was a piece of string. On the string were threaded forty Chinese ears – the cause of the bad smell.

By these and other means the Empire went to great lengths to protect its interests in Malaya. It was a costly operation, but even so the accounts showed a profit. It was all worth it. The reason? Rubber.

*

I had met any number of old soldier johnnies, but I had never met a genuine planter. Now that I was in Malaysia I decided to set matters aright.

'Just one rubber johnny,' I mused aloud, 'just one rubber johnny . . .'

'Did you say something?'

Norbert, clad in a long nightshirt, was standing in the doorway of the downstairs bedroom. For once he was more concerned about himself than about his guest.

'You see we didn't make it to Church after all. Now I suppose we'll catch the dickens.'

'What do you mean?'

'We'll go to hell. Satan will put us both on his bonfire.'
Then he chuckled.
'When it comes to damnation,' he said, 'it's ladies first, isn't it?'
I shook my head.
'That,' I said, 'depends on whether you can introduce me to a rubber planter.'
'Easy,' Norbert replied, giving the matter barely a moment's thought. 'I'll introduce you to Mac. In fact we'll drive over and see him this afternoon.'

If the soubriquet didn't apply equally to Norbert, I would be tempted to describe Stewart McCulloch as a perfect specimen of that endangered species, Commonwealth Man. His house, on the other side of Sitiawan, was a largish stilted bungalow set in an enchanting two-acre garden. Formerly it had been the residence of the Assistant Manager of the Sitiawan Estate. Mac, wearing shorts and a slipover, greeted us in the drive. The skin on his neck reminded me of the Dass's turkey's gizzard, but otherwise he looked young for his years. A big loutish dog called Spot or Chip or Spiv almost knocked me down on the wooden steps up to the verandah. Inside, several small rooms were grouped around a more sizeable living room. The fan spinning slowly on the ceiling was a nasty modern plastic thing. The rattan furnishings, however, were for real.

We sat down, Mac eager to get on with the interview. At four, he apologized, he had another appointment. But first he pushed a clutch of photographs across the table – A5-size colour jobs, taken ten or so years before. Elephants, a near-naked boy fishing, a party of Malays roasting a baby deer over a camp fire. All jungle stuff except a yacht. Whilst I examined them he launched, staccato-like, into his story. Born Canada, but schooled in Scotland. Son of a sheepdog genealogist. Father wrote books, show them to you later. When the war started volunteered for the Indian Army. Went out. 4th Bombay Grenadiers. Tank protection corps. Wounded in Burma. Japanese bloody good soldiers. Thereafter Captain McCulloch of Intelligence. Seconded to the Chinese officer training programme, supervised by the Americans. Fearful business. Chinese permitted a 20% casualty rate. One cadet shot dead on the spot for backing his jeep into a Dakota. To encourage the others. Then back into Burma for the Second Campaign, alongside the Gordon Highlanders. Mountbatten. Gurkhas too. The difference between a wounded Gurkha and a wounded Jap: the Gurkha would attempt to smile, the Jap would attempt to spit. Very difficult to take a wounded Japanese prisoner. Always refused to surrender. Go too near him and he'd detonate a grenade. Had to shoot him sometimes. It was either him or the both of you. Awkward customers. One Japanese taken in unconscious. His guts shot to pieces. Got him properly bandaged in the field hospital. Made no difference, though. When he regained consciousness simply un-wrapped his dressings and bled to death when no one was looking. Preferred it that way. Brave people. Keep my M.C. in a Japanese box. Beautifully carved. Got it at the Battle of Kohima. The Military Cross, I mean. Not the box. Letter from King George VI. Then demobbed, and sent to Edinburgh University to study agriculture. 25 then. Hard work that, much harder than being a soldier. But never finished. Had a cousin already working in Malaya. Why not come out? the cousin said. Came out. Worked for Barlow's. Famous British plantation company. After a year took Planter's Federation examinations in Kuala Lumpur. Boss thought I'd fail. Doubled my pay when I passed. Thanks to India I already spoke Hindustani. That was the thing that got me through. Lucky. Saved my bacon. Plantation workers all Tamils. Six months later promoted Assistant Manager here in Perak. About 6000 acres and a workforce of 2000. Like a little kingdom really. Sometimes the office became a courtroom. Had to sort out their problems. If any of them started lying took him to the temple and made him swear on the ashes. That always broke them up. Religious lot. Couldn't lie on the ashes. Strong sense of perdition. Then, full Manager on plantations in Selangor and Kedah. Emergency in full cry by then. Tough living through it. For 12 years had to sleep between sandbags. Own guard, military escort, armoured cars. Two-way radio in the bungalow. Couldn't go out much. Dangerous. No social life beyond badminton with the local constable. But not a bad life. Kept very busy you see. Spent all day on the estate. And well-paid. About M$4000 a month plus free housing etcetera. Lucky. Remember Stuttering Thompson? Stuttering Thompson went to the St. Andrews Ball in K.L. with his wife. His two children murdered in their cots whilst they were gone. And then there was the Hairy One, a woman bandit. Viciously assaulted a colleague. Got them in the end. Templer did a fine job, though the station masters hated him. Myself, I never married. Came out single and stayed that way. If you married an Asian the company sacked you. But girls no problem, except there was never any time for them. Certainly not what you might imagine. Sitting around playing bridge with a gin sling in each hand – all that disappeared completely after the War. Gin slings before my time.

At 55 Mac was compulsorily retired. There was a new policy. Malay plantations to be run by the Malays. And why not? They're certainly up to it. Which is certainly more than the company accountant was. Balls-up over my pension policy. Bad investments. Actually managed to take out less than he'd put in. Therefore had to go on working. No directorship or anything at the end of the line. Directorships reserved for people back home who never set foot on a plantation. Went to the Philippines. Basilan in Zamboanga. One and a half years there, which was one and half years too long. Bad scene, Moro territory. Had the feeling I was being watched. Had to wear a gun again. Cleared out and went to Sumatra. But Sumatra was worse. Lasted just six months there. Couldn't stand it. Children working a fourteen-hour day for a bowl of rice and a few biscuits. Tiger country. Sumatra tigers with faces as big as bicycle wheels. Chucked it in and came back here. Bought this place, to go with the yacht. Bought the yacht thirty-six years ago, from a colleague's widow. Only cost two thousand five hundred. Old vessel but keep it trim. Called the *Matahari Cendung*, or Departing Sun. Sometimes hire it out. Tomorrow for example, a bunch of Japanese tourists. Otherwise use it to train youngsters. Founded the first troop of sea-scouts in Malaysia. Now involved with the Outward Bound programme. Duke of Edinburgh stuff. Looking for old pirate hideouts in the jungle. Sometimes come across secret villages – illegal Indonesian immigrants. And look after the garden. Take care of the dog. Found him in a sack in a pond. Somebody trying to drown the poor creature. Paint pictures when the time can be found. Which isn't often.

Stewart McCulloch had finished. He had left himself exactly enough time to show me over the bungalow. His father's books – John Herries McCulloch. His krises. His 300-year-old coffee pot. His Burmese bronzes. His carvings from Kashmir. His bottle cabinet. His sweet-smelling, highly polished camphor-wood chest.

'You ever feel like going back to Britain?'

'Scotland you mean? Absolutely not. There's nothing there. Talk to the doctor, talk to the schoolmaster, talk to the lawyer, and that's your lot. This is my home. I've got a red identity card. No vote, but they can't kick me out.'

Outside Norbert went almost mad with excitement. The garden had everything. Curry leaf, elephant's-ear, velvet flower, durian, cladium, jack-fruit, Penang nutmeg, henna hibiscus, even a shrub — *daun palas* — whose leaves could be used for polishing the fingernails. But best of all was the moonflower, which opens in the night, just once, and dies.

FIVE

Onto the skin of Borneo

The next stage I cheated. I should have gone back to Batu Gajah and continued my journey to Kuala Lumpur by train. But I didn't. Instead I took a coach all the way from Sitiawan. In any case I felt like cheating. I had a hunch that I wasn't going to like KL. Somebody had told me that the Kentucky Fried Chicken there was the busiest Kentucky Fried Chicken in the world. I couldn't imagine that a place which boasted that could boast much else.

My hunch proved correct. I didn't like KL. The atmosphere was appallingly humid. The city was drowned in a thick green haze that made my lungs ache again. Also, it was mostly very new – lots of flyways and glass office buildings and modern mosques – but without any of the convenience of the new. The street-map looked like a bowl of spaghetti thrown onto a plate of spinach. The streets themselves snaked around humps and bumps of grass that weren't big enough to be called parks or squares. They merely made it painful for the pedestrian. To get from A to B simply took longer, that was all. The buildings which should have been next to each other weren't. One had to cross six roads to go next door. And because the roads snaked and twisted like vermicelli you never quite knew what was going to hit you, or from which direction. Being there was like being inside the mind of a frenzied moth.

Moths. There were plenty of moths about. And butterflies. And scorpions. And all of them in glass boxes. They were the best of what the city had to sell the visitor. The souvenir shops sold Rajah Brookes by the hundredweight. Alfred Wallace and all that. Why not give Aunt Clothilda a pair of stag-beetles for her birthday? Mounted on a card.

What they didn't sell was cockroaches. But then cockroaches, as I soon discovered, were easy to come by without having to pay for them.

I stayed one night at The Lodge Hotel, an old and perfectly comfortable establishment opposite the infinitely more expensive Hilton, studied a few thousand scorpions, and then moved to the Station Hotel. It had not been my intention to stay anywhere my second night, but the Singapore Express was booked solid. I had the option of either travelling through the night, or going in comfort the following day. Finding myself at the station I checked into the Station Hotel.

At first I thought I had done the right thing. The Station Hotel was a part of the station which, built in 1916 in the style of an Indian fort, was by far and away the most attractive construction in the city. The rooms were upstairs, either side of a corridor carpeted in threadbare pink that petered out into the distance in both directions. And my room was *huge*. Not particularly well decorated, a bit like an empty warehouse in fact, but *huge*. On an extremely high ceiling two genuine late colonial fans had enough thrust to lift a small aircraft.

It was sad that I hadn't brought along a ballet corps. There was certainly enough space for one. A pair of wooden doors led to a covered balcony the size of a parade ground. Its beautiful round arches overlooked the street below. To such a place I could have invited everyone I'd ever met, for Pimm's, or rum punch, or a game of rounders.

The bathroom was less dimensional. Even so, it was the first hotel bathroom where the shower didn't either soak the toilet-paper or leave the toilet seat permanently wet, or where, sitting on the throne, my knees didn't rub up against the rim of the bath.

It was only when I looked at the floor of the bathroom that I began to realize my mistake. It was covered with what appeared to be dabs of red-brown nail-varnish. But for the while I thought nothing of this. Secreting my valuables under the mattress of one of the two beds (perfectly normal beds but, relative to the room itself, ridiculous doll's house affairs), I ventured out. Half a mile away was a new skyscraper.

117

If I could get to the top of it I'd be able to take some photographs looking straight down onto the Railway Station and tell my Hong Kong paymasters that I'd hired a helicopter. A very *cheap* helicopter, but worth perhaps an extra fifty dollars.

The Dayabumi building was quite extraordinary. I had to walk round its base four or five times before I could find a way in. It was 300 or more feet high, and its sides were covered with vast concrete grilles in the Moorish style. On the lower ground, ground and first floors was the usual array of shops and facilities, and a courtyard with a fountain. There were also several security offices. I stopped at one of them and asked whether I could go up on the roof. I was immediately referred to another security office, then another. Uniformed men with guns looked at me as though I'd brought a leg of pork into a mosque. But at last a man with two stripes, after consulting with a man who had three stripes, who in turn consulted with what looked like a field-marshal, indicated that it would be all right so long as I was accompanied and only stayed ten minutes.

From the top of the Dayabumi Kuala Lumpur looked a good deal more appetizing than it did on the ground. The horizon was ringed by some stunning mountains, and to the north a colossal tropical storm was raging among the peaks. The city itself was bathed in light, and the Railway Station, as cute as an architect's model, looked as impressive as I had dared imagine.

'It's okay?' I asked, lifting my camera.

'Is okay,' the corporal replied, adding: 'Welcome to the standard view of Kuala Lumpur.'

This more or less knocked me off my feet. Firstly the man, coming up, had shown no command of English, and secondly I was convinced that taking photographs from the top of the Dayabumi was an inspiration that had JW stamped all over it.

'Do a lot of people come up here?' I asked, as casually as I could.

'Thousands,' the corporal replied. 'Tourists, schoolparties, Japanese photography clubs, everyone. Especially journalists. Everyone want to take picture of Kuala Lumpur Railway Station.'

Blast!

For a couple of hours I went walkabout. Then I returned to the Station, dined in what must once have been a ballroom, and turned in.

No sooner had I stretched out on one of the doll's-house beds than I realized I was not alone. Some friends had come to see me.

To begin with there was just one of them, a lame old thing heading staight across the floor for the balcony. I watched it disappear beneath the balcony door and shuddered. Any more like you, I thought, and I'll scream.

I screamed.

Two of them were now clambering over my hold-all.

I could have done with some coaching. I'd never done battle with roaches before. The enemy had made its headquarters in the bathroom. All night filthy dragoons, singly or in raiding parties, issued forth. They scuttled north, south, east and west. Their main objective was the bed itself. But they made cunning detours, to distract my attention. To gain my stronghold.

At first I was loath to slaughter any of them, but after an hour it became clear that ladling scoops of water across the floor was a hopeless means of repulsion. I was forced onto the offensive. The only serviceable weapons I had were my sneakers. After several misses I stamped on the first of them. Crunch! And then – good fortune! – another. Twist and crunch!

But the enemy was not intimidated. It simply wised up. Now they scuttled about at twice the speed, and it was another hour before I heeled my third victim.

Crunch, you little bastard!!!

And then the counter-attack. Roaches swarming *onto* my sneakers, threatening my ankles.

Get off you creeps!

Avaunt!

Ughhhhhhhhhhhhhhh!

But give credit where credit is due. Come dawn, I had laid out no less than seven of the brutes. Seven!

Not bad for a beginner.

*

Having thus gained my spurs in the war against nature, having thus danced the dance, I sallied south 400 kilometres to Singapore.

For once, travelling by rail was a pleasant experience. The train left Kuala Lumpur punctually at a sensible hour: three o'clock in the afternoon, arriving at its destination well before midnight. Because I had scarcely slept at all the previous night, and because the fare was anyhow cheap, I once again went first class. It was worth it. I could not recall having been in such a well appointed carriage before. Proper air-conditioning, double-glazed smoked windows, broad comfortable seats. But the *coup de grace* was the video screen. I had a choice. Either I could watch TV through the windows, or I could watch TV straight ahead. And by happy coincidence they were running *Mutiny On The Bounty*. Pitcairn and Marlon Brando, dying deathlessly. At last the South Seas were heeding my call.

Singapore, on the other hand, did not inspire. It is a place to dwell in – maybe – but it is not a place to dwell upon. Everything I'd ever heard about it – that it is antiseptic, anodyne and avaricious – seemed true. According to the papers the city-state was in something of a recession, though this was hard to believe from appearances. Christmas was a-coming and Orchard Road was packed with shoppers. Even in Tokyo I'd never seen so many department stores. Unlike their Japanese equivalents, however, the Singapore emporiums had space. The one that particularly didn't grab my fancy was called The Paragon. It might just as well have been called The Epitome. In accord with the anality of Singapore it actually is designed to look like a bathroom fixture: and I don't mean the bath, the shower or the handbasin. And as for the people – the men mainly wore Take Six suits and no expressions whatsoever, while the women, inhumanly clean, and equally expressionless, were all alarmingly well-groomed, as though each and every one of them wished to be chosen to advertise Sony Walkmans. And on all their minds, men's and women's alike, there was just one word; money.

Of course, it isn't very difficult to see Premier Lee Kwan Yew's point. Who wouldn't prefer to live in a modern apartment block rather than a bamboo shack? It is a miracle, what the government has done, so very near the Equator. And again, what the shops have to offer is difficult to refuse. Tomorrow's goods at yesterday's prices. But if only these were just a part of life's rich fabric, instead of the whole of it.

Wallet-moths are the particular plague. One of the reasons for the recession was a sharp fall-off in the tourist trade. People were still going to Singapore, but only to do their shopping. They'd learnt that in modern Singapore there is nothing else to do. Singapore has snake and crocodile farms, but then so does every other large city in S.E. Asia. But the government didn't quite accept this. The government thought that the reason why Singapore was falling behind was that the facilities had fallen behind. The hotels were no longer good enough. So now, according to the *Straits Times*, it was going to invest S$1.64 million *per diem* for the next five years to improve the situation.

Nor does the planned recovery stop there. The government has also pledged to re-open Bugis Street, precisely to bring back the tourists.

Bugis Street was, until its closure on moral grounds in 1983, a place for seeing, meeting, and having drinks with transvestites. Foreign seamen especially would go for a pub crawl down Bugis Street, just to behold and admire. But then some of them would encounter some really rather lovely girls, and their evening progressed accordingly. It was not until they were in bed with these girls that they realised they were boys. But by then it was too late. If they wanted their sailors' uniforms back they had to pay, one way or another.

The fame, or infamy, of Bugis Street spread far and wide, and the street enjoyed top billing with the international gay jet set.

To contemplate re-opening Bugis Street in the current climate is nothing short of astonishing. One couldn't wish for a more craven example of what makes Singapore tick. But Lee Kwan Yew, it is well known, doesn't like gays. First the gays of Singapore were punished for their nonconformity. Now, just when they need protecting against the less fortunate gays of the West, they are expected to resume service.

*

But what was that to me? I was straight, safe and okay. I was merely passing through. And I was on my way to Borneo.

It is, or used to be, the ambition of every Englishman to visit Borneo once in his life. Perhaps if more Englishmen had fulfilled this ambition fewer would continue to entertain it. But because Borneo is so very far away not many do go there, and so it remains a cherished dream.

The two strong components of the Borneo dream are Rajah Brooke and longhouses. Sir James Brooke, whose story has been told a thousand times, was an adventurer and, arguably, a pirate. But a Christian pirate, note. In 1835, aged just 32, and having already seen service in India, Brooke inherited his father's fortune. Rather than do something conventional with it, such as found an Oxford college or build a country pile bigger than the one he grew up in, he decided to start a settlement in Borneo. In 1838 he set sail aboard an armed yacht called *The Royalist*. Arriving in Singapore he learnt that the then

Rajah of Borneo, Muda Hassim, was busy fighting a war against a confederation of (mainly Dayak) tribes. Brooke nipped across the water and, with the help of his superior British weapons, firmly crushed the rebellion. Muda Hassim was so grateful he rewarded Brooke with both the title Rajah of Sarawak and its substance, the province. The Englishman was thus able to establish a small kingdom for himself and his family on the edge of the Empire. In due course he was succeeded as Rajah first by his nephew, Sir Charles Anthony Johnson Brooke, and then by his grand-nephew, Sir Charles Vyner Brooke. It was not until 1946 that the Brooke dynasty finally conceded Sarawak to the Colonial Office, in return for the sum of £1,000,000. Other long-term investments have possibly yielded a greater profit, but for sheer mystique and personal glory none can compare with the money Sir James spent fitting out his ketch.

Longhouses are wooden villages raised on stilts above the often leech-ridden jungle floor. A single roof suffices to provide common shelter for up to sixty families. The dwellings consist of either one large room or two medium rooms. A big longhouse can accommodate between 200 and 400 citizens. In addition, the roof stretches over the raised deck of the construction to form an unbroken verandah, while the uncovered section of the deck doubles as a playground for the children and village high street for the big 'uns. In most cases there is a community hall, which may also house ancestral relics such as skulls captured in the days of headhunting. Headhunting allegedly ceased as a way of life among the Iban and Dayaks who lived in the longhouses in the early decades of this century. However, since some skulls hanging from the beams of some community halls wear Japanese wire-rimmed specatacles, it is assumed that the practice was revived during the Pacific War, and could therefore, in theory, be revived again.

The reputation of the longhouse is partly structural, partly social. Structurally they are strange edifices to find in the midst of the tropical rainforest, on account of their size. Wattled bamboo huts, okay, but why horizontal tower blocks? Yet it all boils down to the immense skill-in-wood developed down the centuries by the Bornean tribes-people. They are among the finest carvers in the world, and for most of them producing planks and beams is a piece of cake. Had they been so minded they could have become one of the great maritime nations. But perhaps this was unnecessary. The longhouse doesn't have to be seen as an unleavened high-rise. It is also a jungle-going pleasure cruiser. Where other seafaring peoples put out upon the oceans, the Dayaks and the Iban put out upon the forests. And this happily suggests the fun-and-games element of their deck-and-cabins lifestyle. At night, when it is dark, and the clamour of the forest swallows up any sounds produced by mere humans, the longhouse enables maximum con-cupiscence. A great part of the entertainment consists in discovering, at first light, whether you have just spent the night with the person you thought you were sleeping with, or whether you have thrown it all away on someone else. The secret is to find out the name of the person your intended partner would prefer if she had the choice. Suppose, for example, she lets slip that she wouldn't be at all upset if your brother, whose name is Jino, paid her a visit. Then all you have to do is say 'It's Jino' at the appropriate moment and you're away.

However, if my own experience of a Dayak lover is anything to go by, it's not necessarily as sweet as it sounds. In the torrid era of my early manhood, when ninety-nine per cent of my energies were devoted to sampling the Fruits of the East, by a great stroke of good fortune I found myself alone one night with a particularly fine specimen of Dayak craftsmanship. What Kanad (which in Dayak means tadpole) was doing forty miles outside London in Haywards Heath remains to this day a mystery, but there you have it, and there I had it. True to longhouse traditions, the friendship was celebrated not in a bed, but on a mat on the floor. A bathroom mat, as it happens. I was not aware of any particular discomfort until around 3.00 am. At first I thought I was being attacked by an especially large insect, which perhaps Kanad had brought with her. Then I realised it was Kanad herself. She was pinching me all over. Her pinches were small, precise and painful.

'What are you doing?'

'Pinching!'

'Yes, I know that. But *why?*'

'Nits.'

'Nits?'

'Nits!'

Kanad told me that back home in the longhouse this was a common routine between not just lovers but also friends and relatives. If you wanted to remove a nit then you had to pinch it hard. If there weren't any nits then you pinched the skin instead, as a way of expressing amicability. What could be nicer than to remove a friend's nit for him, regardless of whether they were real or imaginary?

'But I've never had a nit in my life, so please stop doing that, will you?'

But the girl wouldn't listen to me. She just went on pinching, again and again, until I felt sore all over.

'I'm a Dayak,' she kept saying, 'this good manners.'

'If you don't stop immediately I'm going to start pinching *you*. Understand?'

Kanad laughed, and redoubled her efforts. Soon I could stand it no more. I reached out for a knob of her own flesh and squeezed and twisted it for all I was worth. It was not my preferred method for dealing with troublesome women, but in the circumstances I had no choice. And at least it had the desired effect. After a minute or two Kanad stopped pinching me.

'So,' I said, 'let's get some sleep now, shall we?'

But of course Kanad had now started to cry. Therefore I had to spend another half-hour explaining that I really hadn't meant to injure her, but in my country people didn't have nits, or at least not very many, and that being pinched whilst one was asleep was considered rank bad form.

Eventually Kanad got the message.

'Okay,' she said, 'I go sleeps now.'

Five minutes later she was at it again.

There was nothing I could do about it.

One would be forgiven for thinking, after this unfortunate episode, that I had had my life's fill of Borneo and Dayaks. But not a bit of it. *I'm on my way to Borneo for four reasons*, I noted in my journal as the plane left Singapore. *One, because the opportunity has arisen. Two, because I've always wanted the opportunity to arise. Three, because I'm determined to see a longhouse. And four, because I have to deliver a collapsible walking-stick to an old woman.*

The collapsible walking-stick needs explaining. By an inexplicable coincidence not long after I said goodbye to Kanad (which was not very long after I'd said hello) I became acquainted with some other Dayaks living in southern England. These were a family inhabiting a council flat in West London. Now that I knew better than try to get *too* close, I held myself back at arm's length and became, instead of an anguished lover, something of a reliable friend. Happening to mention that I would be passing through Singapore on my long journey to the Solomons, the mother immediately asked whether there was any chance of my hopping over to Kuching, the state capital of Sarawak.

'There's every chance,' I replied, 'Why do you ask?'

'It's only that my parent, an old woman, recently fell down and broke her leg. She needs a proper walking-stick. It would be very nice if someone could take her one.'

'No problem,' said I. 'Leave it to me.'

As soon as she had my word the mother tore off to Selfridge's and purchased an extremely expensive and highly polished brass-fitted stick that took apart in several places and which therefore could be packed into my suitcase without interfering with the rest of my belongings.

'Do you like it?' she asked.

'I've never before beheld its parallel,' I answered.

It had been my intention to pick up a stick in KL or Singapore, but no matter. From my friend's descriptions I felt sure that the old woman concerned lived in a longhouse, and that, having come all the way with such a handsome present, I would be made guest of honour for at least three or four days.

As soon as I arrived in Kuching I contacted the local family. Several of them were working in Kuching, but the only one who understood my English was a grand-daughter who worked in a home for the handicapped on the town's outskirts. But she knew just who I was. Her relatives in England had written all about me. Could I come along to the home the following afternoon? Then she would take me into the jungle.

'Ah yes,' I murmured, 'the jungle.'

For once I had an inkling of what lay in store. For one thing I'd spent a few days in the jungle, or what I took to be the jungle, ten years before, on my first trip to Thailand. For another, I'd just read Redmond O'Hanlon's *Into The Heart Of Borneo*.

As far as possible I had avoided reading any literature about the S.E. Asian stations of my itinerary. My motives for this were the usual bundle of excuses. I was having a holiday from books. Boning up about places robbed them of any surprise value, and inhibited the freshness of my responses. What justified travel, what legitimated it, was the unexpected – the people met, the stories heard, the connections made. Anything else was mere tourism. But I made an exception of Redmond O'Hanlon, principally because O'Hanlon had voyaged into the heart of Borneo with James Fenton.

Fenton, an established poet (whatever that means) and world-class correspondent (he was now in Manila, covering the trials and tribulations of Cory Aquino's first year of office for *The Independent*), is meat for anyone's curiosity, but particularly for mine. We had been at the same Oxford college together, and had had, at one point, adjoining sets of rooms – rooms that had once been a single suite occupied by the Prince of Wales (Edward VIII). Even as a student Fenton possessed a prodigious personality. He could be totally serious or he could be totally playful, or (rather alarmingly) he could be both simultaneously. With Fenton one tended never to be quite sure where one stood, and I, if only by virtue of proximity, sometimes found myself more miffed than most. For instance, in our second term of being neighbours, I was surprised one night by Fenton's voice bidding me a stern goodnight through the partitioning wall. But as well as the wall there was a door, and Fenton's eye, unblinking, was lodged in the keyhole. 'Goodnight,' I said. And the eye continued staring.

The episode ended, appropriately, in undergraduate giggles, Fenton being his usual charming provocative self. But, like most laughter, mine was motivated partly by suspended alarm. Fenton's caper, executed with an actor's finesse, actually had conveyed an element at least of Big Brother. Even in his frolics Fenton was always a slightly intimidating phenomenon.

Oh yes. My curiosity was exercised by Fenton. And so apparently was Redmond O'Hanlon's. *Into The Heart Of Borneo* describes an eight-week trek up the Rajang River, and its tributary the Baleh River, towards the mountains of Batu Tiban, straddling the frontier between Sarawak and Indonesian Kalimantan. The ostensible purpose of O'Hanlon's and Fenton's expedition was to discover whether the Borneo rhinoceros still survived deep in the jungle. The outcome, however, was the discovery that Fenton survived deep in the jungle, his humour unimpaired. Try as hard as O'Hanlon might, cite as much recondite natural history as he could lay hands on, at every longhouse, at every campsite, at every bend in the river, Fenton stole the show, transforming a horribly arduous safari into a perpetual holiday.

Yet the book gives little or no clue to Fenton's inner thoughts. As I came to the end of it, lying on a creaky old bed in a damp stuffy room on the second floor of the distinctly third-class Borneo Hotel, I felt disappointed, cheated even. And I also felt watched. Outside, a band of young Sarawakians were exploding firecrackers in the parking lot. Inside, a solitary eye, disguised among the scallops of the faded vermicelli wallpaper, was staring at me. And behind it James Fenton was laughing his head off.

'So Wintle,' I could almost hear him say, 'you think you know what the jungle's like?'

Borneo was not about to be a giant success.

At the appointed hour I presented myself at the Sarawak Cheshire Home. The grand-daughter was almost ready. Did I mind waiting fifteen minutes while she finished her duties? She left me sitting in a glass vestibule with corridors leading off to wards and day-rooms. Like most tropical hospitals the Home consisted of several single-storey buildings linked by covered walkways.

My presence did not go unnoticed. When I looked up I saw they were coming at me from all directions; in wheelchairs, hobbling on crutches, some simply sliding on legless bottoms across the floor. There was a sort of race to get to me first. The few who possessed a full count of limbs lagged well behind. They were blind. Among the others, cerebral palsy appeared the chief affliction. In a minute or so fingerless arms and toeless legs reached out to touch me. They wanted to feel the hair on my arms. I was as much a novelty to them as they were to me.

I shook hands with half-a-dozen stumps. The sensation was grotesque. Why pretend otherwise? But it wasn't the tactile peculiarity that confused me. It was the sheer happiness on the faces surrounding me, mainly at waist level, and the fact that I hadn't expected this . . . this confrontation with the unacceptable face of nature. In one way or another each of them was hideously deformed, and yet all seemed radiantly excited. I felt like the Pied Piper, returning to Hamelin after the bomb has dropped.

Shortly afterwards two white-robed sisters appeared and induced a measure of calm. I agreed to play skittles in the dining room. Five minutes later the cast of unfortunates had reassembled on the polished wooden floor. One by one they pushed the putt toward the nine sawn-off truncheons, and one by one they missed. It was getting perilously close to my turn when the grand-daughter entered and took me away. What I would have done if she hadn't I have no idea. Either I could have played to miss, or I could have played to hit. But which would have been the more tactful? I realized how very little I knew about the handicapped. And (to my shame) how very little I wanted to know.

The more able came with us to the door. There was another round of vigorous stump-shaking. Those who could speak didn't, however, ask whether or when I was coming back to see them again. They knew I wasn't, and they knew how to protect themselves from disappointment. In that respect I envied them.

We had walked half a kilometre up the road when it occurred to me that I'd said scarcely a word to the grand-daughter. To cut short my rudeness I asked, as cheerily as I could, where she was taking me.

'To my grandmother's house of course!'

'House?'

The girl nodded.

'Not your grandmother's longhouse?'

She laughed. Grandmother hadn't lived in a longhouse for forty years. Forty years ago she had converted to Christianity. Now she lived apart from the Dayaks she had grown up with.

'In Kuching?'

The grand-daughter shook her head. 'No, in the jungle. I told you. Long way down the Serian Road. Catch bus.'

We reached a main road and waited, beneath a wholly inadequate shelter, for the number three. It was already inordinately hot.

We sat in the bus an hour, and then the grand-daughter indicated it was time to get off. The bus stopped at a dust-track.

'Here,' she said. 'Walk.'

So far so good. Not unlike going to Wat Pa Nana Chat. Except there were no paddis, no water buffalo. Indeed there was no cultivated land of any kind in sight. Just a ring of faintly intimidating, densely foliaged hills, and the incredible heat. But the dust-track was quite okay. It was probably the broadest I'd ever seen.

This time we walked only a quarter of a mile. Then the grand-daughter pointed to an almost invisible path that led straight into the forest.

'There,' she said. 'Walk.'

From that point it was less than two miles to the house. Even so, as an introduction to the Bornean forest, it very nearly did for me. To begin with it was very noisy. Not noisy loud, but noisy busy. It was like seven compositions by Luciano Berio played simultaneously. There were a million and one completely unfamiliar sounds – buzzings and scrapings and flappings and slitherings. Particularly slitherings. With each step that I took I felt my muscles tighten. The abdominal grip. At any moment I expected to be bound hand and foot by vipers. The air was also thick with insect life. Huge beetles that could have been hornets, huge hornets that perhaps were flying scorpions. Indeed it was so thick that it distorted the soundwaves. 'Christ!' I exclaimed, after less than a hundred paces, 'it's like a pair of earphones in here. I think my head's gone a funny shape.' But the grand-daughter, who had carefully positioned herself in the rear, simply waved me on. A black butterfly brushed my nose and I jumped backwards into a brackish puddle. Something long and ratlike nudged my shoe and I jumped forward again, more or less to where I was before. Progress was not so much slow as non-existent.

The grand-daughter laughed. Then she started slapping my back.

'Hey! What are you doing?'

'Mosquitos!'

'And I thought they were daddy-longlegs!'

It was true. They were absolutely vast, and rather ungainly. But there was nothing amateurish about the damage they inflicted. Coming out of the TV for a late lunch they had already made a meal of both my forearms. My skin was coming up, as they say. Wherever my flesh was exposed white plateaux were rising. Not red yet. That would come later. But plenty of isotropes.

Frantically I began hitting them, clobbering my neck and arms. And the grand-daughter continued smacking my back.

'Shirt,' she said. 'No good.'

And how right she was. In a gesture at style I had donned that day a 20-year-old dress-shirt. Wouldn't it be superbly eccentric, I had reasoned, to wander into the Bornean jungle wearing a pair of blue-jeans and a Simpson's dress-shirt? I had had this vision of myself arriving at a longhouse, *the* longhouse, in an outfit that would both put everyone at ease and astound them. Further the shirt had belonged to my father. My father, who was never a well man, had once said to me, 'Junior, you must do my travelling for me.' What could be a greater fulfilment of that sacred injunction than the depths of Sarawak in his own white frills? But after twenty years the fabric had worn thinner than tissue paper, thinner than a wasp's retina. As far as the mosquitos were concerned it just didn't exist. Or rather, because of the heat, it clung closely to my torso, accentuating the target areas for my billion assailants.

'Damn and blast!'

The grand-daughter stopped slapping for a moment and raised a finger to her lips.

'I'm sorry,' I said, 'but honestly . . .'

An image danced in my mind. Or rather, an image of an image. The space probe, sent to spy on Halley's Comet. Its shield. The computer simulation of what would happen to this shield if it encountered too many tiny solid bodies. The shield vanishing in a hail of holes in about three seconds flat.

Somehow I pressed on. Since it was a day for gestures, I thought about taking off my hat in a symbolic tribute to Messrs O'Hanlon and Fenton. But I didn't, for fear of the consequences. The enemy would be at my scalp like a shot.

After half a mile the mosquitos eased off a little. Either they had already inflicted the maximum possible destruction, or they had begun to be afraid. I hadn't succeeded in swatting any of them, but two at least had perished in a pool of perspiration that had formed on my right shoulder, while a third had drowned in an upside-down pool beneath my left nipple. They were beginning to suffocate at their own banquet.

Still I pushed on. Another twenty minutes and I was close to exhaustion. How anybody survived a day of this, let alone a week, let alone a month, was beyond me. But at last I came to a crude gateway, and the grand-daughter told me we had arrived.

The house, now only a hundred yards away, was a two-storeyed wooden crate set in a four- or five-acre garden containing hundreds of bedraggled orchids and a pepper orchard. Having asked me to remove my shoes and shown me upstairs, the grand-daughter immediately disappeared. Nor was she seen again. For several minutes I sat alone on an ancient sofa, glad to have the weight off my feet and glad for the relative cool. Those mosquitos that ventured indoors came singly and could either be evaded or punished for their daring. Under the house a few chickens clucked, and a dog prowled outside among the shrubs. Otherwise there was absolutely no sign of life.

Most of all I wanted to sleep. Even though it was scarcely four o'clock I was overwhelmed with drowsiness. My arms had turned the colour of squashed tomatoes, and it occurred to me that if I did fall asleep it might be for the last time. But that was of no concern. The prospect of sleep was immeasureably inviting, and I had all but given way to it when I heard a baby's cry.

The grandmother appeared through the doorway of an adjoining room. A minute, wizened, crush-featured woman, clad in an ancient sarong, she was not at all surprised by my presence. Since there was no telephone I did not see how she could have been expecting me, but all she did was nod and continue on her way downstairs.

Then another woman appeared in the same doorway, carrying the infant. She also nodded and went downstairs.

One of my friend's sisters, I thought to myself, with one of my friend's new nieces or nephews. But it was pure surmise. There had been no attempt at an introduction. What was wrong? Did they resent my intrusion, or were they incurably shy?

More time elapsed, and then the sister came back upstairs carrying a very small cup of lukewarm weak tea.

'Hello,' I said, 'and thank you. Here!'

A touch desperately I presented the collapsible walking-stick, together with a tin of biscuits I'd bought in a Singapore supermarket.

The sister took my gifts and nodded. Again there was not the least trace of surprise.

'It's a very great pleasure,' I muttered, and sat down again with my tea, which I drank in one gulp.

The sister retired to her room.

I felt a complete and utter oaf. I had never felt such a complete and utter oaf before. Indeed, I felt like the man who answered an advertisement for a penis enlarger and received, for his pains, a cheap magnifying glass.

After a further wait I ventured downstairs, taking my cup with me, hoping for a refill.

The grandmother was sitting on a stool in the corner of the dark wooden kitchen. She did not look up. She was busily occupied sanding a plain wooden walking-stick that she had obviously made by herself. Beside her, leaning against the wall, were two further samples of her handiwork.

I returned upstairs to say goodbye to the sister. In an hour the sun would go down, and I did not intend either staying the night or attempting the path after dark.

It was only then that I noticed what my journal subsequently referred to as 'perhaps the direst object I've ever seen in Asia'.

Apart from the pre-war sofa and a low table the only other piece of furniture was a rough dresser upon which were crowded many family

131

photographs, a radio and a primitive television. Among these, however, was one ornament, a souvenir of London, a thing that I had never seen before, and hoped never to see again.

Cast in an undistinguished alloy it consisted of an almost life-size hand in the palm of which sat a model of the Houses of Parliament. Curiously a part of the roof was cut away, exposing a series of improbable chambers, like the hold of a container ship.

For pure kitsch it took my breath away. Presumably my friends had sent it from England or brought it over on one of their visits. But when? The bric-à-brac had an unmistakeable 1950s quality about it. Yet, when I turned it over, the price marker was unequivocal: *Selfridges*, it said, £5.99.

A noise, and I almost dropped Parliament on the floor.

The sister, who had come out of her room again and was now standing at my side, said just three words:

'Great British Longhouse.'

The slog back to the Serian Road was, if anything, worse than the slog from the Serian Road. In the gathering gloom there were twice the number of mosquitos than before and it was a point of honour among them that they each get a bite. But finally I stumbled, weeping, back onto the dirt track, and civilization was once more within my grasp. On the other side of the highway I now discovered what I had failed to notice before, namely a new *kampong*. At the first glass-and-concrete bungalow I persuaded the occupants to sell me a semi-refrigerated lemon drink at only twice the market value. Then I waited for the bus to take me back to Kuching. I don't know why but I began to feel relaxed, serene even. Perhaps it was the quarter moon, floating unanchored in a cloudless amber sky. Also, at a distance, the tropical sound-effects were a good deal less threatening. Indeed, the jungle now provided a rather melodious background for my thoughts. As I continued waiting I observed two Malay youths taking their evening bath in a nearby pond. When they had finished I asked whether they weren't afraid of leeches. The younger laughed. 'Sorry, sir,' he said, 'no have lychees.'

Once back in Kuching I splashed out on a plate of satay at the Holiday Inn. The Holiday Inn sits on a prime site on the banks of the Sarawak River, and outside oil-rich Brunei is probably the smartest place on Borneo. Everything else I'd seen had a moth-eaten quality:

nothing seemed able stand up to the heat and humidity, the people included. But the Holiday Inn was curiously pristine, curiously clean. So I ate my satay slowly, making the best of my brief encounter with Hollywood *in orientalis*.

Then, to all intents and purposes, I found myself back in Ubon Ratchathani. Close to my hotel was a bar, The Star Express. Surely today I had earned a drink? It was a surprisingly large dive with thirty or forty low tables and even lower lighting. What could be seen looked scruffy, but at least the seats were comfortable. I plonked myself on one of them and five or six waistcoated waiters slid up to take my order. No sooner had my beer arrived than a bevy of ill-clad Chinese women trooped in and occupied a table just two away from mine.

God, I thought, trust me to pinpoint the local branch of the Triad. And sure enough, on my other side the headwaiter, a bespectacled lawyerly-looking man, was already whetting my ear: 'You want I book lady for you? All nice girls, all come Taiwan. One hour, thirty-eight dollar fifty sen.'

I indicated that in about an hour I might just want another beer and the man wandered off in something akin to high dudgeon. As he did so he said something to the girls who began staring at me with a little less coquetry and a little more hostility. In addition the other waiters now lined up across the exit, cutting off my escape. At any moment I expected the fellow to come back to me and say: 'Never mind about lady, just give me thirty-eight dollar fifty sen.'

It was a peculiar tariff – one that had obviously been worked out on the golden abacus. Did it, I wondered, include tax?

But the siege did not last long. Soon a party of Chinese businessmen came in from the street and attention was diverted from myself. A small band materialized and one by one the Taiwanese stood up to sing. They hardly outshone their counterparts at the Pathumrat, but in all other respects there was a material similiarity between where I was and where I had been. The Star Express was a joint, but it was also a place for the general public to gather at. By ten, all the tables were taken, and most of the clientêle were happy youngsters out to enjoy themselves.

I stayed for a second beer, and was soon rewarded. Having nowhere else to sit a party of three girls requistioned my table. A Malay and two Ibans. Hooray, I thought: here's my chance to get to know the other tribe.

The girl in the middle, the Malay, was certainly the most striking of the three, though not the most attractive. Her hair was cropped short and she wore spectacles, a black collarless suit and a bow tie. She also, rather aggressively, insisted on holding her partners' hands. On balance I gave her the benefit of the doubt. In Malaysia, indeed in S.E. Asia generally, women very often do hold each others' hands and it doesn't mean anything. Suits, too, were the fashion. She reminded me of the boy who played the organ at my school, whom the chaplain used to bless with outsize bars of chocolate. She also reminded me of a pregnant melon. She was excessively fat, but somehow kept it all tucked in to present to the world a single seamless surface.

It was this girl who made all the running – who introduced herself, her companions, and suggested I buy everyone a drink.

'You want to join us?' she asked. 'We'd all like a beer!' Adding: 'But don't worry, we don't work here.'

But what they really wanted was for someone, i.e. me, to keep an eye on their bags while they danced.

'Okay,' I said, 'I'll get the beer and I'll look after your things. And don't worry, I don't work here either.'

Visually the most interesting of the three was Linda, an Iban. Her arms were covered with some very untribal tattoos and, as the organist told me, she had formerly worked as a dancer at the Holiday Inn. But the tattoos had put an end to that. So too, probably, had her name. Throughout the world 'Linda' is used to cover a multitude of sins, past, present and upcoming.

The Taiwanese stopped singing – presumably because by now they had all been booked – and were replaced by a disco playing Elvis, Manfred Mann and other golden oldies. Conversation rapidly became problematic, and the three girls left me for another dance. In a trice, however, the organist was back at the table. Before I could flinch she had reached out and grabbed my hand.

'Linda likes you,' she shouted.

'Oh,' I shouted back.

This I didn't want. To change the topic I asked fattie what she did. Fattie told me she worked in the army, though she declined to give her rank. Then, pressing her knee firmly against mine, she repeated her statement about Linda.

'I know. You just told me that.'

'I used to work massage at Feta Hotel. But now I'm in the army, no can massage any more.'

'I should think not!'

'I want to tell you sincere, I want to tell you true, from my heart. Give me ten dollars and I do it for you.'

I said what about Linda, wouldn't Linda be upset?

'No no no. What I mean is, give me ten dollars now, and I do it for you tomorrow. Tonight can have Linda.'

'Maybe Linda will want me tomorrow as well,' I countered.

But the soldier-organist shook her head vehemently.

'No no no no. Linda never go twice one man. Linda real dirt.'

I am not unaware that this sort of encounter can happen anywhere in the world. Hot jelly in Warsaw, or a wax-job in Johannesburg. But why in nighttime Asia is it invariably the only sort of encounter? Although it would have been interesting to discover whether the organist had ten US dollars in mind, or ten Malaysian dollars (approx. £2.70), I curtailed my brush with the military and returned to my hotel. The next day I woke up paralysed. I was quite unable to move. My prophylactics may have spared me malaria, but they could not allay the mosquitos' more immediate effects. There was nothing for it but to spend the entire day in bed, beneath the steady gaze of Fenton's hidden eye.

Just as I had feared, Borneo was proving a disaster. Yet I was determined not to leave until I had seen a longhouse. On the third full day therefore I forced myself back on my feet.

The tour operators did their best to discourage me. All visits to longhouses, they said, meant a three-or four-day trek minimum, and sleeping out in the jungle. But at last I found a Chinese called Sidney with a battered white Mini who assured me the whole thing could be accomplished in five hours flat.

Sidney spoke very good English but was otherwise useless. As soon as he had been paid his fee, 100 Malay dollars in advance, he started telling me that I would have been much better advised to take one of the five-day excursions. The longhouse we were going to was a Dayak settlement, whereas surely what I wanted to see was an Iban settlement?

'But give me 200 dollars more, in advance, and I'll take you visiting Iban.'

'No thank you, Sidney. Dayaks will do just fine.'

'Only Americans and Germans go to Dayak longhouse.'

'That's okay. I like Americans, and I quite like Germans.'

'But you English! You British!'

'I know. And I have sensitive skin.'

'But we go Dayak longhouse five hours no chance find nice girl.'

'Now look here, Sidney,' I began, clearing my throat, 'This may sound funny to you, but as a matter of fact I don't want to find a nice girl. And before you ask, I don't want to find a nice boy either. To let you into a very deep secret, I'm not even sure I really want to see a longhouse. But that's not the point. What I have to do is take some photographs of a longhouse, any longhouse. See? Here's my camera. It's got some film in it. Now the reason I have to take some photographs of a longhouse is to prove I've been there. Nothing else. It's part of my project.'

'Project, mister?'

'Yes. Project. I'm on a sort of Duke of Edinburgh Award Scheme for older children. There are ten of us and we've each been allocated eleven tasks. The first one to complete them all wins. So now, if you don't mind, remove your hand from the handbrake and let's go.'

But Sidney's hand remained firmly where it was.

'What the prize?'

'There is no prize. There is simply the honour of winning.'

'Sound crazy to me. But you like I sell you good photograph any longhouse you want to see. Only cost you fifty dollar.'

'That won't do I'm afraid. Cheating is definitely against the rules.'

'Wrong, mister. Cheating number one rule for everyone.'

'Not for the Duke of Edinburgh, it isn't, and not for me.'

Once he could be persuaded to move Sidney moved very swiftly. He jammed his foot against the accelerator and kept it there until half a mile past Grandma's dust-track on the Serian Road. Then he swung his vehicle into a narrower but well-surfaced turning. Since this road was inclined to hilliness he had constantly to change gears, and this slowed him down somewhat.

'Go easy,' I breathed. 'I'd like to see at least a little of what I'm paying for.'

'Nothing here,' retorted Sidney.

'What's that?'

Sidney blinked up into his driving mirror.

'Agricultural training centre.'

'And that?'

'Leprosarium.'

Vrrrrrmmm! Eeeech! Vrrrrrrrrmmmmm!

And in no time at all we were there.

The first thing I noticed about the Benuk longhouse was that in front of it were a car park and two Malay *restorans*. Fortunately, though, there were no coaches or minibuses in sight.

Funnily enough, the longhouse, or rather series of connected longhouses (Benuk is the closest thing there is to a Dayak metropolis) *exactly* met my expectations. Even if I turned my head in a fresh direction, what I saw was precisely what I had anticipated.

It was all down to the mosquitos. Their poison had reached my brain, and the two halves of my cerebellum were out of synch. The half that registered surprise was being bigfooted by the half that processed the data. My surprise-registering faculty was inadvertently taking its cue from memory, not appreciating that memory had only been charged a split-second before.

'I've been here before,' I said to Sidney.

'So have I,' replied Sidney. 'You want to go now?'

'After we've seen the stream.'

'Stream, mister?'

'Yes the stream, mister. Every longhouse has a stream close by. Nobody builds a longhouse unless there's running water to hand.'

Reluctantly Sidney led me over a small hill. On the other side, sure enough, was a beautiful crystal-clear stone-bedded rivulet.

Better still, a dozen naked children were taking diving lessons from an overhanging tree.

'This'll do,' I said, and took out my Pentax.

At once a woman in a sarong waded into the middle of the water with a washing basket.

'Perfect, I said.

But as soon as she saw my camera she hid her face.

'Lady want five dollar,' said Sidney. 'If not, no take photograph. Give her ten dollar, show breast.'

'I think the Duke of Edinburgh's seen enough breasts for one lifetime.'

I was in a mood to deny my guide everything, mainly because Sidney was incapable of furnishing even the most basic information.

'Any idea how many people live here, Sidney?'

A shake of the head.

'What do they eat?'

Another shake of the head.

When we returned to the longhouse complex I insisted we climb up on deck. The way to do this was not by stairs, nor by a ladder, but on a notched plank no wider than a gymnast's beam. Miraculously I negotiated it while loading my Pentax with a fresh film. Probably if my mind hadn't been on this secondary task I'd have fallen off. Sidney did – twice.

There were not many Dayaks about. A few old folk sitting on mats, mostly naked. But as soon as I appeared a dog tore along the rooms, gathering such youths as there were. These wore jeans and T-shirts. When they saw I was a smoker they started acting very friendly. In return for half a bowl of wood-nuts and a glass of tepid water they relieved me of one and a half packs.

But at least I got to see the spirit-hall. There was a small pagan altar and, hanging from the ceiling like a bunch of onions, some mouldy old skulls.

Also in the spirit-hall, which was of a light, modern, septagonal design, was the communal television. As one of the Dayak youths explained, there had been considerable inter-generational conflict of late between those who wanted to watch *My Fair Lady* and those (the elders) who wanted to have a chat with their ancestors.

'Old people crazy rotten,' Sidney put in, showing unprecedented interest. 'Same my house. Night come, father only want to do accounts.'

Just to annoy him I accepted a second bowl of nuts. Here, at last, was an opportunity to learn something.

'Well,' I began, placing my hands on my cross-legged knees, 'now about those skulls . . .'

But the Dayak youths weren't interested in telling me about their parents' heirlooms. What they wanted to talk about was Christmas.

'What you doing for Christmas, sir?'

'Yes mister, what you doing for Christmas?'

They, it transpired, were planning to spend Christmas in a discothèque.

'Hey tell us, mister, in England have disco yet? Or everybody still have to go ballroom dancing?'

A snigger circulated through the group.

I was still wearing my father's Simpson dress-shirt. Not one of those kids had been taken in by it.

SIX

'Nesia

Indonesia is a heaven-and-hell country. From Kuching I flew back to Singapore, and from Singapore, on December 18th, I flew to Jakarta. As I looked down from the Airbus on a cluster of tiny emerald islands adrift in the Java Sea I smiled to myself. Laut Jawa egad! At last I had escaped the mainland of Asia. I was heading out, I was making progress, I had the Solomons on the end of my line. All I had to do was take the strain and start reeling in. Jakarta, Jogjakarta, Surabaya. A quick jump across to one of the islands in Nusa Tenggara, then back to Surabaya where somehow I would find a ship to take me onwards to Port Moresby; or, if I was lucky, a ship to take me all the way to Honiara. Simple. Easy. Like hitching a ride from Luton to Leicester. And right now I felt lucky. Rightly interpreted, the omens were with me.

The omens, though, had given me a start. It was still mid-afternoon when Sidney dropped me off in Kuching after our drive to the Dayak longhouse. Badly in need of some entertainment I decided to visit the Sarawak Museum. I couldn't have done better. The Sarawak Museum, built in imitation of a Normandy town hall and opened, by the second Rajah Brooke, in 1891, contains more or less everything anyone should want to see in Borneo. The nucleus of the collection is a handsome set of zoological specimens that once belonged to H.Brooke

Low. This includes a great case of many hornbills. A hornbill is a purely fantastic bird that has an enormous and often highly coloured beak in three sections: the lower beak, the upper beak and another bit on top. Of all God's creatures it is the most man-made in appearance: some species are famous for walling-up their young, in the hollows of large trees where they make their nests. Then there are such marvels as the clouded leopard, the tarsier, the grey gibbon and the proboscis monkey – those little fellows who have what can only be described as an elongated nipple in the centre of their faces.

As well as stuffed animals, stretched butterflies and mounted beetles (not to mention flies, mosquitos, wasps, scorpions, roaches, spiders and bugs) the Museum offers a convenient array of human artefacts, and mock-ups of 'typical' tribal interiors. But, unless you have a particular penchant for blowpipes, pride of place must go the the wood carvings. Totems, sickness images, heads etc., most of them with pieces of straw (dried *lalang*) poking out.

The object that particularly enthralled me was a white carved coffin, upstairs in the last corner of the last room. Sizewise it was the same as any other coffin, only squarish (untapered), and somehow very durable. At its base was a small pipe, pointing diagonally at the floor. A notice explained its function. Nobody was actually buried in the coffin. Rather the corpse was left inside until all the body fluid had drained away. Afterwards the remains were taken out and hung in a sack from the branch of a tree.

Awe welled up inside me. But, midway through, my awe was interrupted. Distantly a bell rang. The museum was closing. Anxious to spend a little more time with the coffin I went back next day. The coffin had gone. Noticing that several other exhibits had shifted position I went off in search of the Curator. He was nowhere to be found, but his assistant willingly agreed to talk to me. 'Where,' I said, 'is the beautiful white coffin with a pipe sticking out of its base to take away the juices?' Mr Kedit was unable to help. Nothing had been moved, nor could he recollect ever having seen the coffin as described by myself.

Needless to say there must have been a rational explanation, but further questioning did not reveal it. I left with the feeling that I had made a fool of myself. I also left with the uncanny sensation that what I had seen was a phantom. A phantom casket, a hallucinated sarcophagus.

This appalled me. It was clear evidence that my brain was halfway cooked already. Ordinarily I am rigidly opposed to anything remotely supernatural. There is no God, nor are there any demons – the result perhaps of having once been violently religious, for eight or nine months on end when I was ten or eleven years old. (I saw myself then as a future missionary, creating wonderful pictures of the tortured Christ out of coloured soaps smeared on sheets of glass and left to dry under an African sun.) But this business of the disappearing coffin sliced through my quick. The point about the rational explanation was precisely that it eluded me, therefore the implications were shocking. I have always assumed that one's departure from life, unless effected by something sudden like a motor accident, most probably is accompanied by a certain haywiredness in the upper cavity. But so soon?

Flying over the Java Sea I dismissed such morbidity, but only by resorting to an argument that transfigured rationalism. If the casket had disappeared, I reasoned to myself, that was because I wasn't ready for it yet. In fact the episode was so foreign to any other experience I have ever had while travelling that it was not especially difficult to discount it completely. And yes, in retrospect, it was not an entirely inappropriate prelude to my journey through Indonesia.

I arrived in Jakarta, therefore, in a state of some elation. I had sensed death creep up behind me, but in the nick of time I had swung round and seen the bugger off. My elation, however, was dispelled almost immediately, and remained dispelled until I reached Jogjakarta. In Jogjakarta I fell prey to an unimaginably exquisite treasure of fruit cordials. For a while these restored my spirits. But only for a while. By not paying proper heed to the warnings offered by my guidebook I allowed myself to ingest large quantities of poisoned ice, with which the cordials were chilled. Dysentery followed, and now became my constant companion, if not my mortician. Yet between attacks there were moments of stark sublimity. My thoughts, stripped of discipline, sometimes galloped away with me; yet often they stayed where they were, motionless, dead still, like leaves in a ditch. I was torn apart as never before, to the point where my interpretive faculties were regularly upended and I no longer knew whether I was experiencing the greatest torment or the greatest pleasure, or both simultaneously, or neither. Thus Jakarta, I quickly discovered, contained all the dregs of Asia. So, too, did Surabaya. But while I remained steadfast in my dislike for the one, the other cast a spell on me that I suppose will never quite wear off.

All the dregs of Asia. My disappointment was intense. I'm not the first person to rubbish Jakarta and I won't be the last. But that was the key to my disappointment. When people told me I wouldn't like Jakarta, my instinct was to fight back. It was a city of 7,000,000 souls, surely there must be some good in it? But if there is I didn't find it. All I saw was an endless poverty, interspersed with the occasional modern construction and dark-windowed Mercedes, i.e. a typification of almost any other third-world capital where a reactionary and autocratic government holds sway. And the smell: walking out of my hotel I had each time to wade through a ten-foot swamp of rotting durian and excrement spiced with gasoline. Vermin stalked openly behind, while in front beggars lined up in twos and threes, waiting for the moment when the nut of one's charity cracked open. The young men didn't bother with pretending to make themselves useful, as in *Hey Mister, you want I take you girl?* They just sidled up and said *Money!* or *Dollars?*

At night there was a marginal improvement, if only because the stench-inciting sun was gone and you couldn't see the rats. But it was eerie. The streets filled with food-stalls, called *warung-warung*, and an entirely new population, invisible by day, took possession of the city. Straining my eyes I noticed a myriad of human shadows sitting cross-legged, either on rickety stools or on the ground, all banging away at something: knocking one piece of metal against another, shaving bent stakes with blunt knives, grinding foodstuffs between broken tiles. An imitation of industry, a pathetic madhouse of ill-conceived and misdirected skills.

Fortunately there was nothing to keep me in Jakarta. Nor was I looking for excuses. From day one in Bangkok I had read reports of the Indonesian government expelling journalists. The entire Australian corps, for instance, had recently been given its marching orders. Given that the object of my journey was to get to Honiara on limited funds any brush with the authorities was potentially catastrophic. If I wasn't already under surveillance that was probably because in my passport I had my profession listed as author, not journalist. All I had to do was book a seat on the train to Jogjakarta, to continue the rail journey I had promised to write up for Hong Kong.

I made enquiries at the front desk of my hotel, the Marco Polo.

142

Despite what my guide-book said the receptionist assured me there were no first-class trains to either Jogjakarta or Surabaya. If I didn't believe her I should go along to Gambir station and check it out myself. I went along to Gambir station. There a saronged throng had laid siege to the station-master's office. The station-master himself, when at last I spoke to him, broadly agreed with what I had been told, although the *times* of the trains to Jogja, he said, were quite different.

After a great deal of overwrought agitation I persuaded him to give me a copy of the state railway timetables. As he handed over the booklet his face shone with indescribable glee. The tables were absolutely free, he insisted, he couldn't think of taking a single rupiah for them. Simultaneously the same face – big, curly-haired, moustachioed – exhibited symptoms of a profound dolour. The cat was out of the bag now. It could only be a matter of moments before I discovered that Gambir was not the only station in Jakarta, that there was a Kota station as well, and that from Kota there was a first-class express that goes to Surabaya via Jogjakarta. This meant that I would almost certainly not be buying a ticket from him, and therefore he would not be in a position to accept a bribe for selling me my ticket.

The mechanics of this became apparent as I got to grips with Kota station. Thither I hastened, intending to book a seat on the Bima (as the express is called) for the following day. At Gambir I had seen a string of cattle trucks masquerading as troop transports, so no way was I going to take anything less than the best. At Kota, however, the station-master explained that if I wanted a seat for the morrow I would have to come back on the morrow. Advance purchases were impossible, as was advance *baksheesh*. For the 1600 train I must come again at 10.00am when the ticket counter opened.

By 9.00 am I was there, armed with *Catch 22* and a bottle of water. I was getting used to queues. At 10.30 a rustling among the hundred-odd people in front of me indicated that the ticket clerk had finally got out of bed. By 11.30 I was within striking distance of the counter when the cry went up: *Habis! Habis!* Finished! Try again tomorrow!

I knew just what to do. Stuffing Joseph Heller into my pocket I belted for the station-master's office. I didn't protest, I didn't incriminate. Calmly I laid my money on the table and calmly the station-master wrote me out a ticket.

In fact I needn't have bothered. I would still have got a seat on the Bima. What I hadn't understood is that most of those in the queue were buying up blocks of tickets to sell off later in the day, to those who quite properly have an aversion to standing. And the premium – 2000 rupiah – would have been about the same.

But how much is the rupiah worth? For the curious I offer the following clue: one rupiah in 1987 will buy approximately what one Italian lira would have bought in 1967.

The Bima left on time. The first-class carriage was hardly caviar to Mussolini, but the air-conditioning was effective enough to compel me to hire a blanket from the steward. To make up for this extortion as soon as the train pulled out of Kota station he strode up and down the aisle distributing freebies. These included a face freshener and a State Railway keyring. The keyring you threw out of the window into the hands of small boys who lined the tracks for several miles through Jakarta's suburbs. Presumably the boys then sold the keyrings back to the State Railway, ready for the next trans-Java express.

I now beheld, for the first time, and for as long as the light permitted, the central plains of Java, those legendary emerald-green paddis that send the most inured soul reeling and spinning in a sustained aesthetic swoon. But like most treats it was over ere it had begun. By six o'clock darkness had descended and the train, which had been fairly rattling along, slowed to a crawl, giving villagers a chance to leap out of its path. Dinner was served – a slab of what I took to be elephant meat cunningly endowed with the aromas of beefsteak. Then the lights were dimmed and there was no alternative but to sleep. At midnight I stirred myself in readiness for Jogja. According to my map, however, there was still another hundred-plus miles to go, and I did not arrive until after dawn, a mere five hours late.

Four days later I returned to Jogjakarta station for the last leg of the rail marathon which had started in Bangkok. I'd had a ticklish decision to make. Either I picked up the Bima, or I boarded a more local Surabaya-bound train coming from Bandung. If the Bima came on time it would mean travelling through the night again. On the other hand the second- and third-class-only Bandung train, while hypo-thetically promising more daylight, guaranteed discomfort.

Foolishly I opted for the latter, on the principle that the station-master would be less likely to demand a royalty.

Normally I like a sauna, but I am strictly a ten-minute man. To find myself condemned to a seven-hour sauna was punishment for sins that, to the best of my knowledge, I had never even dreamed of committing. Wedged in between a crowd of other people's bags and boxes I now learnt what it must have been like for Shadrach, Meshach and Abednego. Immediately I sat down I was surrounded by a miasma of my own sweat. My breathing became at first pronounced, then desperate. The two halves of my brain took it in turns to faint. Sooner or later they would synchronize, and that would be that. My only hope was: this journey must end, and perhaps before I do.

In such circumstances the only salvation is work. By a stroke of great good fortune sitting opposite me was a Dutch woman who had grown up in Solo and was now returning *pour rechercher le temps perdu*. Her father had been an engineer with one of the Dutch-run railway companies, and she had with her a selection of books and pamphlets about the Indonesian rail system. In other words she had at her fingertips nearly all the information I needed for my article, but which so far I had failed to research. I took out my notepad and began scribbling robotically as she generously dictated a précis of the literature. My sweat glands ached with depletion, my breathing worsened by the minute, and my brain began toying with schizo-phrenia. But at least I no longer had to think about these things.

As the train drew into Solo my companion, with continental precision, finished the tutorial. She was replaced by a parched octogenarian whose wristwatch was actually thicker than his wrist. Each time I caught his eye he thumped his chest proudly, wheezed the word Sumatra, and coughed hideously. After a while, with a hauntingly polite attempt to shake my hand, he disappeared to the washroom.

Ominously the Sumatran did not come back.

And then came one of those astonishing transformations that do betimes engulf the beleaguered traveller . . . The train was an hour out of Solo when I said to myself, Exercise or die! What I needed was to stretch my limbs. I got up, walked to the end of the car, pulled back the door and started a short programme of disguised calisthenics in that small boxlike area where passengers find themselves when first climbing aboard. Blissfully the carriage door itself was open, letting in a refreshing wind. More, the afternoon rains had begun. Hanging on to a bar I was able to clean first one hand, then the other. By a more precarious balance I was able to clean my face.

When I had finished cleansing myself I turned to discover I was not alone. A man, maybe twice my age, was sitting on the floor on a piece of printed cloth. He was gripping his stomach tightly, and his features wore an extraordinary concentration. There was nothing particularly Japanese about his face, but I recognized the expression at once. I had seen it before, countless times, in Japanese films, just prior to the moment when the hero slits his belly open.

The Dutch woman had described what happened to the Indonesian railways during the Japanese occupation. The Japanese, finding themselves short of steel back home, had taken away all the track and rolling stock not needed in *situ*. The ghastly thought now came to me that here was a Japanese, artfully disguised as a Javan, returning to atone for what Indonesians still regard as a national theft.

I closed my eyes. When I reopened them I realized my mistake. The man was not a Japanese, he was a Moslem. The piece of cloth was his prayer-mat. On it was a compass, to enable him to stay facing Mecca.

I listened to his whispered incantations. Whenever the train swung round a bend and altered course he stopped his prayer in mid-sentence, peered at his compass and shifted position.

After a while I decided it was rather rude of me to stare at the man, and turned back to the open doorway. The scenery and weather had changed out of all recognition. Now the horizon was obliterated by a vast tropical storm. To the east, where the train was headed, the land was swallowed up in mist. To the west the sun had carved a channel through the bank of purple cloud and exhibited itself in a powerful splash of livid crimson.

All hell let loose. To my amazement, when the lightning came, I saw we were passing a volcano. It was not a large volcano, indeed I would describe it as a kitchen model, yet its slopes, illuminated with each blaze of light, made for a perfect cone.

The sun and the storm were making a fight of it, and I was spellbound. But it was more than those two ancient adversaries, it was more than the mountain. I was transfixed by everything: by the wisps of smoke rising from the villages (I am and always will be a sucker for smoke trailing above tropical vegetation, whatever the weather); by the kerosene lamps lit prematurely, and hanging from the beams of the wooden houses; by the buzzing of ten billion crickets; by the zing of the telegraph wires along the track; and of course by the semi-naked people, soaking themselves in the downpour, some with soap, watching the train pass by.

Local Suzy Wong

(*Above*) An Austrian and an Australian monk drawing water at Wat Pa Nana Chat monastery

(*Above*) The Abbot of Wat Pa Nana Chat beside his crematorium

(*Above*) Relief at Borobudur

(*Above*) Headless Buddha at Borobudur

Tanjung Perak: the Port at Surabaya

War Hero: Bill Bennett in his garden

District Officer Bell in 1916–17, courtesy of the Bell family and OUP Melbourne, from *Lightning Meets the West Wind* by Roger Keesing and Peter Carris (1980)

Bill Guinan in the remains of the Execution Block: Bell and Guinan – an unmistakable case of elective affinity

J.W. on Kennedy Island in New Georgia

The diesel pulling us now had its head-lamp on, a strong beam that pierced the murk ahead like a rapier. We were gathering speed all the time, yet even so I leant out to take a look at what was coming.

I was truly on my way to Surabaya. But more importantly I had reached a conclusion about Indonesia. It was already a country that I craved. Simply being there was not enough.

*

But I've missed out Jogjakarta, I've missed out Borobudur.

Jogjakarta, sometimes spelt Yogyakarta, is the showpiece of Java, the very stuff of which travel-guides are made. Its principal streets are wide, airy and ancient. Although twenty miles from the coast, its light is sea-light. A thousand years ago it was the capital of the first Kingdom of Mataram, arguably the most successful of the feudal hegemonies. When Islam and the Dutch arrived it remained the most important provincial sultanate. The Sultan of Jogjakarta, an hereditary entitlement, is still a figure to be reckoned with. Prince Diponegoro, a hero of the 1820s, led the most effective of the mid-term revolts against the Dutch; and from 1945 to 1948 Jogjakarta was the headquarters of the Indonesian Revolution's provisional government.

Today Jogjakarta is a centre for such learning as Suharto's régime permits. It is a city stuffed full with universities and schools, museums and libraries. It also contains countless galleries. The leading feature of Jogjakarta is a city within the city, dominated by an eighteenth-century *kraton*, or palace. This tumbled-down fortress, imposingly lofted on a rock, is connected by underground passageways to vast kitchens and an elegant complex of bathing pools, where in times gone by the sultan sported with his harem. Around the *kraton* is a maze of narrow streets, lined with single-storey whitewashed houses. Formerly these were the living quarters of the royal hangers-on. Now they are inhabited by batik artists, whose extraordinary and sometimes baffling works hang on display in the front parlours.

After Jakarta all this was a sort of music to the eyes. Relatively there was very little dirt. Even the main market had an appearance of ordered cleanliness. And my other senses were equally well provisioned. A twelve-piece gamelan orchestra played almost continuously in the lobby of my somewhat superior hotel, The Garuda –

where I stayed out of deference to the Revolution, which had used The Garuda as its base. The restaurants were special, too, and I have already referred to the skill Jogja barmen have in mixing cordials. Hourly I tested novel combinations of guava, papaya, melon, pineapple, peach and mango. By day two I was a confirmed fruitoholic.

By day three I began noticing the side-effects of my addiction. Regaled with such appetizing liquids my stomach fast forgot the meaning of solid. As I have said, the culprit was the ice, manufactured from unboiled water. I awoke to discover a fire in my rectum – a fire that I soon raised to the status of a blaze, by attempting to douse it with yet more of the treacherous cordials. But there was another side-effect as well. Despite the discomfort, I recognized that within a remarkably short space of time Jogjakarta had utterly beguiled me. I didn't want to do anything except moon around the streets in a state of intense dulcification, asking myself whether I really needed to go to the Solomons.

The best antidote, I resolved, would be a spot of strenuous sightseeing. Because by temperament I don't like sightseeing, in the conventional sense, it nearly always has a purgative effect on me. Seeing the sights demands effort, tolerance of one's fellow-sightseers, and ultimately constitutes a duty performed.

At 40 kilometres outside Jogjakarta, Borobudur, a massive terraced stupa, looked just the ticket. To get there I befriended a young batik painter with a motorcycle. His name was Supri. It was not until much later in the day that I realized he was not quite the innocent his slightly girlish, Javan face suggested.

Borobudur was a good choice, though I should not be too disingenuous here: it is one of the great monuments of S.E. Asia, and no one can visit Indonesia without at least hearing its name. I had scrupulously avoided looking at any pictures of it in the copious tourist literature made available at the hotel and at the tourist office on Jalan Malioboro, for the simple reason that I wanted, if possible, to see Borobudur with fresh, unprogrammed eyes. I wanted to be unprepared.

These are the facts. A stupa is a Buddhist shrine, a place of meditation, often housing relics connected with the Buddha or one of his disciples and usually shaped like a flattened dome surmounted by an umbrella. Although clearly the offspring of pre-Buddhist burial mounds in India, the stupa as a specifically Buddhist enterprise is vindicated by several Buddhist legends. According to one of these the Buddha himself determined the structure of the stupa when he placed his upturned begging bowl on a square of cloth and then crowned the top with a twig. According to another, a divinely-inspired master-builder recognized the necessary form in an air-bubble floating on the surface of a golden vase filled with water. 'He who considers the world as a bubble, as a mirage, will not be noticed by the King of Death.' A third elucidation likens the stupa to the cosmic egg, an omphalos slowly rising through the waters of chaos: nirvana in the making.

Ideally every stupa has a square base, a semi-sphere, and a pointed superstructure. Borobudur conforms to these requirements, only it does so on the grand scale. Built on a hill, its dimensions alone are enough to ensure its place among the wonders of the medieval world. The base measures 123 metres across, and its height is 31½ metres. Over 1,500,000 stones were used in its construction, and its volume works out at 55,000 cubic metres.

The main dome is but a small part of the whole, sitting atop nine terraces. Of these only the upper three are circular; the others are square. Taken all together, the terraces form a mandala, or systematic model of Buddhist doctrine. As a vessel of instruction Borobudur is articulated firstly by a remarkable series of stone reliefs, installed in galleries that run around the lower terraces; and secondly by no less than 504 individual statues of the Buddha. Each of these is one and a half metres tall: 432 of them are displayed in open niches on the lower, square terraces, while the remaining 72 are housed in trellised mini-stupas on the upper, circular terraces.

The symbolism is magnificent. Take first the reliefs, which one analyst has compared to a 'static cinema'. The bottommost of the five sets of reliefs is actually hidden from view, being carved on the covered foot, or plinth, of the monument. Past excavations have shown that, in 165 sections, this depicts scenes from the *Karmawibhangga*, a scripture that describes the causes and effects of good and evil among men and women. Then on the first visible level there are scenes from the life of the Buddha, from his birth in the Garden of Lumbini to the first sermon at Benares (the equivalent in Buddhism to Christ's Sermon on the Mount). The second balustraded gallery illustrates the *Jatakas*, fourth-century poems narrating the self-sacrificing activities of the Buddha in his previous incarnations. In the third gallery (fourth terrace) come the *Awadan*: like the *Jatakas*, these show the Buddha's disciples, bodhisattvas, doing what has to be done to attain Buddha-hood. The fourth and fifth galleries illustrate the *Gandawhyuha*, a key writing that tells of Sudhana, the son of a merchant, who forsakes the world and pledges to follow the example of the Bodhisattva Samantabhadra, who in turn is linked to the Maitreya, or (in Mahayana Buddhism) the future Buddha.

There the reliefs stop. Above them, on the circular terraces, are to be found only images of the Buddha himself. But the whole of Borobudur is covered with Buddhas, all facing outwards and all in the lotus position, but differentiated by their hand positions, or *mudras*. On the lower terraces 368 Buddhas are divided into four sub-sets, according to the cardinal points of the compass. Those facing east have adopted the Bhumisparca *mudra*, or right hand pointing down toward the earth, which is thus called as witness. Those facing south have the right hand stretched out openly, gesturing charity. Westwards, the two hands are joined by the fingers, palms upwards, symbolizing meditation. Northwards – ('. . . but destruction cometh, it cometh out of the north . . .', The Book of Jeremiah, 46.20) – the right hand is raised, signifying fearlessness (and not wholly unlike a policeman forbidding the traffic).

Above these the Buddha icons assume just two poses, exhibited in all directions, north, south, east and west. On the sixth terrace all the Buddhas demonstrate the Witarka *mudra*. The right hand is once again raised, but this time the forefinger bends to touch the thumb: the gesture of reason. Finally, on the three circular terraces, the fourth finger of the right hand touches the fourth finger of the left hand, the one hovering over the other. This, the Dharmacakara *mudra*, symbolizes the Great Wheel of Law, and man's eventual release from it.

These topmost buddhas, however, sit inside stupas of their own. They can be seen only through square- and diamond-shaped holes in their hoods (where the hoods still exist). This indicates the overall cosmogenic concept of Borobudur. The nine levels are composed of three distinct 'spheres'. The lowest, the Sphere of Desire, ends at the upper level of the base. Then comes the Sphere of Form. Finally there comes the Sphere of Formlessness (enlightenment), dominated by the main stupa itself. Kamadhatu, Rupadhatu and Arupadhatu. The square terraces suggest earth, the circular terraces represent heaven (nirvana). But because in heaven there is no form, the Buddhas in the circular terraces are covered, partially hidden (echoing the invisibility of the reliefs on the plinth). They are but a speculative hint of that which lies beyond representation.

Form in the service of formlessness: there can be few other buildings or monuments in the world that embody a philosophy so ambitiously or in such detail. And that after all was the probable purpose of Borobudur: to furnish mainly illiterate pilgrims with a wondrous exemplar of Buddhist teaching. Up each side of the decorated stone hill runs a staircase, enabling visitors to ascend and descend from terrace to terrace, giving them a sense of the great chain of being, of karma and reincarnation, and progress, quite literally, toward a higher good. But this progress is not merely vertical. The galleries, in all 1300 reliefs, are essential to the passage. One enters at the eastern gate and walks round the entire edifice. Then, back where one started, one climbs the eastern staircase to the next tier, and so forth. If one is diligent one has covered 2½ kilometres by the time the summit is reached.

Yet the best of the modern scholars tell us that any unity suggested by Borobudur is accidental, illusory. The monument was not constructed according to one master-plan, but in four discrete phases, between 780 and 850, during which time important architectural and doctrinal changes were introduced in central Java; so that the final assemblage was almost certainly far removed from the conception of the first master-mason. And to add to this confusion, there are as many books and papers written about Borobudur as there are individual Buddhas on Borobudur – more than 540 at the last count.

'The present state of the monument,' wrote the archaeologist Jacques Dumarçay, perhaps the severest of the stupa's critics, 'is an adaptation of an old idea to a new design.'* Yet the wonder of it is it still stands at all. A century after its completion, as Buddhism was displaced by Hinduism, Borobudur fell into disuse. It was not properly rediscovered until 1814, when Stamford Raffles instructed Cornelius, a surveyor from Semarang, to carry out an inspection. By then Borobudur was little more than a pile of rubble. Land subsidence and earthquakes had long obscured its lines and, because of this, much of the stone, a hightly porous andesite, had become waterlogged. The original conduits for carrying away the rains had become dislodged, so

*Jacques Dumarçay, *Borobudur* (O.U.P. 1978)

that the fabric of Borobudur was infested with corrosive mosses, ferns and other vegetal growths. The stucco covering the reliefs, painted over in blues and greens and reds and blacks and probably enhanced with gold leaf, had long since vanished, as had whatever relic the topmost stupa originally contained, looted by thieves unknown.

Since 1814 Borobudur has twice been rehabilitated, once cosmetically between 1907 and 1911 by the Dutchman Van Erp, and again, within the last decade, comprehensively by an international team assembled by UNESCO. This second restoration cost in excess of 14,000,000 American dollars. But if this sounds exorbitant, it should be remembered that the burden of the original construction was even greater. Most historians are now agreed that the labour and resources that went into building Borobudur were responsible for an economic decay in the surrounding countryside that persisted several centuries after the monument's completion. While the stupa went up, the rich volcanic soil in its vicinity was neglected.

My own impression of Borobudur was not especially sanguine. When I first saw it, from the back of Supri's motorcycle, sitting plonk in the middle of a now revitalized plain, I was of course surprised by its dimensions. But it looked like nothing so much as a huge dark wedding cake, made with too little yeast: an image that, as I later conceived, might well stand for Indonesia itself.

There were several possible reasons for my dismay. It could have been the heat, which was ferocious; it could have been the first stirrings of dysentery (as opposed to mere diarrhoea); or it could have been the fact that, as an atheist, my religious experiences are never prompted by religious settings. It could also have been the westerner in me, accustomed to an architecture that manipulates volume. In Dumarçay's words, at Borobudur 'the designers readily acknowledge the laws of gravity.' There are no hollows, no ingenious spaces, no cavities: only a devastating carved compression of heavy substances.

Nonetheless I dutifully traipsed all over the thing until, feeling somewhat sorry for Supri, who on his own admission brought visitors to Borobudur on average once a fortnight, I agreed to return to Jogjakarta. We did not, however, return directly to the Garuda. Supri wanted to take me beforehand to what sounded like Kota Geda, five miles to the south of the city. Aha, I thought to myself, remembering my guide-book, he's going to show me the silverworks. But the Kota Geda Supri took me to had nothing to do with *South-East Asia On A*

Shoestring. It was a village surrounded by paddis consisting of 50 or 60 adobe dwellings. And in every one of them were seven or eight young women.

I had been wondering how much I should pay Supri for his guidance. Now I knew. I thought about giving him a lecture on sexually transmitted diseases, but, when he proudly pointed to one of the girls in the house where we had stopped and told me he liked to visit her three or four times a week, I thought better of it. If not today then yesterday. So instead, as Supri went about his business, I sat drinking tea while down a passageway half-clad prostitutes endeavoured to entice me into the Sphere of Forms.

Supri had brought with him the Sphere of Desire. As for the Sphere of Formlessness, that I suppose was represented by the far-off wheeze of another man's orgasm. When Supri reappeared he was a good deal happier.

*

In Surabaya I went immediately to Tanjung Perak, the port area. This had long been an ambition. As a youngster I used to listen to a recording of Lotte Lenya singing *Surabaya Johnny* from the Berthold Brecht/Kurt Weill operetta *Happy End*. It is the sort of song that makes you want to run your fingers through your hair. Or, now that I'm going bald, through someone else's hair, say the hair of one of Degas's beautiful but bedraggled dancers. It's the death-wish at its most erotic:

> *Ich war jung, erst sechzehn Jahre,*
> *Du kamst von Burma herauf.*
> *Du sagtest, ich solle mit dir gehen*
> *Du kamest fur alles auf*
> . . . .

The woman sings of her passion for the bum who has just jilted her, as surely he has jilted many others before. Surabaya Johnny is famous for his roving, famous for his sailing. In my youth I imagined Surabaya to be full of such men, and such women. I also imagined that if I ever went there something of the same free-and-easy heartache might rub off on me.

This of course was the promiscuous fantasy of a shy student

concocted between the shelves of school and university libraries. Just when I should have been outgrowing it, however, along came Bette Midler and her version:

> *I was young, I was just sixteen then*
> *When you came up from Burma one day*
> *You told me to pack up my suitcase*
> *And I did and you took me away*

And then the refrain:

> *Su-ra-ba-ya Johnny*
> *Is it really the end?*
> *Su-ra-ba-ya Johnny*
> *Will the hurt never mend?*
> *Sur-ra-ba-ya Johnny*
> *How I burn at your touch!*
> *You've got no heart Johnny*
> *But oh! I love you so much!*

In English not perhaps the greatest lyrics ever penned, but even so Better Midler succeeded in turning the original German, enthused with the bitterest ironies, into a red-blooded blues. The remorse was simplified, the yearning amplified, and Surabaya once more assumed high-ranking on the list of places I wished to visit.

Sailing and roving. Fifteen years later I was finally there, squashed up in an overcrowded bus and bearing down on Tanjung Perak. What had I done in between? Edited a few dictionaries and written a few books. Nothing that would have interested Johnny. But now I was making up for it. Now I was swinging into the Harbour Master's Office. Johnny himself could not have stopped me. I would have pushed him aside.

The Harbour Master was not on duty, but the Assistant Harbour Master was. Captain Moninkan, large, handsome and immensely reassuring, shook my hand and winked. If he nursed the slightest suspicion that here was a fellow who knew nothing about ships and passages he kept it to himself. 'You want a berth,' he said. 'Tell me where to?'

'Port Moresby,' I answered. 'I'm headed for Honiara.'

Captain Moninkan nodded. Then he shrugged. As a matter of fact there were not many boats bound for Moresby these days, about one every five to six weeks. Honiara was an even longer shot. He couldn't remember when the last Honiara boat came by. But I was not to worry. Captain Moninkan would find me a berth. In January, after New Year, he knew for certain of a merchantman steaming from Singapore. The master was Scottish. I'd have to meet him of course, since it was the master's decision whether any passengers were taken on board. But (Moninkan winked again) I wasn't to worry: he'd put in a good word for me.

He reached for a piece of paper and produced a well-chewed pencil. 'Here's the name and address of a shipping line,' he said as he wrote. 'They may have a vessel sooner if you're in a hurry.'

'Thank you,' I said. 'January suits me very well. Your English if I may say so, is excellent.'

Captain Moninkan acknowledged the compliment with another wink and a laugh. He'd put into London a thousand times. Did I know the Bell and Anchor by any chance?

'Good heavens yes,' I lied, 'I know it well.'

'How do you say, I used to get pissed out of my breeches there. Before I became a captain of course.'

We all but slapped each other on the back.

And January did suit me very well. It gave me more than enough time to visit Lombok and research my second commission for Hong Kong. I'd have a few days left over to explore Surabaya and East Java as well.

My brief was to write about an Indonesian island that wasn't either Bali or one of the big five, and which nonetheless was accessible to the routes flown by Cathay Pacific. Since Cathay was now flying to Denpassar, the capital of Bali, it seemed both logical and economical to select Lombok, one along down Nusa Tenggara and also within easy range of Surabaya.

It is a conviction of mine, dating back to student wanderings in the Aegean, that any island larger than a tennis court must have something special to offer. Whether the visitor finds it or not is another matter – it depends on his luck. On Lombok I thought for a while my luck had run out. But finally, at Otakokok, Lombok came good, and my faith in islands was preserved.

It was a close call, though. The very name was disconcerting: Lombok, hard-edged and meaning, in *bahasa Indonesia*, red chilli pepper. In the state my stomach was in that was no advertisement. But more, just because of its proximity to Bali, that paradise packaged for western consumption, Lombok suffers a certain stigma. People wishing to disparage it say that it is like Bali without the culture. The riposte to this, that Lombok is like Bali without the hassles (i.e. thieves and rip-off artists), carries rather less force.

That at any rate is what I had picked up from back-packers on the Java trail. In fact Lombok and Bali are very different. Lombok's people, almost 2,000,000 of them are predominantly Moslem, not Hindu. Life for them is not a perpetual celebration of birth and death. Denied the tourist pickings of their neighbours they must derive their livelihood from the land. There is also the matter of the Alfred Wallace Line, drawn across the narrow but very deep straits separating the two islands. According to Wallace it is here that nature doffs her Asian gown and assumes her Australasian mantle.

Yet this is a good deal less apparent today than it was in the mid-nineteenth century. What I actually found in Lombok was an extension of rural Java. Nearly all the island is now cultivated, and the crops are the same crops you would find anywhere between Jakarta and Banyuwang: rice, sugar-cane, tobacco, pepper, coffee and cassava. And there is the same densely populated jigsaw of paddi, plantation and village.

The leading physical feature is Mt Rinjani, which rises almost 4000 metres from the central plain, making it the third highest volcano in all Indonesia. Although it last erupted in 1901, it is still classified as potentially active.

As an object in the landscape Rinjani is spectacularly attractive. In the mornings, before the inevitable clouds obscure its higher reaches, it stands bathed in majesty. By night dynamic electric storms rattle around its summit. Yet precisely because I had just come from Java I had had my fill of volcanoes. Rinjani was just another terribly beautiful lava-heap. Its spendid moods were second-hand. And what went for the mountain went for most of what else I saw. Everything had a *déjà-vu*, forlorn quality to it. As well as dysentery I was experiencing a sustained bout of traveller's surfeit. My article looked in distinct jeopardy of being stillborn, or of not being born at all.

To begin with, like most visitors, I found my attention concentrated westwards. The road that runs right across and bisects Lombok, some 80 kilometres long, begins at Ampenan. This small town is the home of a few small hotels and guesthouses, and is backed by a fishing village from which, at sunrise, a fleet of gaudily painted outriggers sets sail. Alas though, as pretty as these craft were, they were oddly familiar. They reminded me of some equally gaudy outriggers employed by fishermen in the islands of Hawaii.

From Ampenan the road strikes east along an uncommonly broad avenue lined with waringin trees. These raised my hopes somewhat. But not for long. Ampenan becomes Mataram, Lombok's administrative capital, and Mataram becomes Cakranegara, the commercial centre. The needle on my durian-meter was soon dancing dangerously up my nostrils. Taken together the three towns that form the urban heartland of Lombok were no better than any other Indonesian provincial capital.

Not, of course, that Ampenan-Mataram-Cakranegara was entirely devoid of merit. No place is. It offered several good remains. But these, too, had a borrowed quality. They were mainly Balinese.

To explain this I should explain something of the history of Lombok. The indigenous population is Sasak. The Sasaks arrived on the island somewhere between 1500 and 1000 BC, a part of the mongoloid-melanesian migration then sweeping through the whole of S.E. Asia. some of their ancient customs, or *adat*, still survive. The most interesting of these concerns marriage, and is known today either as 'elopement' or 'kidnapping'. Three days before his wedding the groom literally steals his bride from her family. To atone for such wanton misbehaviour he sends personal representatives to her home, to negotiate a bride-price. Once a deal has been struck the wedding proper proceeds. Attired in traditional Sasak costume the couple are paraded in a sedan. An important feature of the elaborate rituals that follow is a 'walking on eggs', performed after a ceremonial bath.

Such procedures have become rare, however. The majority of weddings are conducted according to Islamic law. Islam arrived in Lombok in the fourteenth and fifteenth centuries, and it is this that helps give the island its Javanese identity. But in the eighteenth century there was a disruption. The Balinese came.

What happened was this. There had long been a war between Lombok and the next island eastwards, Sumbawa. To put an end to the fighting the Sultan of Lombok, Datu Selaparang, enlisted Balinese help. In the very next battle the Sultan was slain and the Balinese decided to stay. After further bloody contests Moslem rule was eventually reimposed, but by then the Dutch were effectively the new masters, and the Dutch only packed their bags with the coming of Indonesian independence in 1946.

Such old buildings as do remain belong, nearly all of them, to the period of Balinese suzerainty. In Cakranegara I stumbled upon a complex of shrines called Pura Meru, still the focal point for those Hindus who have stayed on in Lombok. I also visited the Mayura Water Palace, in both senses of the word a stilted hall built on a lake in 1744 as a safe assembly place for Balinese barons. The star turn, however, if star turn it can be called, lay ten kilometres to the east. This was the ornamental garden of Narmada, a series of broad terraces and ponds carved out of a steeply banked hillside. The lowest pool is shaped after Segara Anak, the lake in the caldera of Mt Rinjani. According to legend the design was commissioned by King Anak Gede Karanagasan, another Balinese who, in old age, found he could no longer manage the long climb up Rinjani where, each spring, he was expected to make offerings to the Fire God. Legend also has it that he had constructed a secret chamber next to the Segara Anak lookalike, where, from a hidden window, he observed the younger female bathers. Those that took his eye soon joined his harem.

As I paced about Narmada, falling frangipani blooms kept hitting the ground like empty fruit-juice cartons. The sound was emphasized by the silence of the place, and the silence of the people in it. But this was not a silence occasioned by awe. It was occasioned by lethargy. As lovely as they were, the gardens of Narmada had about them an air that was at once soulless and disconsolate, and I decided they were not the reason I had come to Lombok.

I also decided that Pusa Lingar was not the reason I had come to Lombok. Close by Narmada, Pusa Lingar is yet another temple complex, only this time one that contains both Hindu and Moslem shrines. Once a year its rival congregations stage a mock battle, pelting each other with *ketupat*, or rice wrapped in banana leaves. The spirit of faction, though, is no match for the spirit of tolerance, and the distinguishing feature of Pusa Lingar is a divided altar. Here Hindus and Moslems can and do kneel down together.

Remarkable, even interesting, but still not quite what I was after. So next I hired a motorcycle and drove along the arterial to its eastern extremity. There, at a small but crowded port called Labuhan Lombok (ferries across to Sumbawa) I stared at Mt Rinjani and asked myself why.

Then I tried a couple of beaches. These were perfectly pleasant, but still left me feeling perfectly spare. Was Lombok after all going to prove an exception to my Law of Islands?

In desperation I swallowed my pride and called in at the not very large and not very busy tourist office. There I availed myself of a guide called Harris.

How Harris acquired his name I cannot tell. When I asked him he said it had something to do with his father and 'the war', but wouldn't expand. He was a Sasak, intelligent, eager to oblige, and in some need of a shower. He spoke good English, though, and, with a little push from myself, he delivered the goods.

To begin with all did not go well. Clambering aboard my bike, which had now lost one of its brakes, Harris took me to three villages, rather as though I were being asked to choose between three potential brides, each of whom was blemished.

At every stop we had minor altercations about which of us should drive. As events were to prove, it was eminently reasonable that Harris should take the handle-bar every time. In the first place he was used to the altogether lethal machines available in Lombok, and in the second he knew the no less lethal roads. Pitted against this compelling logic, whenever I rode pillion I was subjected to the full blast of Harris's pong. Rather than explain this to him I told some fib about having taken part in cross-country rallies. Harris didn't believe me for a moment, but was too much the gentleman to argue. In fact Lombok was the first time I'd driven a bike for sixteen years.

The first village was Sengkol, in the south. Perhaps Wobbly Village would have been a more appropriate name. Some tall, Hansel and Gretel-style rice huts were the main attraction. They swayed dramatically at the merest hint of a breeze. The inhabitants of Sengkol, a band of Sasaks still awaiting the nineteenth century, swayed of their own accord. They were a diseased, undernourished lot who could easily have made a killing for Oxfam or Christian Aid. Not only were they without electricity, most of their bamboo and rattan dwellings lacked kerosene. Their overriding problem, however, was their language: they spoke a tongue indecipherable to any other Lombokian, and even Harris seemed nonplussed.

Show me some more, I said.

The second bride was scarcely less primitive: Rungkang, a pottery-producing enclave on the road to Rinjani. All the work was done by women. The technique used is known as 'stone and paddle'. Locally quarried clay of the coarsest kind is mixed with sand and water, then moulded by hand and stone into the desired shape. No wheel is employed. The outside of the pot is beaten with a wooden spatula (the 'paddle') until a more or less even surface is achieved. Finally the pots are fired on an open compost heap, for approximately twenty minutes. Then they're ready. A small one cost 50 rupiah (roughly 3 US cents), a big one (football-size) 100 rupiah.

As Harris explained, the reason the industry survives is that its product undercuts anything made of plastic, and, for holding water, the pots do have their uses

Let's see Number Three, I said.

So Harris took me off to Sukarare, alledgedly a weaving village. There was but one weaver's shop and but a single weaver plying her craft. The cloth was passable, but it didn't move me. Good news for a moth, I thought, but bad news for a wedding.

I told Harris we'd try again in the morning.

I collected him at eight o'clock and the first thing that happened was the remaining brake fell off. I was swinging round a bend at the time and there was a group of children dead ahead. An urgent warning flashed in my brain: if you kill one of them they will kill one of you. Since there was only one of me I improvised a spectacular slide. The bike keeled over at 30 mph. Incredibly neither Harris nor I was badly injured, though we were both shaken.

I started wheeling the bike toward the garage I'd hired it from. Harris by now was of the opinion that we should call it a day, but I knew that if we threw in the towel now it would mean throwing it in for good.

'There must be something else for me to see,' I asserted.

Harris thought hard about this and finally replied:

'Otakokok.'

'Come again.'

'Otakokok. A medicinal waterfall. But you won't like it.'

'Who says?'

On condition that I never again sat at the handle-bar Harris agreed to chaperone me.

It took almost two hours to get to. The journey took us over some very rough dirt tracks made even rougher by the fact that the replacement machine, while it had a good pair of brakes, was minus its suspension. It was also one of the hotter days of my travels. By the time we arrived I was a cross between a burst watermain and a squashed prune. Harris meanwhile had been telling me that I definitely wouldn't enjoy Otakokok. Though much visited by Lombokians, it was not a place for foreigners.

But Harris was wrong. For Otakokok I would return to Lombok any day of the year.

As my guide intimated Otakokok was very much a local institution. Some way from the nearest village, water cascaded down the face of a 25-metre cliff, shooting out of the hillside above in great volume and with great ferocity. At the foot of the fall the water collected in two or three shallow pools before draining into a stream. On the cliff face itself were several ledges, and here a swarm of people, old and young, some of them dressed, some of them not, stood beneath the torrent, shrieking and yelling and laughing.

'Too many people,' Harris observed.

'Not at all!' I cried, stripping to my underpants.

Of course, as soon as I climbed down from the road I was the centre of attention. A dozen naked children wanted to touch my peculiar European skin, and I could tell that their elder sisters were undecided whether I was the handsomest villain they had ever laid eyes on, or the most brutish. When it was realized that I intended to immerse myself there was a general jubilation. Everyone scrambled to clear a passage for me, and everyone rushed to join me beneath the falling water.

It was wonderfully cold. About ten gallons of ice-cold liquid cascaded over me every second, and there was a seat hollowed out in one of the rocks where I could just sit and be drenched.

Also, the water tasted good. I drank and drank and drank.

'But why,' I asked, when finally I came out, 'is the water medicinal?'

Harris, who had been amusing himself with my camera, explained. The water, he said, had a magic diagnostic power. If you stood beneath it and it turned white that meant you were sick. But if the water didn't turn white you were well.

I laughed. What an old wives' tale I said, or words to that effect. But Harris insisted, vehemently, that it was true. And he quoted two examples to prove it.

A month before, he'd brought an Australian to Otakokok and the water had whitened. The Australian hadn't believed Harris either, but a week later he saw a doctor and learned he was really very ill indeed.

Then there was the case of the Big Shot from Java. This man, formerly a minister in the government, had come with an entourage and ducked himself most ostentatiously. He wanted to show the world how clean he was, but instead the water turned to milk. A short while after he was forced to resign. The rumours of corruption in his department had simply got out of hand.

I smiled, and told Harris that in any case it was his turn now. But Harris wouldn't. If perchance his water turned white all his friends would get to hear about it.

'Too many people,' he repeated.

I agreed to change the subject.

'By the way,' I quizzed, 'did my water . . .'

A little glumly, Harris assured me nothing at all had happened. The water flowing off my body had remained perfectly clear, and I had no right to be feeling anything but on top of the world. Which, as it happens, I was.

Those who know about Indonesia may well smile grimly at Harris's second anecdote. Although I was in the country first and foremost as a traveller in transit, and only secondarily as a journeyman writer contributing the odd piece of soft journalism hither and thither, it would be wrong, I believe, to progress further without offering some account of the real goings-on.

In recent years the Indonesian government has striven hard to attract foreign visitors. It has witnessed the immense economic benefits derived from tourism by Thailand, Malaysia and Singapore, and somewhat belatedly it has sought to join the carnival. And why not? The Indonesian cornucopia is as bottomless as its contents are varied. The emerald ricefields of Java alone make Indonesia one of the most stunning visual experiences in the world, never mind about the volcanoes, Borobudur or Bali. No true hedonist could ever be disappointed, however badly his stomach behaved. Yet the beauties of the Republic pale into insignificance beside its brutalities; and beside its President, General Suharto, most other long-established dictators appear distinctly bland.

Probably there is only one thing to be said in Suharto's favour, and that is that Indonesia is ungovernable at the best of times. Indonesia is the classic case of a post-colonial state whose boundaries were determined by colonial administrative convenience and little else. Her frontiers are unnatural and her peoples ethnically, culturally and linguistically diverse. But rather than accommodate to these conditions, Suharto's New Order government (replacing Sukarno's Guided Democracy) has pursued its own neo-colonial policies. In East Timor and Irian Jaya (western New Guinea) the military has imposed Indonesian rule by main force.

The modern Republic consists of 13,700 islands, of which 9000 are inhabited, spread over a vast area of sea. The five larger islands consist of Java, Sumatra, Sulawesi, Kalimantan (the Indonesian lion's share of Borneo) and Irian Jaya. Among the smaller islands are the Molaccas and what used to be called the Lower Sunda Isles, now Nusa Tenggara, including Bali, Lombok and Timor. There is an equally vast population, the fifth largest in the world, presently estimated at 170,000,000 of whom over 120,000,000 live on Java, which accounts for less than eight per cent of Indonesian territory. By contrast Irian Jaya, huge and still partly unexplored, is the least populous area in the tropical belt. The native Melanesians, racially distinct from all the other peoples of Indonesia, are plagued by malaria and, as though that were not enough, by a régime that intermittently practises genocide.

Given the scale of this demographer's nightmare, logic would seem to require political forms of unusual flexibility and tolerance, of federation rather than centralization. What Indonesia possesses, though, is a racist oligarchy that has institutionalized corruption and stymied, perhaps permanently, both economic and cultural growth. While the other nations of the Orient – Japan, South Korea, Taiwan and Singapore in the front rank, Thailand, Malaysia and the Philippines in the second, and China somewhere in between – are jockeying for position in the Pacific Century Derby, Indonesia is kicking herself unconscious in the stalls. To give just one example: Indonesia, as it happens, is the world's ninth largest oil producer. For most third-world countries this would have been a godsend. But not long ago, thanks to a combination of embezzlement and mismanagement, Pertamina, the state oil monopoly, actually went bust. Among other malpractices, Ibnu Sutowo, formerly the president of Pertamina, siphoned off company money to open a restaurant in New York. Today, 40 per cent of the value of all exported commodities is spent servicing interest payments on Indonesia's foreign debts.

Needless to say the origins of what at least one commentator, Brian May, has dubbed *The Indonesian Tragedy* lie buried deep in history. A thousand years ago Java and most of the other islands were ruled by local kings, some of whom were Hindu, some of whom were Buddhist, and some of whom adhered to older homespun animistic religions. These feudal overlords, often immensely rich, fought wars with one another, but rarely in such a way as to interfere with local trade. Periodically a particularly successful dynasty would spread its hegemony across the seas, but none of these promised to last forever. Mini-empires waxed and waned. Meanwhile the great mass of village-bound subjects continued working the land for a subsistence living.

The two climactic changes were the advent of Islam, and the arrival of European traders. Islam, carried by Arabic and Indian merchants, came first to Sumatra in the thirteenth century, and then spread eastwards. By 1596, when the first Dutch ships put in to land most of Java had converted, as had Lombok – though interestingly Bali remained a Hindu enclave, which explains its cultural 'uniqueness' in modern times. Yet the intensity of conversion varied from area to area, even from village to village. In contemporary Java, although Islam is the official state religion, there are broadly two kinds of Moslem: *santri*, who practise Islam to the exclusion of all other religious elements, and *abangan*, who combine Islamic elements with older indigenous beliefs. It is this distinction that explains how it is that, in recent years, a nominally Islamic government has managed to persecute followers of Islam without appearing, to its own people, irredeemably two-faced.

But of that, more anon. In 1596 the Dutch arrived, not initially as a force for invasion, but singly, as seaborne pedlars. What dictated colonization was the rival presence of other Europeans (the Portuguese and English, later on the Germans, French and Danes) coupled with the very broad charters granted by European powers to their trading organizations, the great Companies. What enabled colonization was the superiority of European weapons which the Companies deployed without restraint. Eight thousand miles away in Amsterdam what mattered was profits, and profits depended upon the success of the Dutch East India Company. If the DEIC needed to arm its ships against interlopers from the British East India Company, that was a matter of Company policy; and if the DEIC decided that outright dominion was a more effective way of protecting its interests, that too was a matter for the Board, and nothing must be allowed to stand in its way.

Over the next two hundred years the Company spread its tentacles through the islands, thus creating a unity of sorts where none had existed before. Sometimes it used brute force, sometimes diplomacy, preferring indirect rule through client princes. A central garrison was built at Batavia – modern Jakarta. But it was a costly enterprise, despite the rich return on spices, and in 1796 the Company, weakened by successive conflicts with British and Danish 'pirates', declared itself insolvent. It was at that point that the Dutch Government intervened directly. The Dutch East India Company was bought out, and Indonesia formally became a colony.

The colonial period in Indonesia was not entirely static, nor was it wholly repressive. During the nineteenth century plantations tended to replace small holdings, to force the mass production of agricultural produce. But hand-in-hand with this economic rationalization came a partial relaxation of imperial ideology. The way forward, according to the new liberal creed, was to encourage native participation, which effectively meant advancing native education. The general idea was that select Indonesians, once they had been enlightened in the ways of European liberalism, would assist in the colony's administrative and economic affairs to the extent that they would reduce both the running costs and the threat of insurrection.

History, however, had other ideas. Even before the Second World War there were several dissident groups that, with varying degrees of militancy, pursued the notion of Indonesian independence. What was lacking was a united front. On the one hand there were neo-Marxists, on the other Islamic fundamentalists. Even during the subsequent War of Independence (1945–49) these parties not infrequently found themselves at odds with each other. But the event that made independence a realizable ambition was the Japanese Occupation. Firstly the colonial power was, temporarily at least, removed. Secondly the Japanese, facing defeat themselves, saw that the long-term interests of Asia would be better served by an independent Indonesia than by the return of European empire. A crucial factor in the early victories of the Indonesian independence fighters was their possession of rifles, small cannon and other military equipment. These the Japanese obligingly left behind when they departed for their own shores.

The man who co-ordinated the revolt, and who steered Indonesia through its first two-and-a-half decades of independence, was none other than Sukarno, the Republic's first president. Born in Surabaya in 1901 this formidable and charismatic individual acquired prestige early on. At school he was known as Djago, which translates as Champion or Cock. Later on he became known as Bung Karno, Brother or Comrade Karno. While attending secondary school he lived in the house of Omar Said Tjokroaminoto, a Surabayan political leader who financed Sukarno's higher education. Tjokroaminoto kept something of an open house for East Javan intellectuals, and through them Sukarno acquired something of the breadth of vision that subsequently informed his own political programmes. Yet even as a student Sukarno shone in his own right. Among his other talents he had an exceptional gift for languages. As well as Javanese, Sudanese and Balinese he mastered Arabic (the language of the Koran), Dutch, German, French and English. He was also fluent in Malay, which, with hardly any changes, became the basis of *bahasa Indonesia*, the Indonesian national language – a development that Sukarno himself contributed to.

From Surabaya, having married Tjokroaminoto's daughter Siti (the first of seven wives), Sukarno moved to Bandung, to study civil engineering. Two years after taking his degree (1927) he found himself in prison, on charges of sedition. His political career had begun in 1926, when he published a book called *Nationalism, Islam and Marxism*. This was no dry academic study of three contending, and largely exclusive, ideologies, but an exhortation to all Indonesians to bury their differences and come together in a common cause. Sukarno saw that the way ahead for an independent Indonesia lay precisely in blending the three forces alluded to in his title. Elsewhere in the East countries were to be torn apart by them. Sukarno though, either by an excess of hubris or because he understood something other leaders did not, chose what on paper at least was the most difficult path available; and in the end it was not the impossibility of his dream that thwarted him, but the army he had done so much to organize during the struggle against the Dutch.

From 1933 Sukarno was exiled, first to Flores, a predominantly Catholic island in Nusa Tengarra, then to Sumatra. He returned to Java only in March 1942, following the Japanese invasion. Throughout the occupation he collaborated with the Japanese, because he knew, or sensed, that the Japanese were unlikely to stay forever. In return for the services he had rendered them (which included recruiting prostitutes) the Japanese 'granted' Indonesia independence in 1945. Sukarno used the occasion to proclaim the *Pancasila*, or five-point national philosophy, stipulating (1) belief in one God (though it didn't matter which) (2) a just and civilized humanity (3) national unity (4) representative democracy, and (5) social justice. Four years later, after the Dutch finally conceded defeat, he made his triumphal entry into Jakarta.

Today the *Pancasila*, engraved on tablets in every marketplace and on every public building throughout the country, is about all that remains of Bung Karno. The Five Principles are universally revered by order, and universally ignored by those best placed to observe them. To be fair to his successors, however, it was Sukarno himself who initiated the rot. At first his policies were hampered by his fellow-generals, who from the beginning disliked his ideological sympathy for communism. By 1956, however, he had outmanoeuvred his rivals and assumed dictatorial power. Parliament was disbanded, and replaced by what the great patriot lovingly called Guided Democracy: a council of state packed with his own supporters. Sometimes he ruled through the council, sometimes by direct decree, which, as President For Life, he felt himself entitled to do. Meanwhile the economy stagnated, corruption spread and social conditions worsened.

The end, when it came, was sudden, dramatic and, even by Indonesian standards, obscure. On 1st October 1965 a group of junior army officers staged an attempted putsch. Seven senior officers, including six generals, were seized at dawn and assassinated. Their bodies were unceremoniously dumped into what has since become known as the Crocodile Hole, a well at a military base on the outskirts of the capital. But that was as far as the young Turks got. General Suharto, mysteriously overlooked by the assassins, moved like greased lightning to restore order. As though by magic his tanks were already waiting in the best counter-offensive positions; and by the end of the week Sukarno was critically indebted to his subordinate.

Suharto, however, did not rush his own *coup d'état*. He was aware that the army contained many cadres loyal to Sukarno, and his new ascendancy would be imperilled if he assumed power abruptly. For a while he let it seem that Sukarno was still the effective ruler, while in reality he appropriated, one by one, the reins of government. At the same time he orchestrated the beginnings of what was to become a full-scale and very bloody purge of communist elements. Thus it was not until March the following year that Sukarno publicly delegated powers to Suharto; and it was not until March 1968 that Suharto formally became President.

Most independent historians and Indonesia-watchers today take the view that Suharto, the supreme tactician, engineered the abortive October putsch, i.e. that he 'arranged' for a small section of the army to revolt in order to give himself the chance to smash a rebellion. Certainly, if his subsequent actions are any guide, he was capable of it. The clever deployment of *agents provocateurs* would seem to be the hallmark of Suharto's rule. It is also generally believed that he deliberately exacerbated Moslem dissent in the mid-1980s, again to furnish himself an excuse to display the iron fist.

The iron fist, though, was first unleashed against the communists, members and affiliates of the PKI, or Partai Kommunis Indonesia. It was claimed, with no proper justification, that the PKI had master-minded the putsch. On this flimsy pretext one of the great witch-hunts of modern times was launched. Somewhere between 250,000 and 750,000 so-called rebels were openly murdered, often by gangs of 'young Moslems' whose activities the authorities 'overlooked'. Thousands more were slung into prison, usually without any form of trial. Yet there were trials, too, and these set the pattern for subsequent government assaults – for example, upon the Melanesians of Irian Jaya, the inhabitants of East Timor, and latterly those termed Moslem extremists. Confessions were extracted under duress (torture) and then read out in court. If a defendant tried to retract anything he had said, he ran the risk of being further indicted for perjury. He was also lucky if he secured counsel of his own choice, though even that didn't help much: in many cases the judges refused defence lawyers the right to call key witnesses. Finally, there were few, if any, acquittals. Suharto's judiciary, in blatant disregard of human rights as defined by the United Nations, dealt out (and continues to deal out) sentences regardless of anything the accused may or may not have done.

The purge of the communists, in addition to subverting the courts for political ends, also consolidated the position of the military, not just in government but throughout the land. To tighten security officers were posted to every village on every island, with the result that the army has largely replaced traditional local leadership (i.e. the village headman). Commonly the army's resident representative is engaged in some business of his own, to supplement his modest pay.

Perhaps he runs a grocery counter; in which case the local people are well advised to purchase at least some of their condiments from him, even though his prices are higher. Thus, the government permits a protection racket staffed by members of the establishment.

But what happens at the village level is only a microcosm of what happens at the national level. Here retiring generals are routinely paid off with state monopolies. Before retirement they can make their millions through Chinese intermediaries (called *kukongs*), into whose hands all important state business is placed. In addition Suharto's wife, Mrs Tien Suharto, has worked assiduously to ensure the financial security of each and every member of the presidential family. She may not look as fancy as Imelda Marcos, but she is quite as deadly.

All this is a far cry from the syncretic unity Sukarno envisaged for his people. As Brian May puts it in his book, Suharto has pursued 'harmony by elimination'. This has been made possible by the continued goodwill (i.e. aid) of the United States, the Dutch, Britain and Saudi Arabia (among others) who have recognized in Suharto a staunch enemy of communism. Indeed there is even evidence that Suharto had American support before October 1965, and the CIA certainly did everthing in its power to assist in the communist purges – it was after all the period of escalating conflict in nearby Vietnam. Without American dollars it is difficult to see how Suharto could have maintained control of the army so effectively so long. Nor is there any sign that the dictatorship is relaxing or otherwise running out of steam. The present crusade against alleged Moslem hardliners demostrates that Suharto is as virile as ever.

In September 1984 in Tanjung Priok, a docklands area of Jakarta, a peaceful protest of Moslems was ruthlessly butchered by army units, brought into the district some while before the 'trouble' started. Between 100 and 300 protestors are reported to have been killed. Since then hundreds of Moslem leaders have been hauled up before the courts throughout Java and beyond. The usual judicial standards have applied, and the public prosecutor has enjoyed his usual hundred per cent strike rate. And once again the real evidence points towards government complicity in the origins of the so-called riot itself. Suharto, or one of his most senior colleagues, instigated a crisis to legitimate draconian reprisals.

The secret of Suharto's success lies in knowing where and when to apply the pre-emptive poultice. In 1984 Moslem dissidence was probably no greater than it had been five years before, or ten years before. Yet the fact remains that, having previously disposed of any possible danger from socialists and communists, the most likely source of militant opposition was organized Islam. This was so for two reasons, one internal, one external. Internally, come 1984, Islam was the only broadly based organization in Indonesia not under government control. All political parties not directly sympathetic to the government had been outlawed. Externally, Islamic fundamentalism had already shown its power to topple governments elsewhere in the world, notably in Iran. Suharto could argue, therefore, amongst his fellow-generals, that there always was the possibility that Islamic extremists might get ideas above their station in Indonesia.

It is conceivable that Suharto may for once have over-reacted. Because of Indonesia's religious diversity it has until now been historically unlikely that any one sect, however extreme, would gain political ascendancy. Given the level of repression achieved by Suharto's government, however, it is no longer inconceivable that Islamic fundamentalists could find themselves in the vanguard of a genuinely broad-based anti-Suharto movement, which they alone have the capacity to organize.

On the other hand it is also possible that Suharto's latest poultice has drawn what poison there is. Either way the outlook is grim. An Islamic revolution – the only possible revolution available – would almost certainly be a protracted and bloody affair: after all, the fundamentalists' human rights record is also abysmal. The long-term sufferers would most probably be the *abangan*, those half-Moslems who, according to Koranic tradition, are guilty of impiety. Or Suharto stays, at least until another like-minded general, another *dalang*, ousts him in a palace *coup*. Meanwhile the economy stumbles backwards. In a few enclaves, the main streets of the big cities, there are all the trappings of a fake prosperity: big new department stores, designed according to the Japanese fashion. But for the vast majority of Indonesians, finding themselves more and more in debt, life was certainly better forty years ago. Forty years ago they could take pride in having overthrown their European overlords. Overthrowing their Javan overlords is likely to prove a stiffer task.

*

On Lombok, however, none of this was readily apparent. It was not until I reached Jayapura, the administrative capital of Irian Jaya, that I observed at first hand incontrovertible evidence of oppression. Rather I continued in the hedonistic mode. After Otakokok I stayed on the island a few more days, mainly to avail myself of the beach at Sengiggi, ten miles north of Ampenan. There the proprietor of the beach huts, an old man dressed in dazzling batik shirts, sang Japanese songs at night. But I did not sleep in his huts. I stuck to the Wisma Melati in Ampenan, a *pension* within striking distance of the Garden House Ice Cream Palace in Mataram, where travellers of all sorts congregated for their meals. Half the people I met were working or had worked for the BBC in some capacity or other. There was also a sterling fellow called Morton Klein who, despite his name and his Californian accent, claimed to be a native of Southampton. His favourite trick was to throw bits of fish at me, saying 'Have a prawn cracker!' One afternoon, at no great expense, we hired a driver and a Mercedes Benz to explore the southern coast. Each village we passed Morton waxed lyrical about the richness of life. Also waxing lyrical was an immensely stout woman from Flores called Margaretha. Margaretha loved all foreigners, but especially she loved Englishmen. I wasted no time showing her a photograph of my wife, which I kept on me for just such emergencies. Morton, alas, was less well equipped, and bore the brunt of Margaretha's attentions, which included a medley of lines from various Scottish ballads which she shrieked into his ear. In no time at all she took to slapping Morton's thighs, back and neck, hard, and with both sides of her considerable hands. Yet by the end of the day the two were almost friends. For Morton's benefit I directed the driver to take us to the gardens at Narmada. Somewhere between the third and fourth terraces I separated from my companions. Soon I espied Margaretha garlanding Morton's head with frangipani blooms, and Morton, looking lost and bewildered, tentatively holding Margaretha's hand.

Conceivably Morton was responsible for the second anonymous and bizarre telephone call that came my way during my travels. I had just laid head to pillow in my room at the Melati when the plastic rattled beside my bed.

'Would you like some Dover sole?' dinned an exaggeratedly British voice.

'Do I have any choice?'

'If you're feeling fussy I can arrange a porterhouse steak.'

'Sorry, but who are you?'

'I'm the toothpaste man.'

'Toothpaste man?'

'Yes. I'm the man who sells toothpaste to the Indonesian hookers. You know what they use it for?'

'I'm afraid you've got me.'

'It's got me too. Either they use it as a contraceptive cream, or as a disinfectant. I never have been able to discover which. But every time, toothpaste, right up.'

'Gosh.'

Next morning I interrogated Morton, but he denied all knowledge of it. All he would say was, 'Sounds like you got the prawn cracker there, mate.'

Then I returned to Surabaya, in time for New Year, greeted in by several hundred thousand youngsters blowing paper-made golden trumpets in the streets. Captain Moninkan welcomed me like a lost son, but gave me the bad news that the boat from Singapore was now not expected to dock until the 19th or 20th of January. Still determined to continue my journey by sea I said I would wait, even though that meant the complicated – and expensive – rigmarole of renewing my visa. But not to worry. In my naivety, in my loyalty to Bette Midler and Lotte Lenya, I considered that if I had to be holed up anywhere Surabaya was the place for it. I set about exploring the city as best I could. A lot of the time I just hung around Tanjung Perak, drinking bottles of chocolate-flavoured soyabean milk sold to me by doleful young men pushing wheeled ice-boxes. Away from the port, though, I realized that the city and the song had very little to do with each other.

> *You said a lot, Johnny,*
> *It was all lies*

Make no mistake, Surabaya is a great city, but only in the sense that Liverpool, Frankfurt and Turin are great cities. It is a vast and filthy metropolis. Since no one stays there unless he has to it has rightly earned the nickname Transit City. The primary sensation is the smell of diesel. The air has to be drilled for oxygen. And if it's not diesel it's our old friend, rotting durian.

Another Jakarta. Foodstalls, or *warung*, are endemic. There's scarcely a street where you can't buy your breakfast, your lunch or your dinner from the gutter. The city also abounds with markets, where fruit, vegetables and meat are piled up, as often as not, on the ground, making Surabaya into another paradise for rats. But more than this, pollution-wise the canalized river that runs through the heart of Surabaya, the Kali Mas, and its many canalized tributaries are in a class of their own. Constantly one risks toppling into the world's biggest open sewer.

Driven by the sheer stink of the place you run for cover. But the visitor is lucky if he makes cover. Another negative aspect of Surabaya is its traffic. An incredible assortment of trucks, buses, jeeps, taxis, *bemos*, motorbikes, cars and trishaws, very few of which would pass the most rudimentary roadworthiness test, somehow manages to keep on the go at breakneck speed. Attempting to cross a road is like attempting to play an advanced computer game. If you don't get zapped from the left you'll certainly get zapped from the right. Nor are the very few sets of traffic lights any guarantee of safety. Mainly the drivers ignore them. It is said that when they were first introduced the police considered arming themselves with bricks to throw at offending drivers. But then it was calculated how many bricks would be needed, and the project was abandoned.

Not that there is much incentive to brave such hazards. For a conurbation its size – 50 square kilometres and upwards of 3,000,000 people – Surabaya offers woefully little to do and see. Tanjung Perak is one of the few musts: the sight of up to a hundred white-painted engineless Madura schooners, or *prahu*, along the wharf at the sea-end of Kali Mas will appeal to anyone who has read a word of Conrad. There is also a large, cheerless zoo, in the south of the city, reputedly the biggest in S.E Asia. Its special attractions are the Komodo Dragon, a pair of dugongs, Sumatra tigers and a genuinely exotic collection of tropical birds, although for my money first prize went to a couple of orangutans whose love-hate for one another was expressed in a seemingly infinite variety of manoeuvres culled from some *ballet fou*. Otherwise zilch. A small museum, and not much of a night-life. A smattering of good restauants, and the usual discothèques for the sweaty young, but these are dispersed, and there's hardly what could be called a city centre. Jalan Tunjungan is where the best shops are, including two new Japanese-style department stores, but even this thoroughfare quickly degenerates into the usual low-rise concrete alley.

Yet there were two mitigating circumstances that made Surabaya, for this detainee, a welcome experience. The first was its history. The second was its people.

Roughly, Surabaya has been in existence for five-and-a-half centuries. No one is quite sure, but the city was probably founded in the early 1400s by the Moslem Raden Rakhmat, a cousin of the then King of Majapahit. Very soon the new town, blessed with a huge natural harbour, was trading with Sulawesi, Borneo, Malacca and China. For two hundred years it retained its independence until at last, after a long siege, it fell to Sultan Agung, ruler of the central Javanese Kingdom of Mataram, which in turn was fast becoming a client state of the Dutch.

In all this period Surabaya prospered and expanded, exporting, as it does today, rice, teak, sugar, tapioca, sugar, spices, textiles and tobacco. Yet just because of their success Surabayans tended not to become involved in politics – they had too much to lose. But when the moment came Surabaya contributed as much as, perhaps even more than, any other city to Indonesian independence, thus vindicating its name, City of Heroes.

After the Japanese were defeated the British temporarily took charge, meaning to safeguard Indonesia for their European allies. But the Surabayans had other ideas. Famously, when Britain sailed into Tanjung Perak, in October 1945, Surabaya resisted. For three weeks, in the Battle of Surabaya, and armed with Japanese rifles, the citizens fought for their rights. Although the battle was finally lost, an important point had been made. For the first time the Indonesian national flag – a segment torn from the old Dutch flag – had been raised in defiance.

Thus was the war of independence launched; and under the leadership of Surabaya's most famous son, Sukarno, it was pursued to fruition.

I was lucky. The staff of the Garden Hotel in Jalan Permuda, where I stayed, virtually adopted me when they learned of the delay to my ship. Several charming and well-educated young men and women took it upon themselves to show me the real Surabaya. With some zeal they took me round the many statues and monuments commemorating Surabaya's history. These scarcely held much aesthetic appeal – every one of them was cast in the universal social realist style employed to celebrate the birth of most new nations. But, accompanied by my new friends, I managed to see beyond their excessive vulgarity. I was also invited by the Garden staff to their homes. Mostly they were young marrieds, and lived modestly in the so-called suburbs – mile after mile of single-storey dwellings separated by paths rather than roads. Here, away from the hurly-burly of the big streets, I was able to observe Javans at rest. What struck me was the obsessive love they have for one another, and the great beauty of their faces: the simple, child-like features of the Orient, but substantiated by an over-whelming warmth of spirit.

Two memories stand out from my Surabayan days. Inevitably some of the young men wanted to drag me off to the red-light district, 10,000 square metres of it, at Bandarejo. I protested strongly, but finally agreed on condition I went only as an observer. At this they laughed. Whatever I wanted, they told me, whatever my desire might imagine, I would find it at Bandarejo. There were girls of twelve there, and likewise there were women of sixty. And they would do whatever I wished.

This boast was amply justified. Bandarejo consisted of hundreds and hundreds of *wismas*, each containing an extraordinary selection of women. They were indeed of all ages. The parameters I had been given were, if anything, conservative. In the house where we eventual-ly stopped for a beer the youngest can have been no more than ten, while the oldest was seventy if a day.

'Come on, mister,' plied the boldest of my hosts, 'what you want?'

Putting on my best confessional voice I answered:

'She's not here, I'm afraid. What I would really like is a 22-year-old without arms and legs.'

My friend looked at me quizzically. Then he spoke to the mama-san. At last he turned back to me and said:

'You are right. She not here. But tomorrow, come back. Have girl no arm, no leg.'

I did not return to Bandarejo. Instead I returned to the ordinary suburbs and sat with the less adventurous. It was a hot, stormy, rainy night and people darted from open door to open door in pursuit of society and conversation. In a while a very small girl came walking up the track beneath an umbrella. When she saw me she stopped and asked if she could come in. My hosts welcomed her at once. But she wouldn't drink any tea. What she wanted was to practise her English. Apparently my fame had spread, because she lived many lanes away, and would shortly have to return to her own home.

She was no more than eight or nine, but her English would have done credit to a university student.

'So,' I said, 'what shall we talk about?'

The little girl frowned, then suggested we talk about her brother.

'But I haven't met your brother,' I said.

'That's all right,' she replied, 'I will tell you about him.'

She told me about her brother. She told me everything there was to tell about him. He was tall, good-looking, and had beautiful eyes. But the best thing about her brother, the girl said, was his voice. At night his voice helped her to sleep.

'Is he very much older than you?' I asked.

'Oh yes. My brother is sixteen.'

'And what does he do now? Does he go to college?'

The girl looked at me and smiled.

'Oh no,' she said. 'My brother doesn't do anything. He's dead.'

That broke me up. That, and the girl's continuing smile, a hopelessly wise smile for one so young.

*

After ten days, for the sake of my lungs, I decided to leave Surabaya. But what was I to do instead? Dr Indiarta, a senior official at the Department of Telecommunications who had sponsored my visa renewal application, and who was also responsible for promoting tourism in East Java, had just the answer. 'Go to the mountains,' he said, 'go to Tretes.'

Since almost everybody else I met offered the same advice I went to Tretes. The bus from Joyoboyo terminal to Pandaan (pronounced Panda Ann) cost around 20p, and a minibus from Pandaan up into the forest was the same again. It was 40 kilometres from the city and immediately the cool air awakened my spirits. I checked into the new Bath Hotel, ate some chicken satay, and set off to explore. Within ten minutes I had discovered everything about Tretes that the good Dr Indiarta had omitted to mention. Every other house was a brothel. There were literally hundreds of young women smiling through their make-up behind enlarged plate-glass windows. Prostitution on the Asian scale in a mountain resort. *Hey mister! You have cigarette?*

I pressed on. Close to the *wismas* were elegant villas set in elegant gardens. These belonged to the rich of Surabaya, who like to drive up from the sweltering sea-plain of an evening to spend a few hours with the lasses. There were steep, narrow, winding streets and little shops selling cold drinks, *kropok* (nibbles) and, of course, toothpaste. It was a place that properly belonged on the coast.

Later it was explained to me: there is a White Tretes and a Black Tretes. Or, if you like, a Moral Tretes, and a Not So Moral Tretes. Where the one ended and the other began, however, was a matter of pure conjecture.

I still pressed on. Not the least of Tretes's charms were the clearwater streams gurgling between the houses and the cobbled lanes. I wanted to see where they came from.

I climbed, and eventually arrived at the top road. A sign board said Dirgahayu Indah Hotel. I climbed a little further, and reached the Dirgahayu. When I saw it I raced back to the Bath and checked out. I had found the perfect answer to the vapours of the city.

The Dirgahayu deserves to be better known than it is, which is hardly at all. For comfort it's nothing much – my tiny chalet was damp, ill-lit, and I was much exercised by ants. But the hotel itself had a quality that its newer concrete rivals in Tretes can never aspire to. It was like a cake upon which the cake-maker had practised all his different skills. But where taste should have predicted a chaos, luck had wrought a palace. It was the sort of affair Fellini could have used for one of his set-pieces.

The central feature was a truly large bathing pool, compartmented into five discrete levels: one for small children, one for older children, two for intermediate adults, and a proper four-metre deep trough for serious swimming. The joy of it was that you could set off on a crawl and not have to think of turning round for fifty strokes or more.

Around the pool was pitched all the cake-maker's art. A bar and dining areas with preserved knotted tree-trunks for pillars, and ceilinged with dark bamboo; a corner gazebo overlooking the valley (saddled ponies waiting on the road below); a long two-tiered loggia, red-tiled, in size and tone like a spectator-stand on a polo pitch; stone staircases walled with serpents; an onion-headed mosque; a wall covered with geometric Spanish-style ceramics; and the *coup do grâce* – at the top end a terraced façade reminiscent of the 'house' in a Greek theatre. In its centre a vast and gaudy garuda, supported by a plinth fantastic, spouted water; beside him, round-eyed elephants squatting on skulls; to his right, in the corner, a three-storeyed square turret of green; and, flanking him, four giant reliefs, depicting nymphs and heroes.

But it was the pool, not its surrounds, that monopolized my attention. Thirty-five years old, the pale blue-green paint covering its sewing-box floors was peeling everywhere, revealing the black and brown rock beneath. As the water rippled in constant diamonds (the effect of the garuda fountain) all manner of shapes and images welled up to the surface. Depending on where I sat I could discover almost anything. From one chair I studied a bizarre bestiary of creatures that were half-animal, half-bird. A peacock's head on the shoulders of a bullock, for example. A horse with the legs of a turkey. A bear spreading its wings like an eagle. Or, from another chair, a terrible array of military machines caught in the mangle of destruction. Or again, from another side, a peasant woman (the face so exact, so precise, so forlornly winning) lifting her skirt as though to run faster, her head turned backwards in fear, observed by a funny-nosed but equally Goyaesque Russian soldier, snow clinging to his furs. And these two figures contained within a larger composition of a Chinese coolie, a beturbaned and bearded Arabian prankster grinning on his shoulder . . .

Accident is a fine creator. Unwittingly the cake-maker had surpassed himself. No conscious stroke of the brush or chip of the sculptor's chisel could have achieved such a rich and elusive gallery. Hour after hour I watched the Dirgahayu water, happy to be distracted from my work, and always finding something fresh.

On the fifth morning, however, the pool was empty. Several of the hotel staff were down in its rectangular hollows (like the hold of a ship) with stiff brushes. As they scrubbed, a few more flakes of paint came away. The Russian soldier's nose, I could see, would no longer be funny, but diseased, grotesque.

When they had finished I climbed down the rungs and walked across yesterday's illusions. For a joke one of the barmen, grinning like a cut lychee, played *Don't Cry For Me Argentina* on the poolside speakers. No voice, just a cornet.

I think he wanted me to dance. I obliged.

For six monastic days I remained at the Dirgahayu, dropping thoughts into my notebook as they occurred. Except at the weekend I was the only guest. I had a staff of fourteen or fifteen to look after me, at approximately 50p a head. I also began writing a novel that I knew would come to a halt after twenty or thirty pages, but which I nevertheless persevered with if only to tap the creative juices mysteriously released by the pool. It belonged precisely to that category of writing which, a few weeks later, I was to disparage so vehemently in my conversation with Dr Key. In it I assembled a network of characters at the huts on Senggigi Beach in Lombok. These were semi-invented people inspired by those I'd met at different stages of my Indonesian journey. Morton Klein, though, presented a problem. His name was too good to alter, and he resisted the transforming processes of fiction. In the end I left him as he was, finding a space for him between Bill, the hero, and Rosemary Bush, the heroine. Deliberately I began without a plot, other than a vague notion that Bill and Rosemary should be brought together, the way Caucasians often are brought together in the Orient, only to discover an enduring (but not endearing) incompatibility. But because I already knew of their incompatibility the project was doomed from its inception. And that's just how I wanted it. When I left Tretes I didn't want to have an unfinished novel hanging round my neck. What I did want was an abandoned novel in my shoulderbag. And so it was.

I began work each morning at seven o'clock, and continued until five or six in the afternoon. Most of the time the temperature was exactly right for composition: between 54ε and 58ε fahrenheit. Sometimes the rain mist came rolling down the mountain, so that quite literally I had my head up in the clouds. If I got stuck I dived into the punishingly cold water. What I didn't do was dive down into Black Tretes. Black Tretes was beneath me, and I intended keeping it that way.

Except on my fifth night. On my fifth night in Tretes, perhaps because the pool had been empty all day, I had a relapse. Suddenly the restrictions I had imposed on myself no longer made sense. I looked down the mountainside after dinner and saw a hundred lights inviting me to resume the pleasures I had canvassed so throughly on my first visits to Asia. Why shouldn't I? I asked myself. Why in hell's name shouldn't I? And it must be safe, I argued. Since coming to Tretes I had seen not a single white man, not a single potential carrier of the plague. And if there were consequences, so be it. I had to die sometime. What I couldn't stomach any more was the new goody-goody identity I had manufactured for myself. It didn't suit. It didn't ring true.

My blood was up, the dam of celibacy was about to burst. My heart pounded as it has seldom pounded before. Yet I had resolved quite clearly what I was going to do. I was going to go down, I was going to find a friendly *wisma*, and I was going to have not one, not two, but half-a-dozen women, just like the good old bad old days when I first went to Bangkok in a state of advanced, post-adolescent cacoethes. I was going to put an end to my scruples in the most extravagant way possible. If anything untoward did happen afterwards I would ascribe it to the 'East' (a casual waft of the hand) and walk away from life in a blaze of riveting memories. But, for now, I was not going to be denied.

Had I stuck to this course probably I'd never have reached the Solomons. Probably I'd never have come home to England either. A man can soak himself in the fleshpots of Asia once or twice in his life and still resume his ordinary activities. But the third or fourth time is dicing with destiny. I've seen men, good men, with university degrees and high prospects, go back when they shouldn't have gone back, and prisoner themselves to the carnal. In no time at all they become limp shadows. They have severed every link with their homes, their families, their pasts. They have nothing to think about except the next girl, and the next drink. But one day, much sooner than anticipated, their money runs out. They also find the capacity for decision-making has deserted them. They can't go forward, and they can't go back. So instead they hole up. A few pennies will always buy a whisky, but one by one the women become unobtainable. And so they rot, western destitutes amid the plenty of the Orient.

As I left the Dirgahayu I thought about this, but refused to let it interfere with my immediate plans. Below me, soon right around me, the myriad-mouthed honeytrap snapped its jaws invitingly. Girls crowded in doorways, flashing smiles and making suggestions. I began making notes of their faces. To which should I return? For I was in no hurry. In delay is added sweetness. Before I committed myself I wanted to check out each shelf of the supermarket, to ensure that my eventual choice was the wisest, the most rewarding available.

But for once the East conspired against concupiscence. I was about halfway down the mountainside, halfway down Black Tretes, when I heard the strains of a gamelan orchestra. The next thing I knew I was standing on the edge of a medium-sized crowd ringing the front court of a house at the intersection of three lanes. In the middle of the clearing two dancers were encircling each other, tapping their feet in

180

time with the music. Tied to their ankles were bells. They had stocky powerful legs, and stocky powerful breasts, which showed in the boxlike decollétage of their peasant costumes. When they sang their voices were correspondingly low, almost deep. But their lines were often disrupted by shy, self-concious laughter whenever an onlooker shouted out a compliment. As performers they were neither particularly skilled nor particularly disciplined. Sometimes they were unsure of their steps. But their faces were adorable. Both possessed beauty, and both enjoyed what they were doing.

Yet the dancers were only a curtain-raiser. The main course was to be a *wayang kulit* performance, or Javan puppet play.

In Jogjakarta I'd declined several opportunities to watch *wayang kulit*. They were shortened versions for tourists, staged in purpose-built auditoriums, and as such were only to be avoided. But in Tretes the circumstances were disarmingly authentic. A full moon hung overhead. Dogs prowled hither and thither, rubbing themselves against the spectators' legs and sometimes sniffing at the musicians' instruments. From the windows of the surrounding *wismas* sullen-faced girls stared at the proceedings, angry that some of their custom had been stolen. Sometimes they ventured out, pushing themselves against the men in the audience, hoping to distract their attention. Sometimes their own attention was distracted, so that they stayed to watch the drama unfold. Motorcycles whipped past, temporarily drowning out the words and the music. In the distance an occasional cry of '*wayang! wayang!*' was heard, followed by a fresh influx of spectators. And all the while the *dalang*, or puppet-master, kept up his incredible incantation, oblivious of whatever else went on.

Wayang kulit is traditionally played before a divided audience. The puppets, flat stylized characters made of paper or leather and mounted on a stick, with wires to operate the heads, legs and arms, are moved by the *dalang* in front of a white sheet, or screen, with perhaps only a single light to illumine his actions. The male audience sits behind the *dalang*, facing the screen, while the women sit on the other side, watching the shadows. In the middle of Tretes, however, there was no space for such a segregation. The sheet was pinned across a shuttered window, and everybody looked on from the street. Above the puppeteer's head shone a single light, directed down onto the playing surface. Ranged on each side of him, flat against the two ends of the screen, and in strict order of appearance, were the puppets, at least a hundred of them.

The show started at a little after ten, and did not finish until an hour after dawn. I stayed to the end, mesmerized by what I scarcely understood. What was being enacted were scenes from the *Ramayana* – with the *Mahabharata* one of the two great epics of Hindu literature. Rama, an avatar of the god Vishnu, wins the hand of Sita, daughter of King Janaka, but soon she is kidnapped by Ravana the demon-king. Rama's efforts to recapture his bride form the bulk of the narrative. In the end he succeeds, but only with the help of an army of monkeys, led by Hanuman, the rumbunctious monkey general. Either the forces of good were ranged exclusively on the left or exclusively on the right, but because of the subtle complexities of the plot it was difficult to tell which. Even those near me, appreciatively applauding each fresh scene, were unable to offer certain guidance.

It was astonishing to watch, not least because of the extreme unwillingness with which the *dalang* began his marathon. He sat cross-legged on the ground, immediately below the screen, so that, for the next seven or eight hours, his arms were constantly upstretched. At first he was scarcely inclined to move at all. Croaking, spitting, clearing his throat, he felt tentatively for his voice. After twenty minutes he leaned forward and actually dared touch one of the puppets. At once his hand recoiled as though given an electric shock. It was another fifteen minutes at least before he could bring himself to repeat the move. The puppets, images of gods and devils, were too sacred to handle. But little by little the *dalang* overcame his fears. Soon, propelled by the gathering strength of his incantation, he found the courage to rearrange a head, or adjust an arm. Just a centimetre here, a centimetre there – and as often as not he returned the puppet to its original position. But once he decided that the realignment of a character on one side of the screen was permissible, then he had to readjust the character on the other.

And so, with infinite trepidation, infinite deliberation, and infinite wiliness, he invested his two-dimensional cut-outs with blood and charisma. He created the illusion that, far from obeying him, his simple artefacts had a power over him. His posture was one of veneration and deep servitude, and after a while it was obvious that the *dalang* had entered a kind of trance. He had become like a child playing with scraps, pretending they are real objects in the adult world. Yet unlike the child the *dalang* was obliged to communicate the meanings he discovered to all those watching.

This he did by speechifying. For seven, eight, nine hours, he poured out a narrative, sometimes in harmony with the gamelan, sometimes at odds. In this narrative he had also to take all of the parts, the women and the monkeys included. As well as a narrator, therefore, he was a prodigious impersonator. For each one of the hundred-odd characters he supplied an original throat. Only occasionally, when he needed to slake his thirst, did he allow an old woman, seated among the gamelan players, to take over, for two minutes here, three minutes there.

Shortly before midnight the *dalang*, grey-haired and missing several of his teeth, an old man not unlike the proprietor of the beach huts at Senggigi, came to the first big battle. Until then he had scarcely allowed the antagonists to appear in the centre of the screen together. But suddenly, in a great flurry of arm-movements and beaten gongs, there was an explosive commotion of leather and wire. For the first time the puppets were lifted clear of the sheet, which was filled instead with their grotesque and elongated shadows. Simultaneously the *dalang's* voice broke into a high-pitched cackle. Then, before the audience could properly take account of what had happened, silence. The puppet-master was collapsed in upon himself, in an exhaustion that was both physical and spiritual. It was another half-hour at least before he resumed the pace of his narrative.

Thus my night of projected abandon was supplanted by a night of exquisite theatre. Sometimes my thoughts wandered, but mostly they remained fixed on the cross-legged man in front of me. His artistry was matched only by his stamina, and both were a lesson to me. There was just one serious interruption, and that was towards one o'clock, when a blanket covering a window in an adjacent brothel fell down. For a fleeting moment the audience was treated to the spectacle of a naked behind and a wriggling moustache. Then the blanket went up again, and the *wayang kulit* continued. Indeed it had never stopped. But the next time he paused for liquid refreshment the *dalang* did permit himself a hasty look round. His audience was still there. Nothing could have tempted me away.

Part Three

PARTICIPATING WITNESSES

SEVEN

Smelly feet

Needless to say my ship never arrived. Or rather, when it did put in at Tanjung Perak, it was going in the opposite direction, from Port Moresby to Singapore. Captain Moninkan apologized profusely and laughed. I knew then that I would only reach the Solomons by other means, i.e. by air. The surest route, and the one that all the agents recommended, was via Bali and Brisbane. Instead I chose to fly first to Jayapura, stopping at Ujung Pandang in Sulawesi and Biak, then to Vanimo, then to Port Moresby. Australia had never been on my itinerary, whereas Melanesia was my target. Yet as an introduction to Melanesia, Jayapura, the administrative capital of Irian Jaya, or Western New Guinea, was grotesque.

New Guinea is the world's second largest island, a vast terrain of rainforest, swamps and, on the high mountains forming a central cordillera, equatorial glaciers. Today it is divided arbitrarily in two, down the 141st degree longitude. To the east is Papua New Guinea, an independent state that still depends heavily on Australia (its former colonial master) for money and technology. To the west is Irian Jaya, since 1969 officially a province of Indonesia.

The indigenous people of New Guinea are Melanesians, sometimes called Australasian negroids, sometimes negritos. As their name implies they have dark skins, ranging from dull coffee to ebony black.

How they came to inhabit the islands of the western Pacific is something of a mystery. To look at they clearly have something in common with some African negroes, yet in every other respect they constitute a separate race. Their culture, in as far as there is a cultural homogeneity among Melanesians, is distinct, as are their many languages, although there are linguistic links with the aboriginal inhabitants of Malaysia and the Philippines, who have survived in small isolated pockets and probably come from the same stock. The most plausible explanation is that the Melanesians originally migrated from the Asian mainland between 2000 and 4000 years years ago, perhaps being pushed out to sea by the more advanced mongoloid peoples, who were also migrating southeastwards. The Melanesians in turn confronted the Polynesians, now broadly confined to the Eastern Pacific, and with them one or two other groups, notably the Micronesians and the Pygmies. The Pygmies fared worst of all, only surviving in near-inaccessible highlands in the interior of New Guinea.

The vulnerability of Melanesians lies in their social organization, rigidly and at times fiercely tribal. Even with modern communications pan-Melanesian solidarity remains a distant dream. In an inhospitable environment tribalism had great advantages; but in the face of European and Asian expansion the odds always were with the aggressors. Whereas Melanesians had evolved relatively sophisticated agricultures, in other key respects they lagged behind the rest of humanity. There was never, for example, any move toward townships. They developed extensive trading networks, but these always operated from village to village, or island to island. Individual artefacts might travel immense distances, but only by passing through an equally large number of hands.

Transmigration is of the essence of human history, and it is only within the last hundred years or so that mankind has begun to take proper cognizance of the human suffering that must occur when one population is forced to give way to another. A crucial contribution to this awakening has been made by the anthropologists. Broadly – there always are exceptions – anthropologists, where they permit themselves to enter into political debate, uphold the view that every race and every culture deserves the right to exist without interference from any other race or culture, and that any interaction should be by mutual consent. Central to this proposition is a profound appeal to our sense of empathy: how would *you* like an alien people to come and lay a pipeline through your back garden, imprison your leaders and rape your wife?

The high-minded and laudable assumption here is that, even if historically homo sapiens is not distinguished by the fair treatment of his fellows, he is nonetheless amenable to persuasion and can reform his ways. Man, bounded on all sides by codes of honour, may yet live up to the very best of them.

In practice however it's never so simple. The 'anthropological' view, although purporting to be universal in its application, is nonetheless cultural-specific in its origins: the great majority of anthropologists were and are nurtured in christian-liberal and christian-marxist societies. It is difficult to see by what principle, other than an obscure enlightened self-interest, non-christian-liberal-marxists should acknowledge the anthropologists' meta-rule, the more so as christian-liberal and christian-marxist cultures are widely perceived as harbingers of destruction and oppression. Even though liberal anthropologists are frequently at odds with the less-than-liberal elements of their mother cultures, as racial or cultural representatives they can appear two-faced. And there is this further problem: if a tribal culture is to be respected because of itself, why shouldn't this entail the respect (tacit condonement) of other tribes, such as imperial Britain, imperial France, neo-imperial America or neo-imperial Russia? After all, they are doing their own thing, just as headhunting savages are doing theirs. That there are no savages, that those people once deemed savages may be relied upon, across the global board, to exhibit complex social and religious structures is always apt to become irrelevant. Or even the opposite of irrelevant. Savages can be civilized. People with a strong sense of their own cultural identity are more likely to resist and cause trouble. Greater knowledge, therefore, may dictate the preemptive strike. Genocide is not inherently irrational.

This is a real dilemma, and is illustrated by the history of Irian Jaya. In the huge area of New Guinea that now constitutes Indonesia's 26th province there were, when the first Europeans arrived, between 1,000,000 and 1,500,000 Melanesians spread out in the lower mountains and coastal plains, living in small villages that were generally isolated from one another. There was no such thing as a nation. Each village had its leaders, or big men, and generally outsiders, even those from the next village, were regarded as enemies who might or might not merit killing. It was not exactly a peaceable society, but it was stable. Everyone knew what the ground rules were, and everyone got on with the main tasks of life: raising food from the land, placating the ancestral spirits, and celebrating births, marriages and deaths.

In due course the Dutch appeared, but to begin with this caused little disruption. For a long while the Dutch found nothing in Irian Jaya to warrant more than a few outposts whose primary purpose was to remind the British and Germans busy colonizing east New Guinea that the Dutch East Indies was forbidden territory to them. But matters changed when, in the late 1920s and 1930s, geological surveys indicated the presence of sizeable mineral deposits. There was oil there, and copper in the mountains, and nickel, and chromite, and maybe gold as well.

In the decade leading up to the Pacific War the Dutch steadily increased their manpower. They also let in the Americans and the Indonesians. The Americans came under the banner of Standard Oil, to help the Dutch open the first oil fields. The Indonesians were brought over from Java in their capacity as lesser civil servants. But, compared with what was to follow after the war, it was still a small operation when the Japanese invasion forces landed in 1942.

The Japanese occupation was nasty, brutish and mercifully short. It did, however, foreshadow the later Indonesian occupation. Whereas in Java the Japanese sought the co-operation of the resident population, in Irian Jaya they behaved toward the Papuans (as they were then called) with racist contempt. Labour camps, torture huts and executions became the order of the day. Yet, like the Dutch before them, they never established control over the interior. Nor, when they left, did they bequeath their weapons to such nationalists as there were.

In 1944 the Allied Forces, commanded by General MacArthur, regained possession. In effect this gave the Americans an uninhibited opportunity to conduct a more thorough geological survey of the region than had been previously attempted. The results showed that the mineral reserves had been greatly underestimated, and from now on the fate of Irian Jaya was determined by what it is no hyperbole to call American economic opportunism. In its foreign policy Washington gradually transferred allegiance from Holland to the more biddable and newly independent state of Indonesia. Indeed the Indonesian war of independence would probably not have succeeded were it not for covert moves by the Americans to force Holland to concede its former colony. Wearing its anti-colonial hat, the State Department let it be known that Marshall Aid to the Dutch would be withdrawn unless the Indonesian achipelago was allowed to liberate itself. Irian Jaya, however, was excluded. In 1949 it remained under the Dutch flag.

In a sense no other solution was possible at the time. West Papua run by Melanesians was not yet a realistic proposition, therefore the Dutch had to stay. Certainly it was the best guarantee the Americans could give themselves of continued access to the oil and copper deposits. In the meantime the Dutch were expected to nurse the local population towards the point where they could assume government functions.

Indonesia resented this settlement, arguing that since West Papua had been a part of the Dutch East Indies it should now be incorporated within the new Republic. This was a curious claim to make as there were no other substantial links between the two regions, but even so at the end of the day the claim won out. The decisive factor was Washington's growing concern over relations between Jakarta and Moscow. Russia was known also to be supplying arms to Indonesia, and President Sukarno was sympathetic to communism. To keep Sukarno sweet, America delivered Irian Jaya into his hands, knowing that the Indonesians would be even more dependent on American technology and capital than the Dutch had ever been.

This was achieved by thoroughly manipulating the United Nations. In 1962 the UN ratified what is usually known as the New York Agreement. According to the terms of this instrument the Dutch were to withdraw from Irian Jaya and its people to be allowed to choose for themselves whether or not they wanted their independence. But not immediately. A referendum could be held at any time during the next seven years. In the interim Indonesia was to manage Irian Jaya. Indonesia was also to manage the referendum.

Between August 1962 and May 1963 a small UN peace-keeping force was stationed in Irian Jaya, to oversee the transition from Dutch colonial rule to Indonesian caretaker rule. But even in this period killings were reported. The reign of terror had begun.

Those seeking to cock a snook at Suharto by rehabilitating the reputation of Sukarno would do well to remember Irian Jaya, for it was Sukarno who initiated the terror, and determined its pattern. Sukarno's problem was that, on paper, there was no reason why a majority of Papuans should vote to join the Indonesian republic – and apart from Papuans there was nobody in Irian Jaya eligible to vote. His solution to the problem was three-pronged. Firstly he would beat the Melanesians into submission. Secondly he would resettle as many Javans and other Indonesians in Irian Jaya as was logistically feasible. Thirdly, in 1964 he announced that there would be no referendum.

As we have already seen, by 1966 Sukarno had been deposed. But whereas Suharto, basking in the support of the CIA, pursued a very different policy toward Indonesian communists, he continued Sukarno's policy for Irian Jaya, thus protecting American investments in the province. He was, however, forced to give way to international calls for the referendum to take place. Eventually there was a vote, of sorts, at the last possible moment, in August 1969. Predictably the so-called Act of Free Choice resulted in a 'unanimous' victory for Jakarta.

By any reckoning the vote was comprehensively rigged. The new Indonesian settlers were polled individually, the Melanesians collectively. Each district was instructed to send a representative, usually chosen by the military, and the issue was decided at a referendum assembly in Jayapura on August 2nd. Before casting its votes the assembly was addressed by General Ali Murtopo, one of Suharto's most awesome henchmen. If anybody still wanted independence, he told delegates, they should find another island. Or perhaps they should approach the Americans, who had just landed on the moon. Then he gave an assurance that he would personally shoot anyone who voted not to join Indonesia. And so, by 1025 votes to nil, Irian Jaya was incorporated into the Republic.*

Between 1962 and 1969, as the military moved in, an estimated 30,000 Melanesians were eliminated. In line with the rest of Indonesia all political parties not actively supportive of the Jakarta government were banned, which effectively left native leaders without a platform. Frontline government officials, including President Suharto himself, repeatedly warned that anyone who supported separation from Indonesia would be regarded as a traitor. To show that it meant business the army swung immediately into action, arresting and detaining as many 'nationalist' Papuans as it could find. Far from crushing opposition such a policy created resistance where little had existed before. Sometime in 1965 the Organisi Papua Merdeka

*For the full saga see *West Papua: the obliteration of a people*, published in 1983 by TAPOL, the London-based Indonesia Human Rights Campaign.

(OPM), or Free Papua Movement, came into being, and this gave the army virtual *carte blanche* to do as it pleased. It was difficult to pursue the small bands of rebels into the mountains, so instead whole villages were regularly burned to the ground. Sometimes the inhabitants were marched into an open space and shot, sometimes they were ordered to stay indoors, where they were roasted. Later, aerial strafing and bombing also became commonplace. The choice of weapon was the 'Daisy Cutter', a US-manufactured anti-personnel bomb that sprays shrapnel in all directions at waist-height. Napalm too was used, as were other chemical weapons.

Reference to the OPM was officially outlawed. Instead the freedom fighters were called *gerakam pengacau liar*, or wild terrorist gangs. In the eyes of most Javans a Melanesian was, and is, little better than an animal. The term 'stone age' is regularly applied to his customs and culture, and race hatred undoubtedly is a root motivation of the atrocities that have occurred, and continue to occur, in Irian Jaya. Security is not a problem for the ruling Indonesians, except where they have chosen to make it a problem.

Since 1969 it is estimated that a further 100,000 Melanesians have been annihilated, and there is no sign of an abatement. In 1981 the government launched what it chose to call Operation Clean-Sweep. *Let the rats run into the jungle*, goes one of its slogans, *so that the chickens may breed in the coop*. The catalogue of inhumanities documented by Tapol, Amnesty International and other human rights agencies makes dismal reading. Normal torture may involve having a loaded gun pushed into the mouth for hours on end, being made to drink one's own urine, or being forced to swallow live bullets. The rape of women detainees is *de rigueur*. Uncharged prisoners are regularly poisoned. At the notorious Ifargunung jail, near Jayapura, detainees are kept in underground bunkers which, at the touch of a sluice, become drowning tanks. Bodies are cut up into small pieces, packed into drums and dropped at sea.

But the deaths are only a part of the horror. Alongside piecemeal genocide has been an equally determined assault on the Melanesian way of life. To make way for the Indonesian immigrants, whom the government hopes will outnumber the indigenous population by the early 1990s and thus finally legitimize the Repulic's claim to sovereignty, the tribespeople have been systematically relocated. They are removed from the habitats they are adapted to and placed 'out of harm's way' in environments that are foreign to them. A common technique used to dispossess Melanesians of land that is rightfully theirs is to ask them to fingerpoint assignments which they cannot read and which are not explained to them, perhaps in return for a modicum of 'gifts'. Then they may be taken down from the hills they know to the swamps they don't. Famine and starvation have been recorded. Medical attention is deliberately withheld. Aid, in the form of foods and building materials, is confiscated by soldiers and resold in Jayapura and other towns.

One of the more bizarre forms of persecution has involved pigs. Pigs have a special status among nearly all Melanesians, from New Guinea to Fiji. They are sacred animals, to be eaten only on certain occasions as offerings to the ancestors. In a sense, the health of a village is reflected in the health of this livestock. Yet it is known that the Indonesian authorities have deliberately introduced infected pigs into remote villages, to destroy morale.

In short, the situation in Irian Jaya amounts to a vast and calculated persecution. And alas, it is held in place by those who, according their own cultural *nostra*, should be striving to put an end to it. Without doubt the chief beneficiaries of the régime in Irian Jaya are American, European and Australian businesses. Between 1971 and 1976 exports from the province rose from a little under $2,000,000 to well over $350,000,000 pa. While Javan stormtroopers hacked their way through the local populace, a large expatriate community, in charge of extracting the oil and copper, stood by and watched. Worse, their own governments actually supplied the hardware. The helicopter gunships, the Bronco aircraft, the automatic rifles, the grenades – none of these were manufactured in Asia. Even the World Bank is implicated, by providing grants to fund some of the eastward migrations.

For the Melanesians the position is hopeless. The OPM, unlike other freedom organizations around the world, has no overseas support. Many of its cadres are still armed only with spears, bows and arrows or casauri bones. Its most obvious ally, Papua New Guinea, has withheld support because it is frightened of Indonesia's army, and because it cannot afford to antagonize its Australian patrons. For a while PNG reluctantly accepted an inflow of refugees, but since 1980 these have regularly been turned back to face certain extermination. Yet not to fight promises nothing. The Indonesians are not inclined to offer those they despise marks for good behaviour. Only the most cosmetic attempts at accommodation have been made. Schools exist not so much to educate as to divorce young Papuans from the culture of their villages. For 'reasons of security' work opportunities are increasingly withheld, so that Melanesians are denied any share in the mineral bonanza. Such work as comes their way is menial and underpaid, if paid at all. Typically Melanesians are told that to refuse the chores demanded of them is tantamount to insurrection. Pushed off their own land – and hence separated from their protective ancestors – they are crowded out to the very perimeters of life in Irian Jaya. There they can be picked of by the military, or, as seems equally likely, left to die of their own accord. They literally have nothing to live for.

*

Jayapura was slightly phantasmal and very creepy. At the time I had virtually no knowledge of the politics of the place beyond having read that the UN was well and truly duped in the 1960s. I therefore brought with me a certain innocence. Yet within an hour of landing at Sentani Airport I had picked up on Jayapura's pervasive glumness, albeit from a somewhat personal perspective. 'Big shock here,' I wrote in my journal that night, 'upon seeing my first Melanesians. I can hardly say I am filled with wonder. In fact I have never seen such a prune-faced depressed-looking lot. As though all the runts in the Caribbean had been rounded up and dumped at the back of the earth. Something terribly wrong here. They look like negroes, yet they are very small. Most eerie. And none of them have the *élan* that goes, or should go, with being black. The women, even the youngest of them appear incredibly old. Elongated, prematurely wrinkled faces and practically no neck. Sour. All eyes on the ground. Shuffling. Bad smell too, when you get close to them. Like rancid butter. Feel terribly dampened. Hope to God they're a better crowd in the Solomons, otherwise I shall become what? a rancid white prune! Hotel no good either. Dafansoro. Positively evil in fact. What I thought was someone tapping on the room-door turned out to be a rat the size of a cat scratching at the woodwork. Hungry-looking bugger. And all the way down the corridor his brothers were nibbling away at the other doors. Two layers of wire-meshing on the window. Even so I hardly dare open it.'

195

In the morning I got a better fix on Jayapura (formerly known as Hollandia, then Kota Baru, then Sukarnopura). It was a double garrison. In the centre of town were the police barracks, and all around the town were army barracks. I learned later that between the police and the military there is considerable competition, as to which one can detain the greatest number of prisoners longest. In the streets, however, they were anything but rivals. They all but linked arms as they swaggered around. The Melanesians meanwhile huddled together in corners, never raising their voices above a whisper, and clamming up whenever a uniform was nearby, which was most of the time. In the strong equatorial sun their features appeared more forlorn and desiccated than ever. I decided that if I ever wanted to write a vintage Graham Greene novel I had come to the right place. It was Greeneland through and through, only at twice the heat.

As for the rest of Jayapura, that took about two-and-a-half minutes. Apart from the constabulary and the *komplexi militaires* there was the usual spread of government offices, a couple of banks and a few hotels, none of which tempted me to desert the awful Dafansoro. A rat is a rat is a rat. But even the rats, which inhabited every available shadow, were clean by comparison with the filthy attempt at a market that snaked along the bank of a sewer that trickled down the side of a hill where the well-to-do had most sensibly built themselves villas. It was by no means clear that the thick carpet of insects on each and every tressle was not a part of the merchandise. Otherwise, somewhere in between innumerable parade grounds – at 11.00 am it was the army wives' turn to drill, by default an almost voluptuous sight – were a sleepy Catholic chapel and a blind Protestant church. All that was missing in this caricature of the capital of a cockroach republic was the president's palace. But the president of course was a thousand and more miles away, safe and sound in his Jakarta chalet.

A rhapsody in wire and rotting concrete. I turned towards the harbour, a natural basin, almost perfectly circular, and about half-a-mile across. By half-closing my eyes I felt myself pulled back in time, which is what I wanted to be. Say fifty years. The few warehouses were all that old, made of wood, bending, creaking. I could imagine a white-painted schooner dropping anchor plum in the middle. Activity. Dutch officials adjusting their caps in mirrors that had been bought in Antwerp. The roar of hectic chains. Young men, pride coursing through their veins . . .

A silly dream. There was no white schooner. Beautiful as it was Jayapura Bay was empty, like a mouth without teeth. The only vessels were desolated hulks, iron hull'n'huts, dragged half-clear of the water they could no longer serve.

And then a canoe. There was actually a Melanesian woman paddling herself straight across the basin in a dug-out. Wonderful!

A blade twisted without warning in my stomach. It was time to get back to the dreaded Dafansoro where, evidently, I had been poisoned at breakfast.

It was the worst attack yet. My hindquarters gushed like a tap that had lost its washer. In a delirium that lasted ninety minutes I reasoned to myself that, of all the places I certainly didn't want to die in, Jayapura was top of the list, therefore it was the place I *was* most likely to die in. And since I had no intention of ever coming back that meant I was going to die now. Fortunately a small, almost contemporary super-market, the only supermarket in Jayapura, was stationed near the hotel, and I was able to stock up with canned beverages and dry biscuits. A Chinese apothecary supplied me with a yellow powder that, after several hours, seemed to work. Sensing that my demise and the Dafansoro were intimately connected, I once again ventured out. At snail's pace I assayed my best to find something in Jayapura I hadn't already seen. I think I was hoping to stumble upon a branch of the St James's Health Club. What I needed, more than anything in the world, was an ice-cold jacuzzi, a hot lemon sorbet and something white and clean to lie down on.

I was out of luck. What I did stumble upon was a jeep and a big fellow from Massachussetts smoking a black cheroot. We stared at each other with some amazement. Our conversation went something like this:

'Hello!'

'Hi!'

'You working here?'

'Sort of. I run a United Nations development project up in the hills. What about yourself?'

'Passing through. Perhaps you can tell me. Where's the best place to eat?'

'Try the Jaya Grill, under the harbour. But what do you mean, passing through? Jayapura's not a place people pass through very often.'

197

'I'm a writer.'

'Newspapers?'

'On and off.'

And there our conversation ended. Big Massachussetts simply turned his back on me and refused to say another word.

His Papuan assistant, who wriggled out from under the jeep, was more forthcoming. The main problem about running a project for Melanesians, he volunteered, was motivation. No way, he said, could you motivate a Papuan overnight.

'Hey!' said Big Massachussetts. 'Give me that spanner and get back inside. We're going to be late.'

'Late?'

'Yeah, late. You heard what I said.'

The Jaya Grill was not difficult to find. The roof was level with the road that ran around the harbour, and inside the tables were more or less level with the water. The food, though, was decidedly superior – superior to my expectations, that is. A beefsteak that had obviously fallen off the back of a cow, and not off the back of a goat, took me by storm. Afterwards my legs began to feel like legs again. I took an evening stroll, enjoying immensely the relative cool of the air, the slight breeze from where the schooner should have been. I looked more closely at the faces that loomed miserably out the dark.

'Hello!' I said to one of them, before it flitted back into invisibility again.

'Thank you!' came the reply.

I tried this again, and got exactly the same response.

'Hello!'

'Thank you!'

It was habit really. In S.E. Asia, in Thailand and Indonesia, I had become so used to being spontaneously greeted by half the people I passed that, to vary the routine a little, I sometimes said hello first before they could say hello mister. It didn't make life more interesting, but it did make it less wearisome. It was also a way of giving oneself a pinch of protection. In New York, many years ago, I learnt that any street is safe provided you wear dirty clothes and get your 'Say fellow can you give me a dime' in before the hoodlum tries his 'Say fellow gimme a dollar'.

But this thank you I had not anticipated. It was said, on both occasions, with such dignity and such forbearance that I honestly believe a genuine gratitude was being expressed.

198

'Hello!'

'Thank you!'

Just like that.

One of them even endeavoured to raise a smile.

Was he really so ignorant that it is my kind as well which is responsible for his plight?

This was my introduction to Melanesia. Thank you. It could only get better. It did.

*

From Jayapura I flew to Port Moresby, via Vanimo, Wewak and Mt Hagen. The first leg, into PNG, was accomplished on a Trilander, a British-made 12-seater twin-prop that reminded me of a machine that once gave me a bad time at a funfair in Llandudno. The Australian pilot was overweight, red as a lobster and had volcanic boils on his neck. The aeroplane sailed at the right height, though. The weather was good, the scenery ace. Below, the coastline was like a geographical model: all the colours were gently exaggerated, and the scenery could have been constructed from Plasticine.

At Vanimo there was trouble with the Papuan customs official. I signed a form saying that I had nothing to declare, then he confiscated a winged lion carved in wood I had bought in Surabaya. I protested vigorously, but to no avail. 'Wooden objects' were hidden under a category marked PLANTS. The man gave me a lecture on how I should always read the small print. I gave him a lecture on the differences between the living and the dead. Obviously he wanted the thing for his personal collection. He kept saying 'It's my decision, it's my decision'. Either I accepted his decision, or I met him tomorrow at the Vanimo courthouse. I was almost tempted to call his bluff, but my stomach and several Australians dissuaded me. Just thank your lucky stars, one said, that it wasn't a bottle of whisky. In any case the jet that would take me to Port Moresby was already landing. 'Here it comes,' the cry went up, 'the little Fokker.' I boarded angry out of all proportion. I had spent three months in S.E. Asia and had never been robbed of a sen. Then this.

Thereon I slept most of the way, determined to have as little as possible to do with a country I already resented. An Air Niugini lunchbox rattled like a politician's promise on my lap. All it contained were three mouldy biscuits and half an apple.

Moresby, when eventually I arrived there, did nothing to raise my expectations. I found it a big unco-ordinated empty sort of place. Papuans roamed through Australianesque suburbs looking for Bottle Shops. Otherwise, raised bungalows surrounded by wire and picturesque ghettos aswarm with milling hillspeople. At least, though, the state was conspicuous only by its absence, which, after Jayapura, was heartening. At five in the afternoon it was still incredibly hot. The sunlight was bright as silver-foil, the air as dry as tinder.

I stayed at the Papua Hotel. Like everything else in Papua New Guinea this was a rip-off. It was also a brothel. Downstairs was a night-club called the Pink Pussycat, containing, perhaps, the worst-looking women in the world. On the first floor, next to my room, I found a grog cupboard with a hundred male Papuans tanking up on Castlemaine XXXX. Would the five locks on my door be sufficient?

They were. In the morning I rang Tom Palaskas and transferred swiftly to his residence in nearby Boroko. Tom's name had been given to me in England. He and his Thai wife Non, like Norbert and Lucy in Perak, were quiet, unassuming individuals of the sort one longs for on a long travel. They were also another shining example of marital contentment. Tom, a New Zealander, worked at an Elcom Training Centre and wanted to write a potboiler. Non looked after their two children and thought about her pottery wheel, stored under the house in her husband's workshop.

Over a T-bone steak at the Aviat Club, originally built for the pilots in WW2, Tom told me something about PNG. Papuans, he said, rather like to be called fuzzy-wuzzies. Moresby was not representative at all. There was too much urban drift. Men came down from the hills and couldn't hold their liquor. Eighteen months before, there had been an unpleasant incident when a white woman was raped. Thereafter there had been a curfew for six months. But the politicians were reluctant at the best of times to give too much support to the police, though very quick to award themselves high pay settlements, parliamentarians being paid more than MPs at Westminster. This was the Big Man system, which means no ideology in our sense. The various parties can and do stand for anything and everything. The number of Australian administrators had been reduced from 55,000 to 15,000 since independence (1973), but were hardly on the way out. Otherwise, society was dominated by the sects, over 500 of them, representing every Christian denomination under the sun, as well as a few that wouldn't care to see the light of day. And these for a population of no more than 3,000,000.

Outside Moresby, Tom assured me, the country had everything to offer. But nothing that he said could induce me to prolong my stay. I had already browsed through his copy of the *Liklik Buk*, subtitled 'A Rural Development Catalogue for Papua New Guinea', and published in 1977 by the Melanesian Council of Churches. It contained, amongst other items, an abundance of 'Hints on Motivation'. If that's the priority, I thought to myself, I'm off. Still bruised from my encounter with the customs man at Vanimo, I was overjoyed when, two days later, my wait-listed reservation on the once-a-week flight to Honiara metamorphosed at last into an actual seat on an actual aircraft.

*

It costs more to enter the 'civilized' world than it does to leave it. In Moresby I parted with a sizeable tranche of traveller's cheques to ensure that, when I returned, I had a through passage to Manila, from where I had bucket-shop tickets to Taipei, Hong Kong, Bangkok, Amsterdam and London. Air Niugini was the only carrier, so it could charge what it pleased. But at least now my home run was taken care of, so I could relish the Honiara-bound Fokker. With one touchdown at Kieta in Bougainville it was a five-hour journey. Greatly rehabilitated by Palaskan hospitality I stationed myself by a window in the alert position. I wanted to get my first glimpse of the Coral Sea and the Solomons at the earliest possible moment.

That moment was delayed by a prodigious cloud cover. Bougainville excepted, the Solomons eluded me totally until the plane began its descent over Guadalcanal. I landed at Henderson airport without espying a single rotten volcano or coral atoll. The sea, when eventually I saw it, was a grizzly mincemeat grey, and the flat landscape around Henderson looked as lively as a tulip field in December. Outside the aircraft it was warm, but not that warm. A fine rain fell steadily without the least discernible flutter of a tropical perturbation. The ground staff hurried hither and thither in oilskin anoraks. Those that were Melanesian shivered visibly. Voices were muted, and nobody was excited. The airport buildings were functional and small: barely enough room inside the passenger reception area for the forty or so

201

passengers who had disembarked. A couple of minibuses waited beyond to ferry us into Honiara, thirteen miles away. For no particular reason I suddenly remembered what it was like the first day I went to boarding school, at the beginning of the winter term. As the jet turned round and took off again, leaving behind nothing but empty tarmac, I had an image of the tail-lights of my father's car disappearing up the school drive. How soon would it be before I made new friends? Would I make any at all?

For several hours the answer seemed to be no. I got on a minibus and got off again at the Mendana Hotel. In between I saw a lot more rain and a scatter of desultory concrete. Honiara appeared a capital city only in name. The Mendana on the other hand boasted a great deal of wood, and for that reason I stopped off there. Its entrance and lobby had a certain laconic dignity that, after the Dafansoro and the Papua, I found distinctly ritzy. It was also, as I subsequently discovered, strategically well placed, being between the government buildings and the main commercial centre behind the port. The Prime Minister's Office and the best pharmacy were equidistant from the gate. (In fact the Mendana is one of the premier hotels of the South Pacific, but I didn't know that then.)

I saw my bags parked in my room, negotiated a modest discount with the German manager (*Oh mein Gott, ein Verfasser*), and then hotfooted it to the British High Commission, a hundred yards up the road in a small building that also housed the national Post Office. It was Friday and ten after four when I got there, and it closed at four; but John Noss and George Anderson, respectively the High Commissioner and Second Secretary, were still at their desks. Both greeted me with a measured cordiality. Across a wooden counter they handed me a disappointingly thin bundle of mail, then waited for me to say something. I asked whether either remembered Philip Smiley, and both shook their heads.

'Never heard of him,' said Noss, a slightly suave silver-haired man in his mid-fifties who definitely had not taken to the bottle in this former outpost of the Empire.

'Nor me,' said Anderson. 'Tell us about him.'

'I met him in Hong Kong. He worked here, for the Commission. Can't have been very long ago. He's still, er, young, you see.'

'I assure you,' Noss said, 'no one of that name was ever posted in this building.'

202

'Oh well then,' I said, convinced that I was right, 'I've made a mistake.'

Two weeks later I learned my error. Smiley had been in the Solomons as one of the last district officers in the colonial set-up before independence. In Gizo, the administrative capital of the Western District, he is still remembered as the blond bombshell who entertained the entire Solomon Islands basketball team (female) in his residence one weekend. But at the time I felt a complete and utter Charlie. And I must have looked one, too, because Anderson had started giggling.

'Never mind,' he said. 'Come in on Monday morning and we'll see what we can do to arrange some interviews. That's what you'd like, isn't it?'

Oh yes. Interviews. Exactly. Absolutely. But as I dragged myself back to the Mendana, tail glued between my legs, Monday morning seemed as far away as London.

I showered, shaved, unpacked, lay on my bed and opened my mail. Family letters apart, there was only one communication of any interest. Kaori O'Connor had thoughtfully extracted homefront highlights. Harold Macmillan had died with the words 'I think I will go to sleep now'. Iris Murdoch had been created Dame in the New Year's Honours List. And Prince Edward was thinking of quitting the Marines.

'I fondly imagine you reading this under a palm tree, clad in khaki Empire-style long shorts, beard hanging halfway down your by now well-tanned chest. However you may be looking, you are certainly in the Right Place. I've just been listening to a piece on Radio 4 called GOLD RUSH IN MELANESIA. It dwelt on the lost (or imaginary) fortune of Don Alvaro de Mendana, theories of new sorts of gold deposit (molten metal spewed up through volcanic rifts) and more or less made Honiara out to be a minor version of San Francisco in 1849 gold rush days. Isn't this absolutely wonderful for you? Also shows me up for telling you there was nothing in the Solomons but coconuts and rotting World War II hulks.'

I looked out of the window, expecting to see a gang of diggers shouldering picks and shovels. What I actually beheld was a Caucasian woman clad in a zipped-up orange tracksuit exercising languidly on the deck of a yacht at anchor in the mincemeat. Admittedly I had only been in the place three hours, but somehow I doubted her crew was off panning in them thar hills. From what I had seen of it Honiara lagged somewhat behind San Francisco in 1749. Clearly the BBC reporter, strapped to justify his expense account, had turned creative.

I lay back and thought about what I should do. Continue with my Indonesian novel? Hijack the High Commission? Set out on a slow crawl for Australia?

The only realistic possibility was Lord Lucan.

I dozed off, to be awoken at eight by the unmistakeable aroma of burning lamb. Of course! Downstairs was Barbecue Night.

I ate like a vulture at the end of Lent: two hamburgers, potato salad, garlic bread, sweetcorn, pumpkin, melon slices, cow-cucumber and half-a-dozen things all washed down with a large jug of bush lime, followed by apple tart and a commendable attempt at a custard sundae. Yet at the end of this meal I felt, psychologically at any rate, the same as when I had begun it. I was still wondering to myself where the airline office was, and whether it opened on Saturdays.

It was a little after nine by then, and I was considering calling it a day when the music started. Spritely Polynesian stuff. A group of bare-bellied youngsters had materialized in the lobby, and were swaying vigorously in a seated circle. They all had flowers in their coiled hair, and pretty soon some of the girls were standing up. As they continued swaying vigorously I supposed they were dancing.

I found a cane chair and forced myself to watch.

'Gilbertese,' said a voice on my right. 'Their grass skirts, I'm afraid, are made of nylon.'

'I did notice,' I answered, without looking round, 'Still . . .'

'If crop rotation's what you're into . . .'

I glanced quickly at the man and laughed. But it was only when he offered to buy me a beer that I realized it was George Anderson.

'Christ,' I said. 'Sorry. I thought you were trying to pick me up.'

'That's all right,' George answered, waving his hand. 'Where have you been all this time? We were expecting you a month ago.'

'Inodnesia, mainly.'

'That explains it. It takes most people a year to recover from Indonesia.'

'Where is everybody tonight?'

'Everybody? Probably at the Yacht Club next door. On Friday nights anybody who's nobody goes to the Yacht Club.'

204

'So where were you before, if I may ask?'

'Libya. And before that Uganda.'

'And now you're in the Solomons.'

'And now,' said George, with real diplomatic grace, 'I'm in the Solomons. Where the nylon rustles forty minutes once a week, and time, to quote Gavin Young, is like wading through wet sand.'

*

The Solomon Islands as a geographical entity and the Solomon Islands as a country are almost, but not quite, the same thing. According to the atlas the Solomons constitute an archipelago of seven large and innumerable smaller islands lying in a double chain slanting south-eastwards due east of southern Papua New Guinea from 5° to 11° latitude, and from 165° to 162° longitude. To the northwest is the largest island, Bougainville, and then Choiseul, New Georgia, Santa Isabel, Malaita, Guadalcanal and San Cristobal. Bougainville, however, is not a part of the modern state. Formerly a German colony, it was ceded to the Australian Trust Territory of Papua New Guinea. On the other hand the territory ruled by the Solomons Islands Government stretches considerably beyond the archipelago proper into the South Pacific, and includes the Santa Cruz Islands, the Duff Islands, the Swallow Islands and several isolated landfalls, for example Anuta and Tikopia, that belong to no groups at all. These, the non-archipelagic Solomons, are all very small, are usually referred to as outliers and are mostly Polynesian by race and culture. Ninety per cent of the Solomon Islands' population, however, is Melanesian, and therefore it is appropriate to describe the Solomon Islands as an essentially Melanesian nation – although, as I shall endeavour to show, such a formula adds up to rather less in reality than it might seem to convey in print.

Alvaro Mendaña de Neyra, the leader of the first European expedition to set foot in the Solomons, was a Spaniard by birth, the nephew of the Governor of Peru. He left South America in 1567 to find the legendary lost continent of the Pacific, gold and hopefully establish a Franciscan mission. His two middle-sized ships, *Los Reyes* and *Todos Santos*, made heavy weather of it, and Mendaña's arrival in the Solomons was, to say the least, adventitious. He was driven onto Santa Isabel by a cyclone, on 7th February 1568. Within a week his men had begun fighting with the islanders. Within two weeks some had already died of fever.

Thus began the recorded history of the Solomons. Mendaña stayed in all six months in the archipelago, landing on Guadalcanal and San Cristobal as well as Santa Isabel, then set sail for home. Twenty-seven years later he attempted a return, this time with four ships, but died in the Santa Cruz islands. Further Spanish and Portuguese expeditions were mounted at the beginning of the seventeenth century, but not one of them succeeded either in finding gold or in founding a colony. Thereafter, for a century and a half, the Solomon Islands were little more than a name on the hopelessly inaccurate maps of the western South Pacific. Indeed the name was about the only legacy of these early voyages. For centuries men had been looking for King Solomon's lost treasure, and the islands were named after him perhaps as an inducement to further exploration, or, as seems just as likely, ironically – a sailor's joke perhaps.

In 1769 the French explorer Surville suggested a new soubriquet, *la Terre des Arsacides*, or Land of the Assassins. Three years earlier Louis Bougainville had been attacked off Choiseul by men riding canoes and shooting arrows. Renewed interest in the region was a consequence of the discovery and opening up of Australia and New Zealand in the wake of Captain Cook. In particular the Solomon Islands were to become an important source of cheap labour for the new sugar plantations in Queensland, and later in Fiji. But progress was slow and often murdersome. In 1829 twenty shipwrecked sailors were widely believed to have been eaten by Malatians. In 1845, during the first attempt to establish a Catholic mission, Bishop Jean-Baptiste Epalle was axed to death after refusing to trade his episcopal ring for two lemons, one of which was already half eaten.

And so it went on. In 1851 Benjamin Boyd, a respected Australian trader (and founder of the Royal Australian Bank) was murdered on Guadalcanal. Twenty years later Bishop J.C. Patteson, the first Anglican Bishop of Melanesia, was slain in the Santa Cruz group. But these and numerous other attacks were hardly unprovoked, even though the ferocity with which some of them were perpetrated reflected a genuinely warlike society. To begin with many islanders, but especially those on Malaita, simply resented the intrusion of foreigners. Their antagonism was greatly aggravated by the manner in which Australian entrepreneurs set about recruiting men for their plantations. On many occasions natives were simply kidnapped by raiding parties – a practice that became known as 'blackbirding'. To achieve their ends the recruiters sometimes disguised themselves as missionaries, hiding guns beneath their robes, so that soon no white man could be trusted, however peaceable his declared intentions.

Little by little, though, the white man demonstrated his determination to stay, and little by little the Solomon Islanders became more skilled at bargaining. Nails, rum, muskets and later tobacco became the wages of labour. As the missionaries – Anglicans, Methodists, South Sea Evangelists – established a foothold, at first along the shorelines, violence became less endemic. Nonetheless it was to counter the violence, as well as to provide a buttress against German expansion in the area, that Great Britain was pushed towards declaring the islands a Protectorate in 1893. Following this C.M. Woodford, a noted naturalist, was appointed Resident Commissioner in 1896, answerable to the High Commission in Fiji. From Tulagi Island, in effect a tiny colonial bastion between Guadalcanal and Malaita, Woodford did his best to enforce fair play between traders and natives. At the same time several colonial companies, among them Levers, began developing plantations in the Solomons themselves.

Colonization was a gradual and piecemeal process, and always subject to alarming setbacks. The most notorious of these was the Bell Incident. District Officer W.R. Bell, whom we shall meet again, was clubbed to death with the butt of a rifle while attempting to collect taxes on the seaward side of Malaita. Partly as a result of this outrage the British learned to pursue a more constructive policy towards their Melanesian subjects. By 1940 the first government schools had been opened, district courts established, and the way paved for a system of local 'advisory' councils.

It was the Second World War that brought the Solomons to international prominence, for it was in the Solomons that the Japanese drive into the Pacific was first halted, then forced into retreat. While this was achieved mainly by American might, a crucial role was played by a network of 'coastwatchers'. These men, the majority of whom were native, relayed vital information about Japanese troop and naval movements by radio. It is not true, as some would like to believe, that every Solomon Islander remained loyal to the flag during the Occupation, but a sufficient number of them took the ultimate risk on behalf of the Allies to earn the whole colony the kind of respect which, in the post-war period, guaranteed its eventual independence.

The Japanese took Bougainville in March 1942, and by May they were in Tulagi. On 7th August the Americans counterattacked, bombing Tulagi and Guadalcanal. Simultaneously a force of marines landed on Guadalcanal, and on 9th August the renamed Henderson airstrip was captured. All this was but a prelude to some of the heaviest fighting in the whole Pacific. While they lost in the air the Japanese retained control of the seaways. From their naval bases in New Guinea they were able to send an almost inexhaustible supply of ships and men (nicknamed the Tokyo Express) down 'the Slot', the protected waters running between the main islands. At the Battle of Savo the seaborne Allies suffered an early and comprehensive defeat. On land, however, the Japanese, always on the attack, were more vulnerable. In September (Battle of Bloody Ridge), and again in October, they tried to retake Henderson, but failed. Finally, in February 1943, the Japanese withdrew from the archipelago, leaving behind only a few manned positions, the last of which held out until 1944.

It was all good Robert Mitchum stuff. The Japanese lost in excess of 20,000 men, though as in New Guinea a moiety died of malaria and other jungle diseases. They also lost what chance they had of winning the war. For the Solomon Islanders it was a confusing experience. The scenes of destruction they had witnessed were on a scale that was strictly fantastic. They were also treated to another miraculous spectacle: white men upon occasion taking orders from black men, in the ranks of the American forces. The black GI was not a phenomenon any Briton or Australian had prepared them for.

The presence of American troops, with their friendly openhandedness and scorn of all things colonial, made a lasting impression on the islanders. When the British returned they were surprised to encounter organized nationalist elements, manifested in two movements. The first of these was called Marching Rule (a corruption of Masina or Brother Rule, and not, as Whitehall feared, Marxist Rule), and appeared to emanate from Malaita, where plantation strikes had been raised in the 1930s. Marching Rule, although in time undone by infighting and the detention of its leaders in 1947, advocated independence for the Solomons through a series of more or less peaceful acts of civil disobedience. A decade later the separatist and somewhat less peaceable Moro movement was spawned by its eponymous 'prophet' on Guadalcanal (where a new capital, Honiara, replacing Tulagi, had been established). What these two very disparate anti-colonialisms had in common was a cargo cult, based on the premise that one day huge American freighters would sail over the horizon to disgorge vast quantities of consumer goods.

Cargo cults are something of a feature of the Western Pacific. In Irian Jaya, for example, once the Indonesians had dug themselves in, some Papuans fervently believed that a convoy of Dutch vessels would come with a similar motherload of earthly treasure. There, as in Malaita, warehouses were built against the day the cargoes arrived. The forces behind the phenomenon are both religious and secular. A millenarian expectation of heaven-sent bounty is tempered by a tacit admission that events in this world are determined by the powers of this world.

Perhaps because of their cargo cult affiliations neither Marching Rule nor the Moro movement were perceived as grave threats to British rule. Even so the British government acknowledged that independence for the Solomon Islands must be the eventual objective of its policy. Accordingly its officials in Honiara set about working for a smooth transition. A governing council, composed of both expatriates and local representatives, was established, more schools built and communications between the islands improved.

Full independence was accorded in 1978, although the Solomon Islands remain inside the British Commonwealth: the Queen is represented by a Governor-General as constitutional Head of State; a 38-seat one-chamber elected Parliament furnishes the government; a fifteen-man cabinet is presided over by a Prime Minister.

Thus, today, the Solomon Islands would appear to be a cosy, pocket-sized Westminster-style democracy set fair for the future. On the ground, however, things are a little less secure. My thesis, if I had to provide one, would be that the cohesion of this new nation-state will only be guaranteed by the right amount of external pressure. Too much external pressure, and the fragility of the national sovereignty will become immediately apparent. Too little, and the arguments for unity will evaporate.

In respect of this analysis I have a tale or two to tell – traveller's anecdotes as may be, but indicative nevertheless. If the reader is to make any sense of these, however, I must first offer some account of Solomon Islands society, both as it was and as it is.

The first thing to be said is that generalizations are dangerous. Like New Guinea the Solomons are an adventure playground for anthropologists precisely because every island hosts a distinct package of customs and rituals. But at least this provides one clue to the overall tenor of the place. Tribalism rules supreme, or at least did rule supreme until the advent of colonialism, and latterly the nation-building successors to colonialism.

The Melanesians first arrived in the Solomons perhaps towards the end of the second millenium BC. The oldest archaeological evidence points to the presence of a neolithic culture before the end of the tenth century. Yet it is not even apparent that this migration necessarily came from one source. According to various estimates there are between 60 and 90 discrete languages spoken in the Solomons. Some of these belong to the Malayo-Polynesian (Austronesian) language group, others do not. Some have an affinity with 'Papuan', others appear to have no affinity at all. More research still needs to be done, but what is clear is that there is little or no correlation between the different kinds of language spoken and either the different kinds of Melanesian people present in the islands or their whereabouts. Communities living hundreds of miles apart might be able to communicate better than communities that are near neighbours. Again, those with the same colour skins might or might not share a linguistic base.

In the modern era the problems arising from the presence of so many tongues is in part abated by the adoption of pidgin as a makeshift national language, while English proper is also commended in official circles. An example of pidgin is as follows:

Mi swear long God dat olketa toktok wea bae bae mi givim
long cot hem tru wan tru wan evribit no eni bullshit bat tru
toktok nomau.

This is the oath sworn by witnesses giving evidence in a court, and is modelled on the oath administrative in British courts. However, even pidgin is probably not understood by more than two-thirds of the population (currently put at around 305,000)

One phrase that every Melanesian understands is *wan tok*, or 'one talk'. Somebody from your *wan tok* speaks your language, and therefore has a priority claim on your attention. People arriving for the first time in Honiara from outside Guadalcanal will naturally seek out members of their own *wan tok*, who are obliged to offer them hospitality. More significantly, within a *wan tok* mutual assistance is also the norm. An injured party can call on his fellows to protect him, and even exact revenge, which these days generally amounts to pecuniary compensation (another key concept in ordinary Solomon Islands' social transactions). One reason why a high proportion of the police in the capital are Polynesians recruited from faraway Tikopia is that it is very awkward for someone to arrest a man or a woman from his or her own *wan tok*.

The *wan tok* system is a vivid reminder of what life used to be like on the archipelago. While social structures varied from island to island it is fair to say that the clan – I use the word to describe various kinds of descent group – was the common strong unit. In most cases each village, seldom numbering more than 200 individuals, and often a great deal fewer, was a clan. Within the village, or clan, property was owned by individuals, but only vicariously – a point made with inadvertent clarity by Charles E. Fox, an early missionary, when he wrote: 'Everyone owned some land belonging to his clan.'*

Family or kinship ties counted for much, but in nearly every case the clan chief was non-hereditary. The position of village headman was assumed by a Big Man, one who had demonstrated personal prowess by his courage in fighting, and his magnanimity in feast-giving. On some islands he was also a species of high priest, officiating at sacrifices and other rituals held in honour of the ancestors. Commonly the skulls of the valiant dead were kept in special shrines, before which pigs might be roasted in propitiation. Ancestors had *mana*, or spirit energy, and *mana* was the *sine qua non* of success. A Big man was an individual copiously endowed with *mana*, and therefore favoured by the ancestors. But there were other ways to obtain *mana* – by magic, for example, or possibly through cannibalism. The exact role of cannibalism in the Solomons is hotly disputed, but what is not in doubt is that on some islands it did exist. The human menu was usually supplied by an enemy. By eating him you ingested such *mana* as he possessed. Either that, or you thereby expressed a healthy contempt for his clan. And, of course, you offered the best parts to the ancestral skulls.

The importance attached to the skull also explains another

*Charles E. Fox, *The Story of the Solomons*, Pacific Publications, 1967.

'barbarism', namely head-hunting. The people of Roviana were specialists in this. In their long war canoes they frequently sailed long distances to collect heads, though the practice was not unknown in Malaita, Guadalcanal and Santa Isabel. Even more grotesquely, a new war canoe was sometimes launched on a human slipway. Captured enemies would be tied up in a row on the ground, and then cut to bits by the sharp keel of the virgin vessel as it was dragged over their torsos. It was, you might say, a vicious circle. Canoes would be sent out to collect keel-fodder in order that another canoe could be made ready to repeat the process.

Warfare was endemic, but not always deadly. A good fight between members of rival clans could be had without casualties, at least until islanders began equipping themselves with 'Snider' rifles. Nonetheless it was difficult to trust a man who was not from your village. On the larger islands there was particular tension between those who lived by the sea (the 'saltwater' people) and those who lived in the hills (the 'bush' people). Yet, if only for dietary reasons, some contact between these two groups was essential. In the bush the islanders created gardens, farming taros, yams, and sweet potatoes. Down on the coast they caught protein-rich bonito, shell-fish and bêches-de-mer (sea slugs). Foodstuffs were exchanged, but notably the bargaining was done by the women, explaining perhaps why the entrepreneurial spirit is often lacking among modern Solomon Island males. The men simply stood by on the peripheries of the mart, ready to hurl their spears in the event of an altercation.

Throughout the archipelago women were regarded as inferior, even though, outside Malaita, descent was reckoned matrilinearly, not patrilinearly. Usually a village was arranged in three parts. At the top, or in the centre, was the men's hut, often containing the ancestral shrine (which women were not allowed to approach). Then there were the living quarters, smaller huts where the females and children of the clan ate and slept. Finally there was the menstrual hut, an unclean place where women were periodically banished, and had their babies.

In the bush it was the men's duty to clear the land and prepare the garden space, but the actual gardening was again women's work. This left the men plenty of time to prepare their weapons, build canoes, think about war or simply go 'walkabout'. Or, being men, their thoughts might turn to sex. Marriage was a universal custom, and was probably responsible for the origin of such primitive forms of money as existed in the Solomons before the arrival of the florin and the dollar. Shell-money – strings of worked shell-discs woven together into belts – was the most common form of currency, although others included bat's-teeth, porpoise-teeth, dog's-teeth and 'red-feather' money. Every bride had her price (to compensate her family for the loss of her procreative and economic value), and she could not be wed until her husband-to-be had gathered the requisite funds. Polygamy was not excluded, but in practice it was rare since few men could amass sufficient wealth to take more than one wife.

Monogamy has now been institutionalized by the missionaries. With the exception of some districts of Malaita, Christianity has spread throughout the Solomons. Every village has a church or chapel. In many of them each day begins and ends with a service. To the casual passer-by it all looks like God with his sunny side up. People in the streets of Honiara, Gizo, Auki and other urbanizing centres don't say hello, they say May The Lord Bless You. Yet this is deceptive, because there is no one church or mission. Instead there are Catholics, Anglicans, Methodists, South Sea Evangelicals – in other words a new generation of what might be styled religious *wan toks*. Noticeably a disproportionate number of Cabinet members are Seventh Day Adventists, and it is widely believed that these have formed themselves into a special or secret inner cabinet, minded to look after their own. While this is only one among several ways that Solomon Island politics is bedevilled by clannishness, it is worth noting that the emergence of political parties is likely to occur along denominational, not ideological, lines.

The seismic wrench with the past, however, has been economic. As Sir Raymond Firth had intimated, the introduction of wage labour at the close of the nineteenth century and at the beginning of the twentieth destroyed at a blow many traditional values. An important corollary of ancestor worship in the villages (and besides the village there was nothing else) was a deeply held respect for the clan elders. It was the older male who cracked the whip – decided who was going to marry whom and when wars were to be fought, and settled disputes as they arose. But it was the younger males whom the recruiters and plantation managers wished to employ. To begin with payment was made to the clan leaders, but this practice soon gave way to individual earnings. But while the new pattern was good for the missionaries, and ultimately enabled the wider denominational *wan tok* identity, it spelt decay for the traditional community. With money of his own, real money that could buy tobacco and beer and, if need be, bullets, the younger man was no longer dependent on his father and uncles, and therefore no longer answerable to them.

This said, it should also be observed that economic motivation has largely failed to drive tap-roots into the soil of Solomon consciousness. Precisely because of the *wan tok* system, wealth is not an attractive proposition. If a man moves into a new bungalow, for example when he is elected to Parliament, at once a dozen others move in with him. They are members of his *wan tok*, they cannot be refused. Thus Honiara is largely a place of hangers-on, a town that is beginning to attract the same kind of urban drift that makes Port Moresby considerably less habitable than it might otherwise be. Business managers are not prone to criticize their staff for the work they do. A Solomon Islander can put his back to it as smartly as the next. But what they do complain of is an inablility to keep their staff. Sooner or later the employee wants to return to his or her island, his or her own village. And why not? Having earned enough to purchase a few luxuries, why go on toiling? Subsistence living is still deeply ingrained in the culture. In the long run it is better to live where food comes naturally and freely. With his new fishing rod, metal saw or radio cassette player, what more could a man want?

Copra, tuna and timber are the exports that keep the Solomons Islands afloat in the world at large. While the government encourages 'partnerships' these industries are effectively run by expatriates – Britons, Americans, Australians, Japanese, Koreans. The same is true of every other important business venture in the archipelago. Government, too, is dependent on imported expertise. In the legal profession, for example, there is but one native-born lawyer. Every ministry has its overseas adviser. But while these foreigners are in the archipelago either by the grace or the invitation of the government, without them the country would collapse like a house of cards.

And then what would happen? The Solomon Islands could not revert to its former clan and village culture, for that has eroded beyond the point of restoration. Rather there would be an unimaginable anarchy. A predominantly Christian anarchy perhaps, but an anarchy all the same.

For the moment the archipelago is in a twilight zone between one mode of existence and another. The past is past, the future is as yet a blur. There are those who talk about nation-building, and The Way Ahead, and there are those who go walkabout wearing T-shirts that bear the simple yet deeply ambiguous message: KEEP YOUR CULTURE.

Had I been trained as an anthropologist I would perhaps have focused my attention of the remnants of clan life, on the transition from bamboo to milled planks. Being an ordinary writer johnny, however, I concentrated on those whom I could most easily comprehend. For the most part these were expatriates. My excuse? As a *wan tok* in their own right they deserve some attention. They are a part of the Solomons problem. But they would also be, if at times misguidedly, a part of the Solomons solution.

*

In the expatriate *wan tok* George Anderson was a troubleshooter at large. A Scotsman of middle build, he constantly gave the impression of a man who thrived on a mess, and no mess was too big or too small for him to tackle. He was our man in Tripoli when the rest cleared out. He was also an enthusiast in Solomonology. Within an hour of remeeting him at the Mendana he had given me my two most valuable leads. One of these admittedly was circumstantial. As we sat watching the Gilbertese dancing troupe two imposing older expatriates stopped by to exchange greetings with the Second Secretary. One of these was Dr John Edge, temporarily in charge of Honiara Hospital, or Number Nine as it is known. The other man wore white shorts, highly polished black leather lace-ups, long white socks and a crisp white shirt. To complete the picture he carried a cane and doffed a grey Homburg. Whatever he was up to he was doing it in style.

'What the dickens was that?' I asked, as soon as we were alone again.

'That,' smirked George, 'was Bill Guinan.'

'Don't tell me. The resident dinosaur. Did he come first, or did Adam?'

'Not a bit of it. Until a year ago he was Governor of Wandsworth Prison. He's come here as a special adviser to the Government. If you talk to anyone you should talk to him. He's possibly the most incredible man you'll ever meet.'

'How so?'

'You'll find out.'

'Well, I liked the eyebrows.'

Then George dangled the second carrot.

'By the way,' he inquired a few moments later, 'has anyone told you? There are some people over on Malaita who want to sue us for 70 billion Solomon Island dollars.'

'*What?*'

'Yes. The claim keeps escalating.'

'Who *are* these people?'

'The Kwaio.'

Pronounced Koio. This rang a very tiny bell.

'The Bell Incident?'

George nodded.

'Yes,' he said, 'the Bell Incident. But it'll all keep until Monday. For now I suggest we wend our way to the Super Club. My wife's gone to New Zealand to have a baby. One caveat, though. When we get there don't complain. If you get thrown out of the Super you'll have nowhere else to go.'

The Super Club was three miles away behind Chinatown, which looked like the set of a spaghetti western. One broad street lined with spaced-out verandahed stores on either side and posts for hitching non-existent horses. At 10.00 pm it was thoroughly deserted. The camera crew had been sent home, the arc lamps killed. And then the Super. An ordinary-sized European house that somehow contained a discothèque, two bars and a couple of gambling dens upstairs.

'It's only just re-opened,' George explained as we got out of his car. 'Six months ago, thanks to the Seventh Day Adventists, it was closed down. But you can't stop the Chinese, so it's all systems go again. Here.'

George handed me a complimentary pass, so I avoided having to pay the gate fee. Complimentary passes were given to all the embassies, commissions and consulates on the principle that diplomats were the least likely customers to leave the premises still owing money.

'The Chinese have been in the Solomons since Tulagi,' George went on. 'They run the stores , a few restaurants and this place. I think there are about 400 of them, including children. If you're looking for a tin of vintage bullied beef they're the ones to ask.'

We went inside. Downstairs were ten Australians dancing with six

Australiennes, and a comparable number of young Melanesians sitting against a wall watching the wild roundeye antics. The music, mostly Madonna, was horribly loud.

Upstairs was quieter. There was a snooker table, a roulette table, blackjack and, in another room, mah-jong. I'd seen more formal casinos in friends' kitchens.

'Let's wait to see who else comes,' George said. 'They won't start the roulette until there are at least six players. Percentages, I'm afraid.'

George bought himself a beer and we continued our conversation. What, I asked, were the immediate talking points?

'My word, you are determined to grub, aren't you? Well, let's see. Last weekend some American marines went alcoholic at the G Club. The G Club is the Guadalcanal Club, and I recommend it even less than the Yacht Club. There isn't really any prostitution in Honiara, but if a woman needs some money that's where she goes. One of them got her comeuppance, though. She had to be taken to Number Nine at two in the morning with half her labia chewed off. Hungry people, marines. The Americans have also made themselves unpopular by allowing one of their tuna trawlers to be caught red-handed fishing illegally in Solomon Islands' waters. The *Jeanette Diane* was actually impounded by the one and only Solomon Islands' patrol boat. We almost had a war on our hands, but at least now the US is conceding that territorial waters mean something in the South Pacific.

'Then rumour has it that there's an Australian inventor in town. He's supposed to have invented a coconut-dehusking machine, and he's come here to flog it. If it works, the economy is doomed. About half the labour force is employed dehusking coconuts, on the plantations. But probably it won't work. Trouble is every coconut has its own shape and size. I think a human being is the best possible invention for the work. Otherwise there's been a fraças in the Western province. An international incident, no less. A flotilla of canoes from Bougainville rowed across the sea in December and attacked a fishing village in the Shortlands. Fishing off the Shortlands is very good, and Bougainvilleans have been doing a lot of poaching. They use explosives nicked from the copper mines at Kieta. Some while ago a couple of them were caught and thrown into the jail at Gizo. This was their revenge. About 200 of them landed at Kariki and went on the rampage. The police were outnumbered, and had their rifles stolen. Both governments are highly embarrassed, the Solomon Islands and

PNG. It's strictly a tribal affair, and wouldn't look good if the story got out. These things are not supposed to happen any more, but of course they do.

'I should also mention an outbreak of Luddism. Most of the logging in the islands is done by the Koreans. That's how the chips have fallen. The Japanese have the tuna – the Solomon-Taiyo company is the big one here. The Koreans have the timber. The other day there was an incident of machine-breaking here on Guadalcanal. A Korean mill was sabotaged and a lot of damage done. But it's not political, at least in our sense. What appears to have happened is that the Koreans in question had been walking to work across someone else's land and hadn't asked permission. Land tends to be a sensitive issue in the Solomons. Traditionally land and ancestors are inseparable. Therefore no one likes parting with it. That gets in the way of economic expansion, mainly because it's usually difficult to ascertain to whom any particular piece of land belongs. Investing in a new factory is a double risk. The Solomoners are not stupid. Often they'll let a project get way down the road, then an old man will appear out of the bush declaring that the land it's built on belongs to his village. Usually the difficulty can be resolved by offering compensation, but that's not necessarily any guarantee that the next day another old man won't come running out the bush saying the land belongs to *his* village. All of which makes entrepreneurs nervous. The government is trying to create a land registry, but there's still a long way to go.'

'And the gold rush?'

'There isn't one, for more or less the same reason. Gold's there, especially on Guadalcanal, but access is being denied. The hillspeople own the land, and they don't want their ancestors to be disturbed. Wealth really isn't the priority. Of the thirteen companies licensed to prospect only two are active. There's a certain amount of panning that goes on, but it doesn't amount to much. When a panner has found enough gold in the streams to buy a crate of beer he comes down to Honiara and spends it.'

'What else?'

'What else do you want to know about?'

'Cyclone Namu?'

'That was in May last year. A full-scale emergency. Thousands of houses were flattened and gardens destroyed, here, in Malaita and further west. Miraculously less than a hundred people were killed. Aid

218

has been pouring in ever since. It has to be said that if the houses were better built these winds wouldn't do a tenth of the damage. I've known worse along the sea-front at Brighton. But one consequence was that Cylcone Namu saw off the Prime Minister, Sir Peter Kenilorea. Sir Peter rather unwisely entered into a covert agreement with a French agency to send aid to his own village in Malaita. Typical Big Man stuff, but as the government was pushing a let's-all-row-together line he had to go.'

'Law and order?'

'Bill Guinan's the man to tell you about that.'

'Health?'

'In three words, malaria, malaria and malaria. And some tuberculosis. Talk to Dr Edge. One thing I can tell you, though, we're still waiting for our first case of Aids. They've got it in Fiji, so probably it won't be long before it arrives here.'

'Now there's a topic,' I said.

'Isn't it just?'

And before we knew where we were we were deep into Number One Topic. George was almost as paranoid as I was. He'd had a blood transfusion in Kampala once and, although it was many years ago, he admitted it gave him the willies just to think about it. He was interested in what I had found out, or failed to find out, in Bangkok, and took the gloomiest possible view about my shot of gamma globulin. For an hour we became soul-mates. We were unanimous on most points. One of us mentioned castration, and the other nodded sagely. At the very least the Hippocratic oath should be thrown out the window and branding introduced. Not necessarily on the forehead, but somewhere it would be seen at the appropriate time. Which left a choice: the right buttock, or the left buttock. And both of us, I guess, would have described ourselves as nice educated liberals.

But the fever passed, and the blackjack table filled. When George had tripled his stake he let slip a thoroughly Scottish wink and cashed in his chips.

*

Thus ended my first day in the Solomons. The second day I made a preliminary exploration of Honiara. The cloud cover had vanished and the air was saturated with the scent of hibiscus. Close to Point

Cruz harbour (where Mendaña is supposed to have stuck a cross in the ground) I was greeted by a flame tree in full cry. On the wharf I mingled with a sizeable crowd of Solomon Islanders. Many of them had blonde and strawberry coloured hair – a natural pigmentation. There were big ones and little ones, fat ones and thin ones, dark ones, and light ones. When asked they eagerly told me which islands they were from. And they came from all over. From Santa Isabel and Vella Lavella, from Choiseul and the Treasury Islands, from Rendova and Ulawa. Suddenly I realized that Melanesians were not created to be miserable. They were as far removed from their cousins in Irian Jaya as Amazonians are from Eskimos. I did not get the impression that any of them had anything of burning urgency on their minds, but in that they were perhaps blessed. It wasn't paradise, as some visitors to the South Seas like to pretend, but nor was it the other place.

I walked on. The town itself was not impressive. On the main street there were several gangs of dark Malaitans, chewing betel-nut, red-mouthed, eyeing me suspiciously. Beyond that a small market and the churches, the mission headquarters, four or five of them, with the Catholic cathedral – a very modern wood, concrete and glass job, a bit like the Commonwealth Institute in Kensington, only wearing its Sunday best – riding serenely on a hill. Then nothing until Chinatown except a Chinese park with a Chinese gateway celebrating independence. By day the stores looked a good deal better. There were advertisements for calico everywhere, and inside rolls and rolls of the stuff. No poles, but enough cloth to cover a beach ten times over.

In the afternoon I went the other way, northwestwards, passing the full array of government buildings. Only the Prime Minister's Office had three storeys – the rest had just one or two. But what struck me were the signboards. Some of them had wavy lettering, thus:

THE MINISTRY OF FOREIGN AFFAIRS

The Happy Isles! And onwards, along the broad but thickly foliaged road, bungalows hiding behind quantities of frangipani and bougainvillea, until I reached a path that wound off toward the sea.

I took the path, and came to the end of a promontory. Two sights awaited me. The first was a canoe, midway through construction. The trunk of a tree had been scooped out. The constructors greeted me with smiles and a song of sorts, which may or may not have been in pidgin. The second was Savo, the volcano rising out of the sea nine miles off the coast of Guadalcanal. According to the geologists it has the potential to be another Krakatoa. It last erupted in 1840, but its top is still intact, waiting to blow anytime in the next 10,000 years.

For an hour I sat and watched. Nothing happened. What would I say to his lordship if perchance I stumbled upon him?

Lord Lucan, I presume?

Buzz off, and leave me alone!

But I've come all this way . . .

And so have I! But you are free to return, and I am not.

I made my way back to the Mendana. Swam. Wrote letters. Stocked up with Mary Shelley at the hotel bookshop – the blooming cheek of life. Ate. Telephoned to England. And then it was off to the Super again with George.

There still weren't enough punters to set the roulette wheel spinning. This time I heard the magic word straight from the horse's mouth. 'Ah. Solly. Percentages.' And George was reluctant to trust his luck again at blackjack. Instead he talked about his wife, the baby that was on its way. In a week he would be flying down to Auckland to join her. He was growing impatient, nervous.

We parted company earlier than on the previous evening. George had to be up early, to go fishing somewhere in someone else's motorboat. But before saying goodnight we raided the shelves of the High Commission. The prize? Her Britannic Majesty's copy of *Lightning Meets The West Wind*.

*

William Robert Bell, the epitome of the firm but conscientious colonial administrator, was not an Englishman but an Australian. He grew up in the state of Victoria, the son of an impoverished farmer. In 1899, at the age of 23, he enlisted for the Boer War. He rose to the rank of lieutenant. There his military career ended. While in the Cape he damaged his right hand in an accident with a pitchfork. Later on, when he had become the uncrowned king of Malaita, he was wont to describe the injury as a war-wound. Like T.E. Lawrence he needed to see himself as a martyr, the servant of a noble cause. Routine privations had induced a level of masochism. In the Solomons he became an enormous specimen of a man, like the abnormally large species of spiders, butterflies and cockroaches that surrounded him, only in another, almost mythical dimension. Unlike Lawrence, however, he died, as probably he would have wished to die, on active duty.

After the Boer War Bell worked for a while as an assistant manager on a plantation in Fiji. He was punctilious in observing the rules that by now had been drawn up to regulate relations between employers and employees. This brought him to the attention of the High Commissioner, and in 1911 he was invited to become Inspector in the Department of Labour at Tulagi, under Resident Commissioner Woodford.

In the Solomons Bell had his work cut out. The colonial establishment was much smaller than it was in Fiji, and plantation managers and traders alike turned a blind eye to the rules. Worse, Woodford was soon replaced by a man called Barnett, an unadventurous timeserver who preferred not to upset the status quo. In any argument between Bell and the expatriates Barnett sided with the latter, regardless of any transgressions they may have committed. At one point he even tried to have Bell dismissed for insubordination. For Bell this was an intolerable state of affairs, since on his own he had less power than a magistrate. To reprimand wrongdoers effectively he needed sanctions which, as often as not, Barnett refused to provide. But Bell persisted. He was determined that those who had come to make profits out of the Solomons should respect what after all were but the minimum standards of fair play. If they didn't, he would go after them. And it didn't matter who they were. Even the men who ran the Lever Brothers plantations, by far the biggest interest in the islands at the time, became used to Bell the busybody, Bell the teetotalling martinet. As for Barnett, at the appropriate moment Bell reported on him to Fiji. This earned him a severe rebuke, for stepping out of line; but a much greater reprimand was delivered to Barnett in private. Bell stayed, and his authority was never again challenged by his immediate superiors.

Promotion came thanks to the Great War. In 1915 Bell was appointed District Officer to Malaita. All able-bodied men were recalled from the peripheries of the Empire to fight the Hun. Bell, with his injured hand, was ineligible – much to his chagrin. Perhaps because

222

of this he set about his new responsibilities with a singlemindedness that bordered on the obsessional. Malaita, they said, was untameable. It was the most savage place on earth. Secretly the planters rubbed their hands in glee. How long would Bell last? A year? Eighteen months? And then they would be rid of him for good! But Bell didn't last one year, he lasted twelve, and by the end of them the island was all but pacified. Only a cluster of tribes living in the central uplands remained outside the pale. The Kwaio people. It was in an attempt to subjugate them that Bell met his death.

In one respect at least, Bell's job was made easier for him. In 1917 Barnett was replaced by a new Resident, Charles Workman. Workman had already served many years in the Solomons, and he knew what Bell wanted to do. Moreover he was somewhat in awe of the man. So when Bell said he wanted back-up Workman made sure he got it. But there was a limit even to this co-operation. What finally undid Bell were policies determined in far-away Fiji, policies which the Resident had no option but to urge upon his technical subordinate.

Bell believed firmly that savagery was an aspect of circumstance, not of race. This was not a romantic view, but an uncompromisingly practical one. In his opinion there was only one key difference between civilized and non-civilized peoples: discipline. With discipline anything might be achieved. Without it, anarchy and murder were inevitable. When he had been several years at Auki, the administrative capital of Malaita, he was visited, somewhat against his will, by an American photographer, Martin Johnson, and his wife Osa. Twenty-five years later Osa published her reminiscences, *Bride in the Solomons*. In a passage that might stand as a synopsis of William Golding's *Lord of the Flies* she has Bell expounding on the character of the Malaitans:

> They learn to be clean and obedient, and are loyal to death. They have plenty of talent and capacity. I have always believed that our civilization is only skin-deep. Give me a hundred boys from England and put them into this jungle, on their own or with the natives, and they will survive, but will have the same standards as the natives. Take a hundred of these boys and put them through good schools at home and you will have fine English clerks, shopkeepers, and scholars. At least, this is my opinion, and I am making it work so far.

But what Bell did not appreciate, or appreciate enough, was that the Malaitans, and especially the Kwaio, even in their savage incarnation, had a code of conduct to match his own.

To the outside world the Malaitan code was singularly unappealing since it entailed, or seemed to entail, an endless round of killing. In other words Malaita was part and parcel of the pre-colonial Solomons, only more so. And Bell himself undoubtedly contributed to this picture, as perhaps he had to. Overcoming Malaita was his life-work. He had no choice in the matter. Realistically there was nowhere else he could go, nothing else for him to do. Therefore it had to seem like a life-work. And because Bell had a very high opinion of himself it was important that his efforts reflect heroic values.

Unwisely Osa Johnson one day allowed herself to wander out of Bell's sight, to play with some native children. Bell rounded on her in typically headmaster fashion. The American retaliated vigorously, suggesting along the way that 'all this talk about cannibalism' was 'exaggerated'. 'You're a bloody little fool,' Bell retorted. 'That is the mildest thing I can say to you.' Then came the lecture:

> 'There is just one more thing I want to remark,' he
> continued, looking through me with his gaze. 'Your reference
> to cannibalism just now. Exaggerated! I can put down such a
> statement to only one thing – abysmal ignorance. What do you
> think I have been doing here these many years; sleeping? Do
> you think I have built this establishment and trained these
> guards, and that the Government has gone to all this expense
> and exercise, for some mild pleasure? This is all serious
> business, too serious for your inexperience to comprehend. Do
> you know that hundreds and probably thousands of people
> have been murdered within sight of where you are sitting at
> this moment? And that I spend every hour here at my
> peril? . . . Why, this place reeks with murder and head-
> cutting.'

Bell's 'establishment' comprised his house, a tennis court, a barracks and a small jail. In the barracks he kept what amounted to a private army: a force of policemen recruited locally, and armed with rifles. Though they might be paid for by the government, these were his men, loyal to Bell, and drilled by him to exemplify his thesis that discipline is a *sine qua non*. Natives had been recruited for policework elsewhere in the Protectorate, but, as today, they were not generally deployed on their own islands. On his island, however, Bell wanted to do things differently. If other Malaitans saw that the District Officer had the *mana* to control people of their own kind, their respect for him would be so much the greater.

Brute force, while a component of Bell's strategy, was by no means the whole of it. In 1916, soon after the beginning of his term he led his constables on a 'raid' into North Malaita, but this was principally to give an early warning of his intentions. Thereafter he sought, wherever possible, to resolve conflicts peacefully. Particularly he wanted to put an end to the system of blood-bounties that then pertained. A blood-bounty might consist of pigs, or it might consist of shell-money. It was offered by anyone with a grievance, and was payable upon the execution either of the person who had caused the grievance, or of one of his kinsmen. Thus a bounty might be offered where a man's daughter had been abducted, or his wife seduced. But such revenge was never the end of the matter, for invariably one blood-bounty led to another, proposed by the relatives of the assassinee. What Bell discovered, when he began investigating these murders, was that many of them represented merely the latest link in chains stretching back two or three decades. Men remembered the injuries done to their fathers and grandfathers, and honour required vengeance. Strictly speaking it was a nonsense to punish individual murderers. The real culprit was the custom, not the man. Bell endeavoured, therefore, to persuade the feuding factions to come to terms. Let them hold feasts, and let them thereafter acknowledge the laws of the Empire. Where individuals or clans persisted in their deadly habits, he pursued the culprits into the bush, tried them and eventually shipped them off to serve long sentences in Tulagi.

In central Malaita a man who killed for bounty was known as a *ramo* – the most feared fighter in all the Solomons. Comparisons have been made between the *ramo* and the 'guns' of the Wild West, but an equally apposite parallel might be drawn with the Japanese samurai. He was a mercenary in the cause of justice, and his success betokened ancestral approval. He kept his weapons ever ready, he trained hard, and he avenged the wrongs sustained by his clan, by his village, by his people. But he was also expected to set an example of proper living. The true *ramo* did not steal other men's pigs, or their wives, or their daughters. He upheld the customs: marriage, feastgiving, worship of the ancestors. And well he might because in time, if he survived long enough and fought well enough, he would himself become a feast-giver, a Big Man, and ultimately a priest officiating at the village shrine.

For Bell there was no question but that the *ramos* must be confronted and stripped of their power. Their continued existence necessarily posed a threat to any white who set foot on Malaita. Recent history was littered with bloody attacks. The trouble was the bounty-hunters were incapable of distinguishing between the innocent and the guilty. In the final analysis revenge was revenge against alien ancestors, alien gods. Some of the recruiters, some of the blackbirders, had deserved what was coming to them, but that was no excuse to butcher just any recruiter, much less just any missionary. The *ramos'* principle of generic reprisal was not merely unchristian, it was uncivilized – or as Bell would have put it, undisciplined.

The two systems were intrinsically opposed to each other. On the one hand was Melanesian tribal custom, on the other the white man's liberal individualism. In the former a man was judged according to his blood-ties and allegiances. In the latter, according to how he himself behaved within a framework of laws and moral precepts. In dealing with Malaita Bell made allowances, as many as he could, when presiding over the district court in Auki. He did not approve of custom, but at least he recognized it as a disembodied social force. He took care to learn the different customs of different tribes, and his judgements generally took the accused's loyalty to custom into account. Yet ultimately the issue at stake, the rivalry between two distinct cultures, was too great for one person to decide, and had to be settled by *force majeure*.

The Kwaio *ramos* felt Bell's presence keenly. Little by little he was undermining them, forcing them into an early retirement. If he were allowed to have his way blood-bounties would soon be a thing of the past, as indeed they already were on the western coast of Malaita, and then they would find themselves without their traditional means of livelihood. Further, his court in Auki militated against custom. It interpreted sanctioned killing as something called murder, while much more serious crimes like abduction and adultery were treated derisorily. What did Bell give a man if he stole another man's wife? Three months in prison, or at the most six. What had become of the sacred laws of the ancestors?

226

But soon there was another ground for the *ramos'* festering discontent. In 1920 Tulagi, in line with other colonial administrations throughout the Empire, introduced a poll or head tax, to be levied on all adult males. The aim of this legislation was threefold: to raise money; to increase the depth of government penetration; and to force backward populations into wage-labour – for unless they earned money they would have none to pay over. In effect this meant that yet more of the village young would be obliged to take jobs on the copra plantations, thus further weakening the clans. If the village elders had to rely upon their sons to pay their tax for them, society as the Kwaio knew it would literally be turned upside down.

It was not just the *ramos* who were opposed to taxation. Bell was as well. The policy cut directly across his own strategy of conciliation and gradualism. It threatened his authority. Accordingly he complained about it to the Resident, now a gentleman called R.R. Kane. The head tax, he said, would cause unrest and disruption. But Kane was obliged to disagree. The mother of parliaments had decreed the levy so the levy must be raised. Well then, said Bell, you must give me an assistant D.O., a motor-launch and the authority to train more police.

To these demands Kane acceded. For the *ramos* their worst dreams were coming true. Misa Bello, with twice the fire power than he had before, was raising the ante. And when, in 1923, he began collecting the head-tax, more recruiting ships than ever sailed in the wake of his launch. Bell would put into land, set up a tax hut, a shilling a head if you don't mind, and the only way to pay was to indenture yourself to a plantation. Either that or, in a buyer's market, you parted with your valuables – shell-money, bracelets, necklaces – to some of Bell's own police, who had quickly learned the art of brokerage.

Then came the crunch blow. In 1926 Tulagi ordered that all rifles be handed in. The *ramos* were to lose their precious Sniders.

Bell moved cautiously. The rifles were a mainly symbolic deprivation since most of them didn't work – 'Snider' was merely a euphemism for any piece of antiquated rust traded over the past fifty years – but even so he understood the pride involved. In particular he expected trouble from the Kwaio. Reports had reached him that more than one blood-bounty against his head had been posted, and certainly in that part of the island the killings were continuing. But Bell also believed he could vanquish his most dangerous foes. Indeed, he had already twice collected taxes from the Kwaio. Admittedly, a year ago he'd had to track and arrest tax dodgers, but that was no more than a conscientious district officer should expect. It was all a question of preserving one's authority, and holding one's dicipline.

Thus, on Tuesday 4 October 1927, Bell found himself sitting at a table in front of the tax hut at Gwee'abe, an outpost in Sinalagu Bay on Malaita's unkempt north coast overshadowed by 2,000 feet of mountain ridge. Before him was a long line of men, almost 200 of them, waiting to hand in first their five shillings (the poll tax had been increased), and then their Sniders. Among them, standing as patiently as the rest, were several renowned *ramos*. Tagailamo, for instance, of the Furi'ilai people; Maenaafo'oa, of the Ailai; and Basiana, of the Kwaio. Ah yes. Basiana. It was good to see that he had come. If anyone was going to stay away surely it would be Basiana . . .

Beside Bell sat K.C. Lillies, his recently appointed Assistant. Around him stood five armed police. Bell himself had a revolver placed conspicuously at the elbow. And behind him, in the hut itself, were eight more police, also armed. They had wanted to stand outside, with their colleagues, but Bell dissuaded them. The trick was to remind the opposition of your firepower, but not to overdo it.

Basiana reached the front of the line and paid over his money. Bell nodded, and Lillies inscribed his name on the tax ledger. Then Basiana retreated. But minutes later he was standing in front of Bell again. Pressed against his arm was the steel barrel of a Snider. Before anyone could react he had raised it and brought it down, crack, on the District Officer's skull.

Bell was instantly dead. Lillies looked up, reached for Bell's gun, fired once and was shot clean through the chest by another attacker. Simultaneously the tax hut started to collapse. During the tax collection its stays had been stealthily cut. Now the hidden constables were trapped. One by one they were slaughtered. In a twenty-minute fight thirteen of the government's forces were killed, while the Kwaio suffered only the one loss: that of Maenaafo'oa.

When news of the atrocity got out the Protectorate was thrown into immediate confusion. Everybody had anticipated that something like this would happen sooner or later, but nobody was prepared for it today. The expatriate community, some 600 in number, now expected the entire archipelago to be overrun by thousands of murdering Malaitans.

Ironically it was Bell's death that led to the final subjugation of the island he coveted and in all probability loved. Ironically, too, it was mainly Malaitans who carried out the work. Reprisals, by South Sea standards, were swift. A so-called punitive expedition was mounted. In Tulagi a force of volunteers assembled – a wild bunch of planters and their ilk hell-bent on a bit of savage-bashing. These were to be known variously as the Breathless Army, on account of their average age and fitness, and the Whisky Army, on account of the supplies they took – ten cases of Scotch for 28 men. On 10 October they boarded HMAS *Adelaide*, a battlecruiser that had steamed hastily from Australia, bringing with it fifty marines. After some delays the task force came ashore at Sinalagu, where it was joined by another 40 'volunteers', i.e. Malaitan policemen and the kin of those men who had been killed at Gwee'abe. Also included in the party that set off for the hills were 120 carriers.

The expatriate volunteers were less than useless. Several fell by the wayside in a drunken swoon and others had to be carried. The marines discarded them at the earliest opportunity and pushed ahead. But the marines themselves fared little better. They were unused to the heat, the bush-jungle and the mosquitos. Within a week many men had gone down with fever, and finally it was left to the Malaitan contingent to pursue Bell's murderers. And they did so with devastating precision. They swept through the Kwaio villages in an orgy of destruction. Gardens and houses were burnt, women raped, men killed and ancestral shrines desecrated. Skulls were tossed into the menstrual huts and left lying in excrement. Then they went after the *ramos*. Officially they had orders to arrest them only, but as often as not they shot them on sight. Eventually the ringleaders, including Basiana, gave themselves up rather than witness the complete annihilation of their clans.

Between 60 and 70 people are known to have died as a result of the punitive expedition – although the official Colonial Office records have never conceded more than 27. Of these the majority were probably nowhere near Gwee'abe on the day of the massacre. But even there matters didn't end. A further 200 Malaitans were brought to Tulagi. Awaiting trial, another 30 died. A dreadful plague of dysentery swept through their ranks. Six men were found guilty of murder and executed. Fifty-one were acquitted, and the rest sentenced to long imprisonment. In many cases generic justice had triumphed over individual justice. But at least the colonial power could satisfy itself on one score. Central Malaita had been brought within the pale. The spirit of the *ramos* – or so they thought – had been broken forever.

These events are described in most books about the Solomon Islands, but they are described in greatest detail by Roger Keesing and Peter Corris in *Lightning Meets The West Wind**, best dubbed a collaborative venture in pop anthropology. The confrontation between Bell (the West Wind) and Basiana (the Lightning) is perceived not only as the summation of a conflict between cultures, but also as a tragic encounter between two giants. Most useful is the light thrown on Basiana through Keesing's researches among the Kwaio people, which he began in the 1960s. Physically he was small, a wiry, slight, little man. But he was also charismatic, totally fearless, given to aggression and violence, but calculating, intelligent, and efficient as organizer and leader. Indeed in Keesing's reconstruction the onus of the decision to attack Bell falls almost entirely on Basiana's shoulders. The other *ramos* and clan leaders, recognizing that in the long run they were bound to be crushed, argued against him. But Basiana persisted, just as Bell had often persisted against his superiors at Tulagi. He wanted to see the white man banished from Malaita, and the Kwaio left to enjoy their traditional way of life. He knew that the odds on success were a hundred to one against, but he also felt it was better to go down fighting, samurai-like, than meekly surrender.

Not all anthropologists and historians agree with Keesing's version. His account, some say, is too determinedly anti-colonial – *Lightning Meets The West Wind* concludes with a strongly anti-British chapter that seems to have little or nothing to do with what precedes it. Again Keesing is accused of having paid too much credence to verbal reports of events that occurred forty or fifty years before he began his fieldwork. Malaita, in common with other Solomon Islands, boasts a fine tradition in oral poetry, but where there is poetry, there, too, is exaggeration, distortion and deception. While commending his book, Raymond Firth had also told me that in his opinion it was the Kwaio women who were chiefly responsible for the Bell Incident. They saw that their husbands were losing their *mana*, and they goaded them into proving themselves men again.

But these are caveats. *Lightning Meets The West Wind* is likely to remain *the* book about the Solomons for a good few years to come.

**O.U.P. (Australia) 1980.

This is so not just because of the informed verve with which it tells a sterling story, but also because in terms of much of what is happening in the Solomons today it is of the essence, to the extent that several leading Solomon politicians would dearly like to see it banned permanently from their island shores.

*

My journal entry for Monday 26th January begins: 'I am chagrined to discover that the Prime Minister, Ezekiel Alebua, is but a mere two years older than I. Isn't that a sign of age? When one starts overhauling Commonwealth leaders?' Needless to say he went on my list of people to be interviewed. My plan was simple. I'd sample a cross-section of Honiara worthies. Head-hunting *à l'anglaise*. There was not enough time to go tribe visiting. In any case tribe visiting, unless undertaken by anthropologists, is intolerably patronizing.

Good heavens, Rusty, isn't that a piece of shark-bone?

Whereabouts, Ethel?

Stuck through the end of his shlong, you fool!

By George dear, I think you're right. Let's take a closer look shall we?

It's like watching the grand prix motor racing. Two-thirds of the crowd is there for the big crash.

Hey Rusty, you believe they still eat each other?

Of course they do. Always have done, always will. Young maidens by preference. Before the malarial parasites get to them and swell up their bellies. Cooked in their own juices. That is to say, in coconut oil. Wonder around the bush ready basted. Low in unsaturates. Fillet de jeune fille. The tastiest bit. Fillet mignons.

No thank you. Neither was I much interested in the military hardware which even in the middle of town was scattered everywhere. Small cannon sat outside the Mendana and sat outside the tourist bureau. Further away, the carcases of many fighter aircraft bestrewed the jungle floor. Japanese and American howitzers still pointed at each other, lizards poking their heads out of the barrels. And the sea was apparently no better. Between Guadalcanal and Malaita, hundreds of thousands of tons of shipping littered the coral beds. Iron Bottom Sound, it was now called. 'Bonegi One: 6000-ton Japanese transport shipwreck. Bonegi Two: another Japanese transport photographer's dream' – in the words of a tourist handout, opposite a photograph of a Barracuda launching itself out of a torpedo tube. Most of the residents I was to speak to went scuba-diving at the weekends. How else were they to amuse themselves? Two-meter sea-slugs. Humphead parrot fish (a.k.a. coral crackers). Groupers. One woman who had been in Honiara three years showed me her diver's log: 'Went back down with Charlie,' an entry read. 'We stayed close together and I saw some more of the old wreck.' People put on glazed expressions at the very mention of reef. 'The giant rays so tame you could write a message on them.' Salt-based LSD.

One day, maybe, I'd give it a try. But not yet awhile. For the present my motto had to be: people first, fish second.

George Anderson got me off to a flying start. In his room at the High Commission we drew up a list of possibles. Then he picked up the telephone, and in no time at all I had appointments with the Catholic Archbishop, Adrian Smith, his Anglican counterpart, Norman Palmer, and the Solomons' first Prime Minister, Sir Peter Kenilorea. In addition George put my petition to the office of the current Prime Minister. It seemed that all one had to do in those parts was drop one's hook in the water and the line began tugging. But on one point George was less than forthcoming. The Kwaio Claim.

Rightly I surmised that the Claim centred on the punitive expedition that followed the Bell massacre.

'So what form does the Claim take?' I asked.

'It's all set out in a document,' George replied.

'And what is our, I mean Britain's, response?'

'Irrelevant. It's all too long ago. When the Solomons became independent the Solomon Islands also took over all outstanding causes. Added to which there is the small matter of the Statute of Limitations. International Law gives us immunity. And just as well, otherwise every ex-colony in the world would be suing us for every p. we've got.'

'So really it's a demand for war reparations?'

'You could call it that.'

'Do you have a copy of the Claim document?'

'Here in the Commission? Of course.'

'Can I make a xerox?'

'I think not.'

'Oh come on George, don't be so mean.'

George grinned.

'If it was up to me you could take the damned thing away with you. But it's not up to me. The Claim is classified.'

'Catch any fish yesterday?'

'Yes, let's change the subject, shall we?'

But George wanted to help. If I really wished to pursue the Claim business, he suggested – and I'd be a fool not to – I should talk to Stephen Freed.

George picked up the 'phone and told Stephen Freed I was on my way over.

Stephen was an adviser in the Prime Minister's office, sponsored by the New Zealand equivalent of Voluntary Service Overseas. He was also one of the few unmarried expatriates on Guadalcanal, and was making the most of his status. Having overcome any prejudice against coconut oil and pig fat he was thinking of asking for an extension to his two-year contract when it ran out in April. But life wasn't all frangipani. Regularly he received demands for compensation. At the moment he was being harassed by the former boyfriend of his current girlfriend. A Malaitan of course. It seems the man showed up on his doorstep one night and demanded SI$1500 (one SI$ = 32p or 48 US cents). He claimed the woman was his wife.

'So what did you do?'

'Er, bluffed my way out it. I told him the girl had told me she was never married. He replied that he had had a custom marriage with her and that unless I paid up he was going to kill me. He even pulled out his bush knife. So I said okay matey, if that's the case, if you're threatening my life, it's a matter for the police. I shall have to tell them.'

That got rid of the Malaitan pdq, but Stephen's fear is he'll come back with his *wan tok*.

'It's no joke. Sometimes I ask myself is it all worth it, is it all worth it? I mean I'm only on 70 dollars a week. Seventy Solomon Island dollars. Only last month I had to shell out several hundred to the parents of another girlfriend in one of the outer islands. Well, she got herself pregnant, didn't she? On my salary!'

'So you're a father?'

'Er, I suppose you could put it like that. But I'm not going to see the child. It would only confuse me, I think.'

When he talked Stephen was curiously engaging. He affected a certain goofiness. Whenever I asked him a question either his head flopped to one side or his jaw stuck out beneath a pair of wafer-thin spectacles. And by government standards his clothing was outrageous. Bright broad-banded T-shirt, shorts that most men wouldn't care to call bathing trunks, and nothing else. His skin was tanned the colour of crackling. Stephen was one of life's enjoyers, and he was always up to his neck in it. On his own admission he was the first person ever to be put in jail in Wellington for smuggling marijuana. He was sentenced to three years for returning from Bangkok with eight kilos of Thai stick in his clobber.

'Thing was,' he said, ogling a non-existent female outside his window, 'thing was the false bottom in my suitcase. When the papers got hold of that the judge couldn't have been lenient if he'd wanted to be. Made it seem like I was a professional, which I wasn't. But these days I'm a reformed character. Otherwise I wouldn't be here. I mean this is a Prime Minister's office, and, well, I am in charge of the great Solomon Islands propaganda machine.'

'What were you doing in Bangkok?'

'Lived there two years. As who hasn't? Worst part of it wasn't prison, but what happened to my diaries. Left them in a house overhanging a *klong*. When eventually I went back to collect them every last word had been eaten by white ants. That was the real punishment so far as I was concerned. Up to then I wanted to be an author, like yourself. But the ants ate my raw materials, so here I am instead. Many, many years after.'

An hour slipped by. Eventually we got round to the Solomons. Stephen described his job – essentially public relations. His main contribution had been the production of *Solomon Nius*, a government newsheet which is rather better than its commercial rivals, *The Solomon Star* and the *Solomon Tok Tok*. Its facts are selective, but at least they're accurate.

'Now,' I said, 'tell me about the Kwaio, tell me about the Claim.'

Stephen beamed.

'So you're on to that are you? Have you seen the document?'

'I was hoping . . .'

'No chance. Ezekiel keeps it under lock and key and I don't have one. But I'll tell you what I know. You've read *Lightning Meets The West Wind*? Good. The man behind the Claim is the so-called Paramount Chief of the Kwaio, a gentleman by the name of Folofo'o. He's in his mid-seventies, and he's out to cause as much embarrass-

ment as he can. The claim itself is made against the British government, even though the real damage was inflicted by other Malaitans,
and totals 70 billion Solomon Island dollars, or so I'm told. In the
Claim everything is itemised – every desecrated shrine, every slain
man, every raped woman, every slaughtered pig. Although the
massacre took place in 1927, everything that has gone wrong for the
Kwaio since that time is included. That's the way they think. The
power of their ancestors was broken, therefore their ancestors could
no longer protect them, therefore every calamity that has ever befallen
them is put down to the punitive expedition.

'A key man in all this is Roger Keesing himself. The politicians here,
looking for a scapegoat, have pinned it all on our friendly anthropologist. He is accused, informally, of having incited the Kwaio to
lodge their Claim in the first place. When it was first made, about a
year ago, the first thing that Sir Peter Kenilorea did was to invite
Keesing to leave the country immediately. You see the logic? Keesing
spends ten years with the Kwaio investigating their epics. This stirs up
old memories. The Kwaio then make a totally outrageous claim. Ergo
Keesing is the prime mover.

'Keesing of course denies any complicity. I'll show you a letter he
wrote to the *Star*. He says he had nothing to do with formulating the
Claim, let alone writing the document, which is what some people say
he did. And probably he didn't. Equally he's probably wrong to
suggest the Claim was entirely spontaneous. There were also a couple
of American Peace Corps workers in the Kwaio area. They've gone
home now, but there's no doubt they were encouraging the Kwaio to
return to their roots, the way Peace Corps workers do. They probably
went through Keesing's book line by line with the Kwaio – so in that
respect Keesing is involved.

'As of now the Kwaio want Keesing to come back, for a reunion
feast or whatever. And this is the sticking point. The government
doesn't like the Claim, and wants to settle it, wants it to go away. At
the end of the day the Kwaio will probably give up their demands in
return for a couple of schools and a new hospital. That's how
compensation works. You make a claim that's out of all proportion,
then you settle for what's realistic. Magnanimity, chuck, magnanimity. But Folofo'o insists that Keesing should be at liberty to revisit
the Kwaio, and the government absolutely refuses to give way.

'But this may be posturing as well. Probably Folofo'o knows that

Ezekiel Alebua won't give in, just like Sir Peter before him. There's another dimension, namely the Kwaio *fadanga* movement, which is Folofo'o's particular baby. Basically *fadanga* means autonomy for the Kwaio people. If the Kwaio are to drop their Claim then they want greater self-government. And if you push that one far enough it spells the end for central government. In the last few years there's been a push toward regional assemblies. Well, now there are regional assemblies. And they're costing the government a great deal to run. Instead of one parliament, they've now got five. A central one here in Honiara, and one for each of the four districts. And as if that wasn't enough there's also a separate tier of local councils. Without being a snob about it, I'd say that's rather like learning to run before you can walk.

'Folofo'o made his ideas clear two years ago in the general election. He persuaded the people of central Malaita not to vote, with the result that no MP was elected. Six months later a by-election was called, but again Folofo'o emptied the polling booths. Finally the government called a third election, and sent over a suitably large contingent of police to make sure people weren't intimidated from exercising their democratic rights, if you follow my meaning. Anybody caught inciting anyone else not to vote was liable to twelve months in jail. Folofo'o continued as before but was not arrested, principally because this time enough people voted for a member to be returned – Daniel Fa'asifobae. But Folofo'o's real enemy is Jonathan Fifi, a Big Man sympathetic to the government. In the old days they'd have slugged it out with machetes. Now they've resorted to politics. The nomadic pagan from the hills versus the Christian bigshot.

'In a way the situation is strictly comic, in a way it's not. From time to time there are other separatist noises in other islands. The Moro movement lives on here in Guadalcanal, for instance. In the Western District, where a lot of the best resources are, there's also been talk of independence, though there it's more opportunistic than tribal. If the government gives way to the Kwaio, or is seen to give way, that's going to open a floodgate. Which is why everybody wants to give the Claim a quick burial, and also why you may find it difficult to come by a copy. It reflects the big unresolved problem of the Solomon Islands. It's nine years since independence, but still the population as a whole seems undecided as to whether it wants to be a nation or not. Solomoners are a lot wiser than they used to be about the way nations behave, and mostly they don't like what they see. They think that if they don't develop into a nation they won't be beset by the evils that beset the rest of the world.

'That's the uncomic side. The comic side is that the lack of common purpose perpetuates a certain, er, Ruritanian flavour. You'll hear plenty of examples, but let me give you one of my favourites. One of the Western District MPs is a man called, let's say, Jimmy S. Now a few people say some nice things about Jimmy, and a lot of people say only nasty things about him. He's a bit of a soap-opera villain. For example he has a habit, whenever he's in Honiara, of inviting all his friends to a restaurant and then not paying the bill. Because he's an MP the restaurateurs find it difficult to refuse him, but for the same reason he's bad news for the rest of parliament, who by and large do uphold the dignity of their position. On the other hand he does have go, which makes him unique I suppose. The rumour is that Jimmy, who is also the most widely travelled Solomon Islander there is, has access to a quite incredible sum of money, around 90,000,000 US dollars. Nobody knows where it comes from. Either it's hot money, something to do with the Mafia perhaps, or it belongs to a group of wealthy Russian Jews who don't want to keep it in the West. What he wants is to open a bank, bring it into the country and use it to finance local industry. But the government won't let him. In the first place it would give Jimmy too much personal power – he definitely wants to be the next Prime Minister – but more importantly it would expand the economy too much too soon. In some circles the prospect of an economic take-off is distinctly unwholesome.'

'Seventh Day Adventists?'

'Yes, and, er, there again no. They're certainly a force to be reckoned with. I'm not especially *au fait* with religious matters, but I do know the SDA is out on a limb. The three big congregations, Anglican, Catholic and South Seas Evangelical, get along fine with each other. There's an ecumenical organization called the Solomon Island Christian Association, which provides an umbrella of sorts. But the Adventists haven't joined, and won't join. They're a funny lot. Every time there's a motor accident – and despite the small number of vehicles it happens all the time – they crawl out of the shadows and place empty beer-cans on the wreckage, by way of comment. Not just one or two, but dozens. There was also a fuss when SOLAIR first

237

started. The only Solomon Islander qualified to be a pilot belonged to the SDA and wouldn't fly on the Sabbath. They're real sticklers for the Ten Commandments. But it would be wrong to think they're backward-looking. In government it's rather the reverse in fact. They are the ones who want to forge ahead with nation-building. But then again it's nation-building according to an SDA blueprint, so that only adds to the divisions.'

'What happened to the pilot?'

'He was sacked. SOLAIR reverted to Australians. A good example of just why it is that the expats are still indispensable.'

And so on, until at last we reached Bill Guinan.

'Ah yes,' said Stephen, 'Rove Prison. George Anderson's quite right. You should get Bill to give you the full saga. In a nutshell a year ago we had what you might call "a situation" on our hands. Rove is the central jail in the Solomons, and the prisoners had taken over. The warders had been scared off, mainly by outside collaborators in the *wan tok* system. If any of them tried to go near the gates they got pelted with bricks and stones. The prisoners were tearing down their cells and using them as ammunition. And the gates, of course, were open. The prisoners were in total control. Then they started using Rove as a base from which to conduct night-time raids on the town. Looting, robbing and raping. Finally they just absconded. They had us all by the scruff of the neck. Even the Governor General, Sir Baddeley Devesi, was forced out of his shell for once. He went on the radio and beseeched the prisoners to return to jail. He said that if they were too far away to walk the government would pay for taxis to bring them back. Can you imagine? But it was Guinan who sorted it out. He was flown in very quickly from London. He put on a display of force that soon had the prisoners back where they belonged. But the trouble went on, and there was a second attempt at a break-out. At one point he had to pretend to the inmates that the police were armed with machine-guns, which they weren't. It could all have got very nasty. But Guinan handled it well, and here we all are.'

'As bad as that?'

'Er, yes,' Stephen clucked. 'It was as bad as that. Although Guinan was typically modest about his part in the charade. He is on record as having said that, compared to Wandsworth, Rove was a piece of cake.'

*

The Catholic Archbishop, when I visited him the following afternoon, reiterated what Freed had told me about the sects. The Catholics, the Anglicans and the SSEs got along just fine. There was also some dialogue with the Wesleyan United Church. But the Seventh Day Adventists had set themselves apart. They were not as other men. Yet in one respect at least Adrian Smith took heart from this. It meant that being in the Solomons was not like being in Samoa, 'where everything is the same. I find that very oppressive!' In the Solomons there was no one way of doing things. Customs varied according to who you were and where you were. 'Individuals therefore are better able to develop according to their peculiar talents.' On the other hand conversions, where they still occurred, tended to be by the group and not by the individual. For the early missionaries this had made life very easy. All they had to do was persuade the village chief to come to church and the rest followed. Conversely there was not as much personal commitment as one would expect to find elsewhere in the world. What the churches needed to do now was deepen the individual's involvement in worship; to help him understand that he has a one-to-one relationship with God.

Smith was not at all what I had expected. At 47 he was a mere babe among prelates. He had a clean-cut, well-set face surmounted by a pair of black-rimmed spectacles that magnified his eyes dreadfully at a certain angle. A naturally curious, naturally alert brain operated through a soft-spokenness that offset the dogmatism of his faith. He was still a learner. As we talked, seated in the cluttered front room of his bungalow above the cathedral which also served as his office – possibly the smallest archiepiscopal palace in the world – Smith frequently paused for thought. His faith was solid enough, but its shape was a touch indeterminate. He had been ordained in 1966, from a Marian seminary in Whitechapel, and had been in the South Pacific ever since. Yet there was a sense in which he was still a stranger to these parts. Appointed to the archiepiscopate in 1985 he was still finding his way.

We discussed several of the sacraments, my questions directed at finding out what kinds of accommodation Catholicism had had to make with Solomon Island mores. For example, did the Solomoners take easily to the confessional? Yes, said Smith, they did. Confession is, or was, a normal cultural act among many of the islanders. Before coming to Honiara he had worked as a parish priest on Malaita, and there women were expected to confess their faults to their partners, sometimes in front of witnesses, before marrying. The concealment of personal faults, it was widely believed, created adverse situations. In some cases, as in an unwanted pregnancy outside marriage, this was logical enough. But in others there was no reason in it at all. 'The wife is sick, therefore the husband has been unfaithful, or vice versa – that sort of thing I couldn't swallow. Where we ask what's causing the problem, they ask who. And that has to be combated.' And what about the eucharist? Again, the difficulties were of a technical kind. All the islands had taboos of one kind or another: pig-meat or shark-meat could only be eaten on certain occasions, and according to certain rituals. The positive aspect of this was that the islanders were used to rules. They actually liked clear instructions, lists of dos and don'ts. Very few of his flock, Smith added ruefully, were 'remotely theologically minded'. There was even a resistance to the new-style 'post-Vatican' theology, which places a greater burden on individual conscience. Unquestioning obedience, for the Solomoner, was a much more attractive precept.

Of course, Smith went on, one tried to find a common meeting place in the middle ground. For instance, the matter of bride-price. At first he had thought this a distinctly unChristian practice. It smacked of barter. But in time he came to see it as 'a valid method of bringing together families to enable and support the marriage'. Likewise compensation customs embodied 'a great respect for the dignity of the person'. More and more he was coming to see the differences between Christian and non-Christian customs as 'a clash not in values but in the ways of expressing values'. 'Much of what we think of as Christianity is just western manners.' Yet there were areas of genuine conflict as well. Death was one of them. Among Melanesians the distinction between the here-now and the here-after is not well marked. Instead of heaven they believed in the continuing existence of their ancestors all around them on earth. The idea of the Resurrection was a concept they found difficult to grasp. Easter tended to be only a social occasion, and the Christ that he preached necessarily 'a more lyrical Christ'.

'Yet on this point one must be adamant. Ancestor-worship and ancestor-beliefs are an obstacle to faith. God is the only source of spiritual help, and any other source must ultimately be denied.'

Smith paused, worried that he might have overstated his case. He had missed out on the saints, and he had missed out on Mary.

'It's not that we wish to deny the existence of ancestral souls. It's just their continuing presence down here that's unacceptable. We have to say, your ancestors have gone somewhere else. I don't see that Christianity has come to wipe out Melanesian religion, but rather to help it to evolve and develop. The search for the meaning of life goes on but with a better light source, and with values which stand up now more fairly in the face of changes over which the average Melanesian has little or no control.'

'You mean the changes brought by ourselves?' I said. 'To me, what you say makes Christianity sound like the shoehorn of westernization.'

'Yes,' Smith sighed. And then: 'But we all come with our smelly feet, don't we?'

After this startling admission, which was also a rebuke, the Archbishop indulged in a little Marist propaganda. The strength of the Catholic mission, at least in the Solomons, was that its supply of missionaries was relatively broad. The priests came from all over, from England, Ireland, Holland, Germany and America. This meant that their culture was diluted somewhat. It was not like New Caledonia, where all the missionaries were French, and where as a consequence the mission was more stridently centred on one particular culture, one particular civilization. Then we talked, as everybody in the Solomons does talk, about Malaita. Smith had a particular interest in the island. Not only had he worked there, but since becoming Archbishop he had created a new diocese for Malaita, so that now Malaitans had their own bishop. And of course, he knew about the Kwaio. He had nothing new to say about the Claim, though he did tell me a little bit more about the *fadanga*. One extreme section had set up a fenced-in village in the mountains whose special feature was that each hut was connected to the next by a speaking tube. Whenever outsiders appeared everybody retired to his or her own dwelling and began relaying reports of what the outsiders were doing to their neighbours. Very few government people had been there, or even knew about it.

'But then that's the problem with Malaita. It's divided east and west, hills and coast, developed and undeveloped. Generally mission-work in the Solomons is in its second phase. The days of empire-building are over. The people have been converted, and now it's a question of consolidating our position, and of handing over, as much as possible to local priests, of whom we have nine. But in some parts of Malaita . . . there is still much work to be done.'

Much work to be done! I detest God and priests and chapels and sacraments and the Cross most of all. But Archbishop Smith I could pardon, if only on account of his priceless smelly feet.

*

And so I began my rounds. Over the following ten days I became a purveyor of men. Taken together, the characters I met were like a bouquet of enlarged tropical blooms. Each one of them was in some way displaced, yet each one thrived. And each had his work cut out, reflecting the other side of Honiara: a place of patient, often unrewarded endeavours.

Sir Peter Kenilorea for example, twice Prime Minister, until Cyclone Namu blew him off the pinnacle.

But Sir Peter was still busy. He may have disgraced himself, but the government could ill afford to dispense with his experience. At 44 he was very much the senior statesman, a big bull of a man, overgrown with sideburns and wearing, when I saw him, purple shorts, a blue shirt and white socks. His face, like many Malaitans', inclined toward the morose. Yet underneath lurked a convivial personality. From time to time he emitted a shrill pearl-string of giggles. Now he was the Minister of Natural Resources, serving under Ezekiel Alebua, his former protégé. He had also hung onto the leadership of the United Party, the dominant political configuration. His office was at an out-station, high above the capital.

'There can't be many ex-Prime Ministers,' I couldn't refrain from commenting, but choosing my words, 'who continue after retirement.'

'I know. But look, we don't have a House of Lords in the Solomons. What else do you want me to do?'

And then:

'But between you and me I am thinking. I am thinking very hard to introduce a constitutional amendment. We'll have a House of Lord, a small place somewhere between the Prime Minister's office and the Governor General's Residence. Just for me!'

Sir Peter's face radiated magnificently. The idea was obviously appealing in the extreme. But then he frowned.

'You know, though, if I did that I still wouldn't get any peace. Half my *wan tok* would come to live with me. That's the Solomon Island context. No one can isolate himself. From top to bottom we are part and parcel of each other.'

'Even the Kwaio?'

'Even the Kwaio. But the Kwaio have been ill-advised. In some places there is a sincere ignorance on the part of our people. Too much ancestor worship is not good. The anthropologists are partly to blame. Knowing the past is one thing, reliving it is another. It stands in the way of progress. Women's rights, for instance.'

'You're thinking of Roger Keesing?'

'I'm thinking of him. I suppose they told you I kicked him out? I didn't. That was Solomon Mamalone, when he was Prime Minister. Now he's leader of the Opposition. I only told Keesing he couldn't go to Malaita. And Ezekiel agrees with me. He says Keesing shouldn't go to Malaita either. It's an important issue. You must remember what our situation is. When I became the Solomons Islands' first leader in 1978 we were a brand-new island nation vulnerable to every outside influence – economic, political and military. It was a daunting prospect. We had no experience in international affairs, and we had no army. We still have no army. All we have is a small constabulary, a couple of helicopters and one naval patrol boat. We can only survive if we all row together. But if all the *wan toks* started reviving custom we'd fall apart. It's up to the local Big Men to take the lead. That's why we have provincial assemblies, so that the Big Men can advise us, and we can advise them. But you can go only just so far with devolution. Too much devolution and the centre will disappear completely. And then we would be at the mercy of the first frigate that sailed into our seas. That's why, in 1985, when the Claim was issued, I personally went across to the Kwaio and told Mr Folofo'o it wasn't on.'

'But the Claim is still being pressed?'

Kenilorea threw up his arms and gazed at the low ceiling above his head.

'Yes. It is still being pressed. One of the beautiful things about our British predecessors is they at least tried to see things impersonally.'

Seeing things impersonally. Soon after I had finished with Sir Peter I had a long tea with Geoff Dennis, the resident naturalist. Dennis was a slightly-built lizardy septuagenarian who had been in the Solomons for forty years. During that time he had observed a steady increase in the mean temperature in Honiara. It had gone up by at least 7° or 8°, thanks entirely to concrete, bitumen and dearborification – a statistic I think was intended to startle me into a profound misanthropy. Certainly Dennis himself was inclined that way. He lived some way outside town and only rarely came in. His achievement had been to set up the Botanical Gardens and the Herbarium, as well as lay the foundations of the National Museum collection, now housed across the road from the Mendana in a building provided by the Gulbenkian Trust. But the Botanical Gardens and Herbarium were presently in decay. Dennis had looked after them long enough and now it was someone else's turn. Only there was no one else willing to shoulder the burden.

He despised the cocktail circuit. There had been massive soil erosion, he said, caused by logging and the planting of oil palms. Oil palms had exceedingly shallow roots and so were guaranteed to disperse the land. On Guadalcanal most of the small rivers had doubled their width over the last ten years. Dennis had issued repeated warnings, but these had gone unheeded. Too bad. Cyclone Namu had proved him right. Eighty per cent of the damage had been done not by the winds, but by the rainwater pouring off the hills. And another thing. Dietary changes. There was a lot more stomach and intestinal cancer now than there ever used to be. It was because people kept adding sugar to everything. Why, the Gilbertese even added sugar to their drinking water. Someone should tell them . . .

Humankind was good at one thing and one thing only: abusing nature. There were 500 species of orchid alone in the Solomons, and they should be spared extinction. The Kwaio and their kind should be left alone, because they knew better than anyone else how to tend the bush. But people couldn't leave anything alone. Just recently a group of Papuans had shown some locals how to distil the leaves of the very toxic angel's trumpet flower. Needless to say at two o'clock in the morning Number Nine had been deluged with a party of Guadal-canalians gone completely out of their minds. But what use was medicine? And other modern chemicals? Take DDTs. Many village huts were now caked with the stuff, outside and in. It fell off the walls and the ceilings onto the children's food, poisoning them in the process.

But for one group Dennis did have a few kind words to offer. The

Solomon Islands women. They kept house brilliantly, and knew how to look after the children. They didn't spoil them, like western mothers, but nor did they constantly beat them about the head,

'But then you see I'm married to one. A girl from Santa Ana. I found her when I was sixty. We have five children. My third marriage and much the best so far!'

Someone else concerned with the ecosphere was Graham Usher, a 28-year-old East Anglian marine biologist running a giant clam project 20 kilometres up the coast from Honiara. Here the intentions were a good deal more commercial. While the gold in Guadalcanal might be reluctant to come out of the ground, Graham was devising a means to fish it from the sea, in the shape of the giant clam *tridacna gigas*.

Giant clams – *tridacna gigas* is merely the largest of several species – have long been relished throughout Oceania and East Asia. The adductor muscle, holding the two shells of the bivalve together and comprising 10–15 per cent of the total meat content, is an especially sought-after delicacy. In Hong Kong, Singapore and Taiwan it fetched up to $25 a kilo – and a mature clam weighs in at anything up to 200 kilos. It also yields a range of important biochemicals, of use in medical and cosmetic preparations; and the shell of the mollusc, when not employed as an ornament, can be incorporated into building materials or fine-ground into a calcium-rich supplementary animal food.

In recent times stocks of the giant clam have come under attack. Bands of Japanese, Taiwanese and Korean fishermen have scoured the Pacific in blatant disregard of international fishing boundaries. A dramatic growth in Pacific island populations has also played its part, to the extent that the *tridacna gigas* is now listed as an endangered species, even though giant clams are among the most gargantually fecund creatures on the planet. Hermaphrodites all, healthy specimens can produce up to 5 billion eggs a day and a near infinite number of sperm.

The snag is that while the adult, living inside its armour shell, is safe from every predator except man, the juvenile, a free-drifting blob of protein, has almost no chance at all.

Unless of course they can be domesticated. Enter Graham Usher and ICLARM (the Philippines-based International Centre for Living Aquatic Resources Management). With help from the ODA and other grant-aid agencies Graham was busy constructing a pilot nursery on an eight-acre strip of coastal scrub: tanks, laboratories, pump-houses and workers' accommodation. It was early days yet, but within a year he hoped to have his aquacultural centre fully operational. Within three years – the time it takes a clam to reach marketable proportions – he éxpected to show the first returns. And he was confident. So long as the parent clams could be induced to spawn – that was the tricky part – there was no reason why he shouldn't breed as many clams as he chose. At eighteen months the giant clam could be safely deposited on the reef: it was just a matter of protecting it until then. Hence the tanks. Thereafter the marine farmer couldn't wish for a better behaved product. The beast is phototropic, i.e. with the help of common algae called symbiotic dinoflagellates, or zooxanthellae, it feeds on sunlight reaching down through a metre or three of saltwater. Once matured it needs no further attention.

'Think of the *tridacna* as a sort of green cow,' Graham urged, 'animal and grass rolled into one. The idea is to furnish as many islanders as are willing with seedlings to put in their own back coral gardens. By 1992 I hope to generate an extra US$250,000 for the Solomons, and thereafter the sky's the limit, particularly if a means can be found to take clam-meat into the previously resistant western market.'

Light-eaters of the world rejoice! I had a vision of the western housewife, *circa* 2000, tossing bundles of clam-sticks into her shopping trolley. And by the year 2050 Guadalcanal 1987 would perhaps have replaced San Francisco 1847 as a byword for sudden prosperity.

Next up was Bill Bennett, the most renowned of the then surviving war heroes (who sadly died in early 1988).

William Billy Bennett was born in 1920. His father was a New Zealander, his mother a woman from Munda, on the island of New Georgia. His grandfather had been a headhunter, a Big Man. Before the war he had worked as a cookboy and a primary school teacher. When the Japanese invaded the western Solomons Bennett joined District Officer Donald Kennedy, the leader of the Coastwatchers, and quickly became his number two. Although the primary function of the Coastwatchers was to report Japanese ship and troop movements, after the Americans had landed on Guadalcanal they also took part in combat missions. Often they went to battle in Kennedy's boat, the *Wai-ai*, camouflaged with mangrove to look like an island. (One day, however, the island was cornered and had to be set on fire to avoid capture.) Bennett's greatest moment of glory came when, singlehandedly, he took out an enemy landing-barge. Under the cover of dark he boarded the Japanese craft and dropped a grenade into the engine room, where the crew were resting. To make sure none of them escaped he then closed the hatch and sat on it until the grenade had detonated.

After the war Bennett made use of the knowledge of radios he had picked up. He travelled to Fiji and took a wireless course with Marconi's. When he returned to Guadalcanal he worked first as a wireless operator for the civil service – then as now, with very few telephone lines between the islands, radio was the chief means of communication – later as a broadcaster. In 1959 he was a member of the team that started the Solomon Islands ordinary radio service, visiting Bush House in 1960 to receive further training from the BBC. From 1968 to 1975 he was chief broadcasting officer, and from 1975 to 1985 Chairman of the SIBC.

At the compound where he lived midway between Honiara and Graham Usher's clam farm, Bennett greeted myself and Dr Edge (who, an old soldier himself, had wanted to come along) with nothing but a calico towel wrapped around his lower half. As a halfcaste, part white part Melanesian, he appeared distinctly Polynesian, although his facial features were predominantly Caucasian. He moved slowly, as an old man should, but it was not a slowness of body: it was an ease of mind. He had a large stomach but even larger shoulders, resting atop a swimmer's deep chest.

Inside this cavern of a fellow lived a fox. Bennett knew his worth to the last whisker. The day before our appointment I got an unexpected call from him. 'You'll be bringing a bottle of Bacardi,' he said. It was not an order, but nor was it a request. 'Of course,' I replied, as though it were unthinkable I should go anywhere without some rum in my pocket. But the pitfall was obvious. At 30 US dollars a whack if I acquired a reputation as a Bacardi bearer I'd be finished in no time. Luckily Stephen Freed was on hand to come to my rescue. He secured me a litre measure of duty-free Australian Bandeburg from one of the embassies for ten Solomon Island dollars. When I collected it from his office only a small amount had been siphoned off: the Prime Minister's information officer's percentage I supposed.

'Sorry it's not Bacardi,' I said, handing the bottle over, 'but I'm told this stuff's even better. Indeed I couldn't help swiping a drop last night. To help me sleep.'

Placing the Bandeburg out of my reach at the far end of his table Bennett looked at me with dismayed suspicion. This was not how visiting journalists were supposed to behave.

'So is it true,' I asked quickly, 'that you sat on the hatch? Didn't you get your bum burnt?'

Yes it was true, and no he didn't get his bum burnt. Bennett reminded me, as though anybody should need reminding, that grenades explode laterally, not vertically. And in any case it was a steel hatch, so why not?

But if I hoped to hear any further details about Bennett's War it was my turn to be disappointed. 'Here,' said Bennett, passing me a thick sheath of xeroxed type-written pages. 'Some Americans were here last year, collecting war memories. This is my transcript. It'll be appearing in a book one day, but I don't see why you shouldn't use it as well. For now we can talk about something else.'

So we talked about something else. We talked about the Kwaio, we talked about broadcasting and we talked about how the Solomons had changed during his lifetime. But in the end I steered our conversation back to the Japanese.

'And now they're here again,' I prompted. 'Taiyo fishing etcetera. How does that make you feel?'

Bennett looked at me and shrugged.

'Nothing to it,' he said. 'In the war the Japanese came as fighting men. Now they've come in peace. It's as simple as that.'

'And you, I've heard, have been helping them find the bones of their dead in the jungle?'

'That's right. In 1971 the Americans wanted to set up a memorial to their casualties at Henderson Bridge. As President of the Solomon Island Wartime Comrade Association I helped them. So I thought why not the Japanese as well? The Tokyo War Office was surprised at the suggestion, but they sent a plaque. That was for their memorial at Eloha River, in 1972. Then in 1976 they sent a goodwill mission, headed by the Emperor's nephew Prince Takeda. I think they were pleased. At that time no one else in the world had let them commemorate their overseas dead. In any case the Prince immediately suggested they build a bigger monument, on Mt Austen, as a gesture to international peace. There was some opposition to the plan, not because of any bad feeling about the Japanese, but because the money, 300,000 dollars of it, could have been used to build more hospitals. But I said let's have something we can look back upon in the future. We have hospitals. So the Mt Austen monument was opened in 1982. Again Prince Takeda led the delegation. After the ceremony I was invited to Japan. I visited Tokyo and Kyoto. I met Mr Suzuki, the Prime Minister. I was made vice-chairman of the South Pacific Memorial Association. Since then they've come once a year, to look for bones. I arrange everything. Accommodation, food, porters. They pay the costs of course, but nothing else. Some people think I must be very rich, because I help the Japanese, but that's not so. I've never made a cent out of it.'

'But there must be the odd bottle of *sake*,' I teased, 'the odd bottle of Suntory whisky?'

Bennett smiled.

'Oh don't get me wrong. They're not ungenerous. I do it because it has to be done. We respect the dead, they are all ancestors. Besides, this year they bestowed on me the Order of the Sacred Treasure. It's the sixth highest decoration they have, and I'm the only non-Japanese to get it.'

As matter-of-factly as he could Bennett showed me the scroll bearing Emperor Hirohito's signature.

'And what about Japan itself,' I asked. 'Did you like that country?'

'Yes. Yes I did. I was very impressed by the way they look after their shrines, and by the way they look after their streams.'

*

One by one I picked them off. Norman Palmer, the Anglican Archbishop of Melanesia, who told me, perhaps a little smugly, that 'the people look on the Church as the stable element in a society where governments keep changing.' The incredible and most courteous Julian Marryshow, son of Theophilus Marryshow, a six-foot plus Grenadian with a cotton-wool-white beard that might have been designed by Inigo Jones and made him look like a negative of Don Quixote, who worked as a consultant to the tourist board. Dr Penelope Key, and others of the ODA party. Dr John Edge himself, seconded out of retirement (Barrow-on-Furness) to run Number Nine for three months, relishing the challenge, but bemoaning the lack of either a qualified pathologist or an ophthalmologist in all the islands. And others, all of them as though mounted on laboratory slides, to be held up to the light and gazed at, every one of them grist to my mill, and a sufficient variety to keep my mill turning.

Yet, in Honiara, democratic though it may have been by intent, my interest became more and more absorbed by a single person, a single slide-specimen-projection: Bill Guinan.

Conceivably there were good psychological reasons for this. Guinan was an insatiable enthusiast for order, a man of impeccable and spirited public service, and by these tokens very much my antithesis. As a younger son, as a sometime rake and doubter of most social and political necessities, as one who instinctively dislikes authority, I was perhaps bound to take special notice of an individual whose job it was to uphold civil society through one its more formidable sanctions: incarceration. Also my grandfather, who died when my father was still in his teens, was likewise a prison governor. Although I have always found this fact strictly incredible, it may have conspired to trigger my curiosity. Or it could more simply have been the manner in which Guinan recounted his story: bit by bit, over several days, keeping me on tenterhooks, egging me on, egging himself on, reliving events with a real glint in the eye, at times boyish in the extreme, at other times standing back from himself, the actor moulding his speeches, intellectually aware of the worth of a pause, or of a digression.

Or there again, and most simply, it could have been the tale itself; for there are some tales that take possession of the listener . . .

On my second Tuesday in the Solomons I found myself standing on the porch of the Mendana waiting for him. The rain, which had been falling since breakfast, was easing off, but the bougainvillea continued pounding the ground with unwanted water. At ten o'clock sharp Guinan's official car crunched into the hotel forecourt. Guinan emerged from the back seat in his uniform: the shorts, the shirt, the socks, all freshly laundered, and incandescent against the damp tropical surroundings.

Guinan looked up at the sky and said:

'This'll bring the big ones out, won't it? I mean the mosquitos. The ones with the Japanese wing markings!'

Oh God, I thought, here we go!

'It's such a collector's piece, this country,' Guinan continued. 'Such an absolute collector's piece. That's what I like about it. The whole place is a museum. Now jump in, and I'll show you my end of the exhibition.'

We drove the short distance to Rove Prison. There, instead of going immediately inside, Guinan took me round the back. Within minutes we were pushing into the jungle. There was a gang of prisoners hacking away at the undergrowth, but we had soon left them behind. A hundred insects kamikazed at my face with every step I took, and for a moment I thought I was back in Sarawak.

'Come along there,' Guinan called over his shoulder. 'I want to show you something. In a month the men will have cleared all this land, and then it won't exist any more. It'll have been taken away.'

Struggling I caught him up. Guinan was standing beside a tree.

'There! What do you think of that?'

I looked at the tree and I looked at Guinan, but I was none the wiser.

'Have a closer look. Go on.'

I took a closer look. At waist height the tree forked. Buried in the cleft was an unexploded hand-grenade.

'Remarkable, don't you think? The grenade's literally been raised off the ground. The tree can't possibly be more than twelve years old, but that thing was lying on the floor since the war. And now it's back in the air.'

We retraced our steps, myself treading even more gingerly than before. Behind Rove was an acre of open ground, where the old prison used to be. More men, using only their bare hands, were digging out half-buried coils of barbed wire. As Guinan approached they stood smartly to attention.

'Mornin' sah.'

'Mornin' sah.'

'Mornin' sah!'

Guinan nodded and we passed on.

'This bit we're going to use as a temporary football pitch. It's strictly stick and carrot at Rove. If the inmates behave I'll let them have one game a week. If they don't, there won't be any Christmas dinner.'

I was about to point out that Christmas was not for another ten months but Guinan was already several paces away. He came to a halt at the edge of a shallow concrete pit that measured six feet square.

'And this,' he exclaimed, 'is all that's left of the original execution block, where the last Malaitan bounty-hunters were hanged. Next week the men will fill it in. Like it?'

'It's the best I've ever seen,' I said reaching for my camera. 'I'll take a picture if I may. In fact I'll kill two birds with one stone, if you'll pardon the expression, and take yours at the same time. Agreed?'

'Excellent idea,' Guinan replied. 'Excellent idea.'

He moved round toward the front of the pit and stood stiffly with his arms dropped by his sides. His stick was perfectly aligned with his right leg, which he placed very slightly behind the left. I wanted him to turn his head more towards me, but he was oblivious to my direction. Nor could I move round in front of him without risking a flood of sunlight in my lens. Guinan had decided exactly how he wanted his portrait to look, and the artist was powerless to adjust the variables.

I did score one early victory, however. I suggested to Guinan that it would be criminal to fill in the pit and he consented immediately.

'Yes. You're absolutely right. It's a piece of history. It must be kept.'

And so, making our way through the half-finished warders' barracks we came to the prison itself. Around the perimeter were two wire fences – high enough, but not especially imposing. At the double gates were an office and a guardhouse. Inside another guardhouse and the cellblocks: single-storey brick jobs. There was also a refectory and a banyan tree.

Each cell measured perhaps twelve feet by twenty. They were dirty airless holes, crowded out with mats and bundles of belongings. There were, in addition, two isolation cells, attached to the inner guardhouse, used mainly for juveniles.

'It's like trying to bring three pots to boil on two rings,' Guinan commented, pre-empting my questions. 'At the moment it's eight men to a cell, which is a recipe for every kind of mischief. We only lock them in at night, as you can see. Unless there's trouble. The great step forward this month has been to persuade the prisoners to cook their own meals. That isn't to save money, but to give them something to do. Otherwise they'll malinger, and hatch plots.'

The prisoners, at 11 am, were scattered about the compound squatting in clusters wherever there was shade enough to cover their heads. One group was seated on a stone bench that ran around the base of the banyan. Once again my fingers palpitated for my Pentax.

'Any objection?'

'None at all. But you'd better ask them first.'

I walked slowly towards the tree. I raised my camera and let the prisoners have a good look at it. Those that wanted to have their picture taken organized themselves into a group. The rest moved off to watch from the sideline.

Snap!

'What about me?'

A prisoner was running toward me from the kazi, still pulling up his jeans. On his head was a basket, on his nose a pair of sunglasses, and on the upper half of his body a green T-shirt.

'Sure,' I said. 'Just stand still a moment and I'm all yours.'

Click!

'Thank you, sah! And God bless you!'

'My pleasure. But tell me, why are you here?'

The prisoner grinned from ear to ear.

'Too many murder. Sah!'

'A Malaitan,' explained Guinan as we walked away. 'But not a bounty-hunter. Just a rough diamond.'

'They seem a happy lot. Given the circumstances.'

'Yes. And I have to watch that. It's part of the national character. They have a predisposition towards happiness, which makes this place a mockery at times. But it's dangerous, too. If they smile too much I know there's trouble brewing. And look at it! You saw them outside, pulling that wire out of the ground. One determined effort and they'd tear the perimeter down like paper. Rove's still little better than a sardine tin packed with explosive. We're building a new jailhouse, but until it's open it's a terrific race against time. I lie awake at night, thinking about it.'

Guinan's official status in Honiara was 'Adviser to the Ministry of Police and Justice'. Anglo-Irish, he was born in 1925. In the war he served in India with the 2nd Dorsetshire Regiment. In 1946, as Captain Guinan, he went to Japan. Then it was back to Malaya, and on to Austria, Germany, Korea and Singapore. In 1961 he resigned his commission and, on his father's advice, entered the prison service. Promotion came quickly. Before Wandsworth (1981–5) he was Governor of Albany and Chelmsford. But Wandsworth was the supreme test. 'The biggest concentration of evil in Europe,' he called it. One-and-a-half thousand inmates, including terrorists, Iranians, Libyans, etcetera. 'The thing that makes any governor nervous,' he said, 'is a rich prisoner.' Some of his had their national economies at their beck and call. Increasingly there were problems with terminology. Were they gangsters, or were they freedom fighters? Plus the fact that prison staff were no longer recruited from the military. Worse, there was no death sentence to reinforce discipline. Riots, killings. On the moral issue he didn't care to speculate, but from a narrow administrative point of view there was no question about it. 'Take away that fear and you take away ninety per cent of what chances you have.'

'By the time my sixtieth birthday came I'd had enough. I took retirement. But I'd hardly taken my boots off when I had a call from the Foreign and Commonwealth Office. December 1985. Could I get myself to the Solomon Islands as fast as possible? Without thinking twice I said yes. The day before there'd been a vote at the UN. Another resolution on the Falklands. Britain was defeated 147 votes to 3. But voting with us were Belize, Oman and the Solomons. And the very next day I got the summons. I had to come!'

He arrived at Henderson on 27 January 1986, with a brief to 'investigate and rectify' what amounted to a total collapse of the prison system. At Rove the prisoners had been in control for over three months. In April and October 1985 they had staged two mass escapes. Now the warders had been scared off, and Rove was little more than a glorified doss-house. The perimeter had been breached in a dozen places, and at night the inmates simply wandered out to do as they pleased in the town. Moreover the urban drifters had quickly cottoned on to what was happening. Young men who had never been inside started robbing and looting as well, pretending they were 'Rove types'.

'It was inevitable,' said Guinan. 'Essentially it was a problem of management, or mismanagement. It started in 1982, when the Prison Service was separated from the Police. Warders were no longer constables. But nor were they ever properly trained for the job. Long before I came morale had degenerated completely. The *wan tok* system had something to do with this. Seventy-five per cent of the prisoners are Malaitan, so of course a Malaitan warder was at a particular disadvantage when dealing with a recalcitrant. But so was a non-Malaitan. And there was also a problem with alcohol. If warders weren't drinking in the compound they certainly were on the edge of it.

'But the pathology lay deeper still. The last prison construction programme took place thirty years ago. The very fabric of Rove and the other provincial prisons was rotten. Also, since that time the population of the Solomons has doubled. It's now well over 250,000. Then it was closer to 100,000. And Honiara is growing all the time. Village life used to be reasonably law-abiding, or at the very least self-regulating. Now we have a large number of relatively sophisticated criminals. The prison scene is dominated by a new breed of long-term and life-sentence prisoners who are hostile. But there are no facilities to segregate them. They know how to get at the system, and they intimidate the younger, immature prisoners for their own ends.

'The government were doing what they could to contain the situation. Here credit must go to Christopher Saungao, who had been appointed the Acting Controller of Prisons in December '85, and whom I later recommended for promotion to full Controller on 1 June '86. He at least had had the wit to insist that the police be involved. By the time I arrived they had Rove surrounded, more or less. But inside was still chaos. Chaos ruled by Kwanairara.'

By now we were sitting in Guinan's office at the Ministry of Justice. Before him, on his desk, he had a file of many hundreds of pages, which he frequently referred to as 'the documents'. The documents contained everything, every fact, every statistic, every date. As he spoke Guinan constantly checked what he was saying against the record. He was determined not to get anything wrong. But really, since he already had the facts off pat, it was to give himself the excuse to pause.

'Here, do you see. Kwanairara!'

His finger stabbed at a page a mere two inches from the beginning of his paper treasure.

'Shall I tell you who David Kwanairara was?'

'I think you'll have to,' I said.

'Prepare yourself then. Kwanairara was the ringleader. A Malaitan of course. But before he was put inside Rove . . .' Guinan flicked through thirty or forty pages of closely typed reports, and then looked up, his eyes burning. 'Before he was put inside Rove he was the Prison Controller!'

Indeed Kwanairara was responsible for ninety-nine per cent of what had happened. He was a typical Big Man, but run amok. As Controller, in October 1985 he had actually organized a breakout – to show the government that he had complete power over the prisoners. When he ordered them back, back they came.

But Kwanairara had gone too far. He seriously assaulted a recaptured prisoner in police custody. He also engaged in such pranks as throwing teargas canisters into the cells. In due course he was brought to book, tried, and sentenced.

In any other prison Kwanairara would have been lynched on his first day inside. But not so at Rove. Although a large measure of the problems facing the authorities arose out of claims made by prisoners against maltreatment at the hands of their former Controller, when Kwanairara went inside he was almost immediately accepted as the prisoners' natural leader. And many of the warders continued to obey his orders.

'So you see what I was up against? On the one hand prisoners were suing the system for injuries received, on the other hand they were paying homage to the man who had given them those injuries. It was an absolute opera!'

Guinan moved quickly. The priority was to restore control of Rove, and this he accomplished on 8 February. With the full support of the government he mustered an assault force of 140 men – police, those warders who could still be trusted, and a labour gang. At 8.00 am, with Rove surrounded, he advanced on the prison gate. Beside him were Christopher Saungao, the new Controller, and David Jeremiah, the expat magistrate who had sentenced Kwanairara. ('I had learnt it in India – when in doubt take a magistrate!') Behind him were six constables with 3.03 resting on their shoulders.

'As much as I could I let Saungao do the talking. It was critical, if any kind of morale were to be restored, that the Controller himself take charge. Mainly a show of force was what was required, because I already knew every Solomon Islander respects that. So Saungao walked in front. David and I followed. And the miracle was it worked! We had them outnumbered, but only just. And we lied. We told the prisoners that they were completely surrounded by a task force armed with machine guns. But there were hardly any machine guns, and in any case I doubt very much whether the police would actually have opened fire if ordered to. *Wan tok* again, I'm afraid. To begin with the prisoners came through the outer gate like a knife through butter. But we held our ground, we remained steadfast, and when they saw our resolve they retreated. And then the real operation began. We had to secure the perimeter and we had less than twelve hours to do it in. We used rolls of barbed wire left over from World War II. There was nothing else. The labour force went to work, and the police stood guard. I even had the police band join in. And then finally, at seven o'clock in the evening, not a minute too soon, the last link of the new fence was put in place. When they saw it was done the police stood at ease and cheered.

'But that wasn't the end of it. There was another breakout that year, on 15 August. The locking system was compromised. The prisoners persuaded two of the warders to give them the keys, three warders were locked into a cell, and they were out, 138 of them. But within days they were all back inside again. We hunted them all down. And as late as November there was a stoning match. The prisoners started tearing down their cells and bombarding the warders, but at least now the warders knew what to do.'

Gradually Guinan had got on top. He recruited more warders, put them into uniforms and made sure they were adequately trained. He also persuaded the government to release adequate funds. On the pinboard behind him was the architect's drawing for the new jail.

'And it's being built. It's going up some miles outside Honiara, and it'll cost over a million dollars. When it's open Rove will be reclassified as a provincial prison and remand centre like those at Gizo, Auki and Kirakira. As you can see, the new one's designed according to the traditional colonial well system. That was my idea. I wanted the new building to have some dignity – for the sake of morale, the prisoners' as well as the warders'. But no air-conditioning. If you put air-conditioning into a tropical prison the people will never move out. And I want there to be a full schedule of activities. Football if they're good, and plenty of gardening.'

'And Kwanairara? What's happened to Kwanairara?'

'That's another story.'

'Which you are going to tell me?'

'I don't know,' said Guinan. 'I mean I don't know that I can, or if I should.'

'Perhaps I'll ask David Jeremiah. I'm having dinner with him tomorrow.'

'Are you?' Guinan's face lit up. 'Then I shall be there too!'

And he was. David Jeremiah I had met on Sunday. We had sat opposite each other on Robbie Burns Night, a gala banquet staged at the Mendana by the St Andrews Club. I suspect we were both glad for the company of a fellow-Sassenach. A haggis had been flown in via Fiji, courtesy of British Airways. One after another all the members of the

Scottish *wan tok* stood up and recited *My Love Is Like A Red Red Rose*. Then they started reciting *My Love Is Like A Red Red Rose* in their seats. Speeches were made and a great deal of wine drunk. Reels were promised. Boiled whisky was passed from place to place in a silver cup. The only interruption was when someone loudly pondered whether you could catch Aids that way. But I told them, *yure hooch has ay been heat-treated*, and the cup continued on its way. It was like being at the wrong end of Cumbria on New Year's Eve.

Up at Jeremiah's ridge-top bungalow a somewhat more coherent party assembled. As well as Guinan there was a commercial geologist called Bruce, the public solicitor called Ken and another magistrate called I can't remember, but who obligingly wrote down for me his observations on the Penal Code as it relates to sorcery. The idea was less to concede the efficacy of Solomons' black magic, more to prevent some people putting the fear of God into others. Needless to say the observations arose out of the magistrate's experiences in Malaita:

> Course for local court clerks (like Magistrates' Clerks in England). Discussion turned to 'sorcery' – a crime in the Penal Code which falls within the jurisdiction of Local Courts. I asked if they got many cases of this. One of them said no and the others agreed. I said I was surprised as I got many complaints of this in Honiara. They said yes, they got complaints, but that they didn't deal with them under the penal code. I said how did they deal with them? They said – 'As civil cases'. I said, Why? They said 'so that we can award compensation for the harm done by the magic'. (N.B. The crime of 'sorcery' involves casting a spell on somebody in the belief that they will believe it.)

But mainly the conversation hinged upon Rove. Jeremiah's role in the events of 8 February was particularly interesting. He'd come to Honiara only eighteen months before. He was 28 and had just given up his work as a barrister in London. As soon as he arrived, however, one of the sitting magistrates decided to go on leave, so Jeremiah found himself presiding over a court for the first time in his life. Then, in October 1985, he had the unenviable task of sentencing Kwanairara for his misdemeanours. Naturally, when Guinan arrived two months later, he turned to Jeremiah for an informed opinion on what was going on.

Guinan and Jeremiah fell into a heated yet entirely amicable debate about who should take most credit for the successful recapture of Rove Prison. Guinan kept saying, 'It was your idea, David, and a really excellent one.' Jeremiah kept saying, 'No no, it was all you, Bill, you had us spellbound from the beginning.'

I tended to believe Jeremiah, mainly because Guinan had already told me that it was his determined policy to restore confidence in the properly constituted authorities. He had been brought to the Solomons as an Adviser only, therefore it would have been unconstitutional to lead the charge from the front. Instead he had led the charge from behind.

'Desperate measures were called for,' said Jeremiah, 'and Bill was the one to tailor them.'

'Well, let's say, David, that we tailored them together in my room at the Mendana. With quite a bit of help from Christopher Saungao.'

'Saungao? Was he there? I don't remember.' Then Jeremiah went on with what he did remember. 'The night before, 7 February, I spent about five hours deliberating whether or not to wear long trousers. Long trousers are more becoming a magistrate, but I run twice the speed in shorts. I anticipated that if I wasn't stoned to death immediately I'd need to run as far as I could as fast as I could.'

'You wore long trousers,' beamed Guinan, 'and quite right too!'

'I remember as we walked toward the gates turning, seeing a line of six 3.03s behind me, and thinking *this really is a situation*.'

'And it was. At any moment our plan could have come unstuck.'

'Your plan, Bill, your plan!'

'But I could never have done it without a magistrate!'

Jeremiah continued:

'After we had got the prisoners back into the compound one of them came out again. A thug called Manni. Something of a con-man. Manni marched up to Bill, Saungao and myself with a bundle of photographs in his hands. He accused the warders of having torn them, of having damaged them. All the other prisoners were watching. Tension was at breaking point. In fury Manni hurled his photographs at Bill's feet. It was tantamount to signalling a counter-attack. Saungao was about to protest when Bill astutely prevented the confrontation which at that moment would have been ruinous. Touching Saungao and myself on our shoulders he indicated that we should temporarily withdraw. The three of us walked back twenty paces. As soon as we stopped it started to rain. A stroke of pure genius on Bill's part, don't you agree?'

'It wasn't genius,' Guinan protested, 'it was damned good luck.'

'Of course it wasn't. You knew it was going to rain. You saw it coming. We marched back to Manni again. By now Manni was in two minds about everything. His pictures, still lying on the ground, were about to get soaked. But it was Bill who picked them up.'

'That's right,' said Bill, taking over the narrative. 'And I handed them immediately to the Controller. Manni demanded them back. I said, *What do you say? You say Please Controller Sir!* So Manni said *Please Controller Sir!* and Saungao handed back the photographs. Then I said *What do you say? You say Thank you Controller Sir!* And after Manni had said *Thank you Controller Sir!* he was as quiet as a lamb.'

'And where was Kwanairara all this time?' I asked innocently.

'He had been removed,' said Jeremiah. 'The first thing we did, after we had pushed the prisoners back, was send in Hugh Bennett to fetch Kwanairara.'

'Bennett?'

'Yes. Bill Bennett's son. Built like a prop forward. Now he's the superintendant, Saungao's chief warder. He was the only man bigger than Kwanairara. As soon as Kwanairara saw him he went limp, more or less. Like most bullies he was terrified of someone his own strength.'

'And where did Hugh Bennett put Kwanairara?'

'Not where he should have put him, I'm afraid, i.e. in one of the solitaries. He took him instead to the police offices down the road. There he demanded to make a telephone call, and unfortunately they allowed him to . . .'

'Which is where,' Guinan interrupted, 'the story must stop.'

'But why?' I asked. 'Surely you can tell me who Kwanairara telephoned?'

'No I can't,' said Guinan, 'and neither can David.'

'Who was it?' I pleaded, almost jumping up and down in my chair. 'Was it the Prime Minister? Was it the Governor-General? Tell me!'

'No,' replied Guinan. 'I really don't think we can.'

'It was the Prime Minister, wasn't it? Kwanairara's brother-in-law?'

'Who told you that?'

I shrugged cutely.

'Well you're wrong. It wasn't Sir Peter. Nor was it Sir Baddeley. It was someone else.'

'Then who?'

'You musn't even guess.'

It was no use. Guinan and Jeremiah were winking at each other. They had me on the end of their line, and I was dancing for them. The best that I could do was call them both a pair of savages.

Yet the very next morning Guinan rang my room. He was concerned about how much he had told me the night before.

'Now you've got half the story,' he said, 'I'd better give you the rest. Can you come and see me again on Saturday morning?'

'Does that mean you're going to tell me who Kwanairara telephoned?'

'No, it doesn't. Really I can't tell you. If you knew then you'd understand. It would be breach of the trust the government has placed in me. But I'll fill you in on the rest. And you can meet Hugh Bennett.'

*

Saturday was my last day in Honiara, and I'd made an arrangement with Jeremiah to see him that morning. I thought maybe he would spill the beans. But Guinan was irresistible. And in any case, I told myself, it was unlikely that Jeremiah would show any disloyalty to the most admired expatriate in the country.

I arrived back at Rove, and Guinan deposited me immediately with Hugh Bennett. It took exactly two minutes to get the information I required.

'So,' I began, 'you're the man who took Kwanairara out of the compound on D-Day?'

'Yes,' said Hugh. 'Myself and two other warders.'

'And you left him at the police offices?'

Hugh nodded.

'Where I gather he made a telephone call to . . .'

' . . . to Swanson Konofilia. That's right.'

Swanson Konofilia. The Minister of Justice, the man ultimately answerable to Parliament for the prison service, and, as it happened, Kwanairara's cousin.

Guinan was almost as pleased as I was that I had been told. Now he could continue the saga to its end.

'You understand now why I couldn't tell you? This is Swanson Konofilia's ministry. In effect I am working for him.'

'I understand completely. I should have figured it out. But thank you sincerely for not gagging Hugh Bennett this morning.'

'I'm only an Adviser. I don't have the power to gag people. Though I will say this. It's one of the few cases where the media should have been gagged. The day after Rove a radio reporter started broadcasting that there had been ministerial interference. That was a very dangerous thing to do.'

'But there had been, hadn't there?'

'Not exactly. It was Kwanairara who telephoned Konofilia, not Konofilia who telephoned us. At midday on the 8th Konofilia came to the prison to see how we were progressing. I said, *How nice of you to come*. The minister then asked to see Kwanairara. I said, *You're the minister*. So Konofilia spoke to Kwanairara. Somebody had told Kwanairara that we intended to remove him to the provincial prison at Kirakira, on San Cristobal island. He told Konofilia that if he went to Kirakira his life would be in danger. Then the Minister left.'

'And Kwanairara stayed at Rove? Where he has been responsible for all the subsequent troubles?'

'Yes,' conceded Guinan. 'On 9 February Kwanairara tried to convince us that Konofilia had said he could go to the open prison at the north end of Guadalcanal, but that wasn't true of course. But we're rid of him now. He's in Kirakira. He was finally sent there in November. We were able to show that he was behind almost every trouble we've had here, and the Minister at last agreed to his departure, whether or not his life was at risk. There are things I haven't told you. The threat of further breakouts was almost constant. For example Kwanairara put it into the prisoners' heads that in June, on the Queen's Birthday, there'd be a royal pardon for everybody. And the same again on Independence Day, 7 July. And of course each time they weren't released the stones started flying. He also made life very difficult for Christopher Saungao – who I must say has stood up to provocation exceptionally well. His life has been threatened several times. More, Kwanairara was also smuggling messages out of Rove. He still had at least two of the warders in his pocket – though they have gone now. Before Independence Day, for instance, slogans started appearing on the *outside* of the perimeter. *Great Expectations July 7th*, and *Sure – July 7th*. Well, at least we were forewarned. But not for 15 August. Then they all got out again, and for two days we were back to square one.'

Guinan paused, and began leafing through the documents.

'It's incredible. You wouldn't believe what that man's capable of. He's a power to be reckoned with. Here, you see: one of his letters which we intercepted. Unsigned of course, but Kwanairara's hand-writing. A commission to poison Hugh Bennett, myself and Christopher Saungao. Addressed to his *wan tok*. Murder all the non-Malaitans, you see? *Me likem poison these people* it says, for *spoiling the custom belong your island and my island*. And what do you suppose is the promised payment? A thousand dollars? A hundred dollars? Not on your life. What Kwanairara says he'll pay is one block of tobacco. *One block of tobacco!*'

'But now he's in Kirakira!'

'And up to his old tricks! But I've got one surprise in store for Kwanairara. Operation St Helena. Next week the Solomon Islands navy, the gunboat you may have seen, is taking him to Temotu. There's a cell waiting for him there. And it's twelve days' canoe ride away from here.'

Suddenly Guinan shut the file. With his arms crossed tightly in front of him his face shone with defiance.

I glanced up above his head. There was something new on his pinboard. It was the cover of *Lightning Meets The West Wind*.

Guinan had followed my eyes.

'Yes. Kwanairara is Basiana to my Bell. But I'll tell you this. I know Kwanairara better than Bell ever knew Basiana!'

And he meant it. Across the water, through the heat, Malaita had worked its magic on the Prison Adviser. Weeks later, when I had my photographs developed in London, the resemblance was unmistakable. Guinan standing in the execution pit at Rove, William Bell pictured by Martin Johnson at Auki: as alike as two peas in a pod.

*

My apologies to David Jeremiah, for not calling him later that Saturday morning. Perhaps I would have learned something else about Rove, or Kwanairara, or about Guinan himself. But the truth is I didn't want to learn anything else. Malaita had worked its magic on me as well. The tale had reached its natural expansion, and I didn't want to see it destroyed, or belittled, by further detail.

But also, on my last day in Honiara, I had one other, not altogether unrelated, fish to bag. All week I had failed to lay my hands on the

Kwaio Claim. It looked as though I would actually have to go to Malaita, which I didn't want to do at all. In the end, though, I was spared that most unwanted trip. I am not at liberty to say who finally showed me the document. Suffice it to say that at the Super Club one night there was a person who had run out of float. An American perhaps, or an Australian. Whoever, he had a copy of the Claim in his office. I couldn't xerox it – it had his company's or his embassy's stamp on every page – but if I came along on Saturday afternoon, when no one else was around, he'd leave me alone with it for twenty minutes.

Here are the notes I made:

1927 MASSACRE CLAIM – extracts

(Preamble) 'Two notable occurrences that cause incursion disasters in Kwaio territory were CHRISTIANITY & DEFILEMENT cause by the punitive expedition. During the punitive expedition rules of our ancestors was determined to break forever, the ancestrally conferred power of Kwaio, systematically desecrated sacred things and places. This of course a cataclysmic events in Kwaio.

> (signed)
> 'Ubuni Folofo'u
> Silas Wanebeni'

(Wanebeni: secretary to the Religious Fadanga)

(On Bell): 'His duties met with his destiny, due to the fact, that his laws were overruling the home laws. He prepare his legislations faster than what he expect.'

(In Malaita this triumvirate:
a. Lamo (ramo): leader in bloodfeuding, bounty-hunting;
b. Wane Ni Alo: entrepreneuarial feastgiver and peace keeper;
c. Fataabu: priest, mediator 'with thye spirit'.)

(1927 – HMAS *Adelaide*: here the victims of the reprisals numbered in excess of one thousand; the 'incursion' continued 'massive')

'Ancestral skulls were thrown in the menstrual, bark metas from the menstrual were thrown into the shrines, ritual objects the relics were scattered, desecrated and destroyed . . . Several hundred were shot and hunted as wild animals.' (Babies left unprotected, etc.)

(Compensation: of 4 kinds:

1 Firitaa: 'life compensation for dead relative'.
2 Sinnga: 'sacrifice in purification of expiations'.
3 Du'unga: 'for violation of taboos or replacement of damaged properties'.
4 Totonga: payment 'in case of intercourse'.)

'To prove that the empire do maintain her justice, this claim must be settled in form of payment.'

(Limitation of Claim' (sic): 'We do solemnly declared that since the damage occurred, we were told not to say or complain against the war damaged.'
(Because: 1. The [colonial] government threatened to imprison anyone who did complain – 6 months hard labour – 'real prison not as todays'. 2. 1927–78 Kwaio people 'ignored'. 3 Kwaio cultural centre established (at Narinaasuru) only in 1979 (activating 'researches').)

TARIFF (in Solomon Island dollars)

each life   50 million
each shrine   20 million
each holy house   4 million
each ancestral pig   300,000
each village   100 million
each garden   200 million
each Ba'o (big shrine) 1 billion
each economical pig   200,000
each edible tree   50,000
each drum   50,000
woman raped ('fucked') 10,000

TALLY

1,246 dead
537 shrines
204 houses
11 consecrated pigs
59 villages
1,066 gardens
   Ba'o

420 trees
80 shell money (not mentioned above)
170 war weapons   „
13 consecrated yams and taros   „
30 women raped

TOTAL: SI $294,612,000 (say 300 billion, = £100bn)
(follows: schedules and names for each village)

Earlier in the week I had quizzed John Noss about the Claim. The British High Commisioner offered this statement: 'Although our role in the issue ceased with independence, we are prepared to discuss aid,' – i.e. a hospital, a school or two, and some expat manpower. It is worth noting that the Kwaio people have never had the Statute of Limitations shown to them for their approval: in any strict sense they are not a signatory to it.

I also spoke to Warren Paia, the Special Secretary to the Prime Minister. His view was: 'once stone-age people are alerted it's difficult to avoid confusion'. Paia was one of the new Solomon Islanders. With a degree in political science from the Papuan National University in Moresby he disagreed with Kenilorea. The Solomoners were not a united people. However, with a lot of hard work by central government they could become united. Nation-building was the name of the game. Yes, he could see that a Honiara-based élite was in the process of formation, but you could not have the one without the other.

'And what about the Seventh Day Adventist élite?' I asked.

'What about it?' Paia replied.

An elementary and perhaps costly error on my part. Paia himself was a Seventh Day Adventist. After my visit to his office all my subsequent requests to interview senior Solomon Islands politicians, including Ezekiel Alebua, were either rejected or ignored. This may or may not have been a coincidence.

EIGHT

All *quiet* at *Shark* Point

Midway through the writing of this book I was invited to Canterbury to address a class of students at the University of Kent. Dr Roger Cardinal was running a course on travel literature. For an end-of-term treat he thought his students might benefit from coming face-to-face with a real live travel-writer. I was petrified: I had never before spoken to such a large assembly – there were at least twenty of them; since I was still struggling with my first travel book it was, to say the least, premature to be thought of as a travel-writer; and I was reasonably sure that, after eight seminars on the subject, the students would have acquired a refined critical terminology with which, in no time at all, they would catch me out. Death by a thousand thrusts, I said to myself as I entered the seminar-room, would be kinder. But being the last day of term I was accorded a certain goodwill, and the afternoon passed off without embarrassment. In retrospect it was even a somewhat jolly occasion. All I had to do was remain seated in my chair and field questions. This I managed to do with consummate disregard for the substance of anything that was asked, and also without running dry. But there was one question which, at the point in time, did make me think. Had I decided yet, one of the girls asked, where I was going to end my journey?

No was the short answer to that, I hadn't. But, back home in

London, it occurred to me that perhaps by now I should know where my manuscript was going to end. Indeed, the fact that I didn't know probably explained why I was stuck. The dreaded writer's block had tripped me up. I had only just finished dousing myself at Otakokok and knew not how to continue.

I remained stuck for quite a while, until the day I met Pin Yathay, a refugee from Cambodia. At that point the system started clearing itself.

The outline of the recent and tragic history of Cambodia is just beginning to be generally familiar. On 17 April 1975, thirteen days before the communist forces of Vietnam took Saigon, the Khmer Rouge, clad in black pyjamas and Ho Chi Minh sandals, marched into Phnom Penh. Their first task was to empty the city. Within days the entire population was evacuated to the countryside, to await resettlement in rural co-operatives – i.e. rice-growing labour camps. The only exceptions were the highest ranking officials of the ousted right-wing regime of General Lon Nol, who were taken to the tennis courts and beheaded. In a sense they were lucky.

These executions were followed by any number of witch-hunts. The new *de facto* government, a communist praesidium made up of a handful of veteran guerrilla fighters under the leadership of Pol Pot, had no shortage of 'enemies'. All imperialists, all feudalists and all capitalists – the three reactionary 'mountains' of pre-revolutionary Cambodia – were weeded out and slaughtered, regardless of the Khmer Rouge's own 're-education programme'. But the purges went further than that even. From the beginning mere association was deemed a sufficient ground for reprisals to be taken. Death was the new price for old friendships. A whole family might be eliminated on account of the record of only one of its members. Likewise ethnic minorities were also at heightened risk. First the Chinese, then the Vietnamese were singled out for persecution. Finally the Khmer Rouge themselves bore the brunt of their own vindictive paranoia. If the régime was failing, that, according to Pol Pot's logic, could only be because the revolutionary cadre contained rotten elements. One by one the zones into which Cambodia had been crudely divided after April 1975 were 'purified'. *Those who are not for us are against us* became *and some of those who are for us are against us as well*. Not surprisingly when Vietnam, after more than a year of provocation, launched an invasion at the end of 1978 it took less than four weeks to reach the capital. Morale had utterly collapsed and Cambodia's historic enemy was greeted, initially, as the country's saviours.

Since then something like a complete picture of the atrocities perpetrated by the Khmer Rouge has emerged. The society depicted is one in which every kind of humanizing activity was prescribed. Shops, markets, restaurants and schools disappeared overnight. Money was abolished, reading and writing discouraged, religion outlawed. 'Justice' was no longer administered by courts, but arbitrarily by the three-man committees who ran the co-operatives. There was no system of appeal, although special cases might be sent to Tuol Sleng, the house of torture set up by Pol Pot and his cronies in a former school-building in Phnom Penh. There the head-butcher, a man called Duch, ruthlessly extracted bogus confessions from those he was about to murder.

The majority of Cambodians, however, were spared Tuol Sleng. They found death in other ways. Many were taken to the local 'killing fields', and many more died of malnutrition, disease and despair. Nor was there any kind of remission. Hospitals were hospitals only in name. The revolutionary medicines they dispensed were generally lethal. Nor could one look to one's family for succour, for of course the family was a reactionary institution which the Khmer Rouge did what they could to smash. Some children were led away to child labour camps; others remained behind to denounce their parents – of all practices encouraged by the Khmer Rouge the most obnoxious.

As to the number who died, estimates vary between 1,500,000 and 3,000,000, out of an original population of 7,000,000. The Khmer Rouge supervised a three-year festival of blood in which no one was safe. It was the Asian holocaust par excellence. And I choose my words. The Khmer Rouge sought to excel. They sought to excel all other communist régimes, and they sought to excel each other in ideological commitment. But what they actually excelled in was negativity. They wanted to uproot everything, to leave nothing untouched by their hard-won victory. Every thread in the social fabric had to be laboriously unstitched and destroyed. A nation and a culture had to be deconstructed.

Again I choose my words. There was much about the Khmer Rouge venture that smacked of the Left Bank. Nor is this colouring wholly fortuitous. Saloth Sar, alias Pol Pot, was first introduced to revolutionary Marxism in Paris, where he went as a student. In 1949 he enrolled at the Ecole Francais de Radio-electricite. He quickly joined the French Communist Party. In the climactic and acrimonious debates about Stalin he backed Stalin. Some of his French contemporaries later became the intellectual leaders of the Left Bank revolution of the late 1960s and early 70s. The 1968 riots, structuralism, deconstructionism, *épater le bourgeois* and all of that. But in the ricefields of Indo-China the same game, *tuer le père*, was played without blackboards. The pay-off was not prestigious professorships, or the gaining of academic bastions: it was power, and the inconceivable misery of millions. And it all happened against a backcloth of international diplomacy and national rivalries that was equally devoid of the humanitarian impulse. France (the former colonial power), Vietnam, China, the United States and Russia are all implicated in the grim unfurling of events. Each pursued geopolitical ambitions regardless of the local consequences.

I first began to be properly aware of the human tragedy involved when I read *Cambodian Witness* by Someth May. This was the last book I reviewed before leaving England for Bangkok and the journey I have described. Not long after my return from the Solomons Anthony Curtis at the Financial Times sent me two further Cambodian titles: *When The War Was Over*, a comprehensive and brilliant overview by the former Washington Post correspondent Elizabeth Becker, and *Stay Alive, My Son* by Pin Yathay.

What struck me about the latter, originally published in France six or seven years before, was its strong convergence with Someth May's account. Both books were written by young men of good education who escaped to Thailand. Blow by blow they bore witness, at times with the same voice, to the same harrowing episodes: the exodus from Phnom Penh, the first inhuman co-operatives to the south of the city, resettlement in the north-west – the promise of a better life, and the actuality of continuing persecution.

Because I had read, and written about, Someth May's book first I did not give Pin Yathay's as much attention in the *FT* as I must surely have done otherwise. But that was not the only reason. I also felt that, comparing Someth May and Pin Yathay, Someth was the one I would have preferred to be stranded on a desert island with. Each man had to maintain a stance of total obedience toward his Khmer Rouge masters and at the same time do whatever he could to help his dwindling family survive. But whereas in May's case this involved stealing cassava and palm sugar under the cover of night, Pin Yathay ensured survival by, amongs other means, creating an artificial market for American dollars.

Pin Yathay, a civil engineer, was Director of Public Works when the Khmer Rouge arrived in Phnom Penh. As such he belonged to the monied class. He was able to take with him a secret stash of US$3000. In the rice-camp, however, his bills were useless – until one day he persuaded the illicit brokers (former Chinese traders, who else?) that dollars after all had value. What he did was this. Having hoarded or otherwise obtained a few extra packets of rice he offered them for sale. Everyone had a few dollars and they were only too glad to get rid of them. This in due course wrongfooted the campsite brokers. Why was Comrade Thay accumulating dollars? What did he know that they didn't?

Everything went according to plan. Within a few days the brokers were chasing dollars, and nobody had more than Pin Yathay. Thus in a relatively short space of time he was able not only to repossess his original rice, but also much more besides. By a clever ruse he had converted his worthless paper into the most precious commodity of all: food.

Amid the famine Pin Yathay thus guaranteed survival for what was left of his family, for a few more weeks at least. Yet, as I read this passage, a chill ran through me. There was an element of dog eat dog about it. More rice for Pin Yathay's family meant less rice for someone else's. And rice was terribly short. It was just the sort of speculative capitalism that, in Asia, had paved the way for blood-red ideologues. The Khmer Rouge, loathsome as they were, had a point.

In my heart I didn't blame Yathay. He'd already suffered too much, and more was to come. When society breaks down to the extent it broke down in Cambodia it becomes fatuous to blame anybody for anything. But I did see his dollar market as yet another manifestation of the complex pathology that had torn Indochina apart. And in a way it was tearing me apart as well. Writing up my travels through S.E. Asia and in the Solomon Islands was not an unpleasant undertaking. In fact, the temporary block aside, I was enjoying writing more than I had in a long while. But now I was struck by the inconsequentiality of what I was writing, and of anything that I might write. My conversation with Dr Penelope Key at the Mendaña Hotel kept returning to haunt me. I had raised a certain standard, and now I was marching against it. Only I wasn't marching, I was strolling, I was dawdling.

But to return to Pin Yathay. In April 1975 he left Phnom Penh in a family group that numbered eighteen – grandparents, adults, children. A year and a half later only three remained: Pin Yathay, his second wife Any, and son, Nawath. The rest had died of disease (dysentery, cholera, the dengue) or malnutrition, or else had been 'taken away' by the Khmer Rouge. Pin Yathay concluded that the only hope left was to escape to Thailand. But he knew that the journey would be as arduous as it was dangerous. If they were caught they would be shot immediately. But there was also the problem of how to survive, perhaps many weeks, in an inhospitable mountain jungle. He doubted whether any of them could make it. In particular he feared for his son. Nawath was not well. But because he was still a child Nawath had the best chance of surviving if he remained behind. Generally speaking the Khmer Rouge preferred killing adults. Therefore Pin Yathay and his wife arrived at a dreadful decision. They would leave without him.

They left the camp in the dead of night, together with a small band of other escapees. Very soon the party was forced to break up. Every time they heard noises in the forest they had to scatter, lest the Khmer Rouge recapture them all. Pin, his wife and another woman pressed on by themselves. And then the worst thing of all happened. One evening a fire they had made to prepare food got out of hand. All around the forest was alight: the surest way to attract attention. At once they gathered up their few belongings and fled into the bush. But two hundred yards away Pin's wife, Any, remembered they had left behind a condensed-milk can. The can was essential to their survival. It was the only means they had for cooking their dwindling store of rice. Any volunteered to go back and fetch it. Before Pin could stop her she was gone. When she didn't return he went off to find her. She was nowhere to be seen. Then he tried to find his way back to Eng, the other woman. But in the gloom Pin lost his way. Within the space of an hour he had become detached from both his companions.

Alone, Pin Yathay struggled onwards toward his goal, a river that separated Cambodia from Thailand. Without rice he was reduced to eating what little he could forage in the forest – a few wild plants that were edible, the odd mushroom, the odd bird's egg. Once he was able to supplement his diet with some raw bat. And when he reached and crossed what he thought was the border river another evil surprise awaited him. He was still in Cambodia. He knew this because twenty yards away three Khmer Rouge soldiers were pointing their rifles at him.

One of the characteristics of the Khmer Rouge, one of the hallmarks of their style, was their deference towards those whom they had decided to kill. This, in part, explains why for a long time there was initially so little resistance to them. When they cleared Phnom Penh they did so as though it were an act of uncommon humanity. In Pin Yathay's own words, 'All their sinister tasks were accomplished in secret, while in public they always spoke politely, even at the worst of times, preparing death with unfailing courtesy.' His new captors were no exception. They told him he was lucky he had met them. They said he was not an enemy, but their comrade, their brother. Then they escorted him to a camp near the real border river and gave him a large meal. Afterwards he was allowed to rest on a proper bed. In the evening another meal, and more sleep. But this time, for his 'own good', he was tied up. If he wasn't tied up, it was explained, he might stray onto a land-mine.

The next day was the same. More food and more rest. By listening to the soldiers' converstion Pin realized they were waiting for the camp commander to return. Then his fate would be sealed. That night he was trussed up for the second time. Probably he had only a few hours left. But somehow, miraculously, he loosened his bindings and made his second escape. By a stroke of great good fortune a thunderstorm camouflaged his movements, so his guards didn't hear his departure.

The man I met, of all places at the St James's Restaurant in Fortnum & Mason on Piccadilly, bore no resemblance whatsoever to the man whose photograph, taken at the Mai Rut refugee camp in 1977, adorned the front cover of *Stay Alive, My Son*. In the photograph Pin Yathay appeared to have lost all of his hair and most of his flesh. His neck was as thin as a bicycle pump. Ten years on, he looked remarkably well-groomed. His soft, understated features reminded me, if anything, of a Japanese businessman's. His hair was very much thicker than mine. Whatever physical hardships he had been through he had made a spectacular recovery. He was as unravaged as the sitting member for Basildon. He was also, when I spoke to him, remarkably at ease with himself. In his position, confronted with the iced-sundae décor of London's premier grocery store – oh yes, undertones of one or two Thai massage parlours – I would have been distinctly ill at ease.

But not so Pin Yathay. As I was shortly to discover he had an emotional constitution that both explained his survival, and matched it.

We were both there, for tea, at the invitation of his publishers. But although Pin Yathay's book had been published just two days before, it was not his launch party. It was the actor Terence Stamp's, whose first volume of autobiography was just out. Press attention to the two authors had been more or less evenly divided: Stamp on one page, Pin Yathay on the next. At Fortnum's, however, it was the actor who received the limelight. It was sadly amusing to watch booksellers and mediamen beelining for the face they knew.

But it was not for me to complain. I was the beneficiary, for I had Pin Yathay largely to myself. To my immense delight I discovered that, in his present incarnation as Project Engineer for the Manila office of the Asian Development Bank, he had been to Honiara. This spared me from having to ask him any questions about Cambodia in what was a wholly inappropriate setting. And Pin, I think, was pleased as well. He'd spent three days talking to newspapers and radio-stations as a refugee and wanted to be reminded that he did have another identity. In no time at all the spark of friendship was kindled. We both agreed that Honiara was a town neither of us would be sorry never to see again.

Since I had arrived late it was not very long before the other guests began taking their leave. I asked Pin about his plans. He said he didn't have any. Why not come for a sauna? I suggested. Pin nodded in agreement. Within the hour we were sitting beside each other, naked, and very hot.

What my motives were in this I'm not entirely sure. I'd been promising myself a sauna for several days and Fortnum's had transformed a desire into a need. To a degree it was simply a matter of taking Pin with me. But I suspect something a little more devious may have been afoot. I'm not altogether sure I wasn't thinking to myself: let's get this fellow in the heat, and then quiz him about his dollar market.

Perhaps if I'd had a tin of mosquitos on me I might have succeeded. But as it is I didn't, and if either of us got the better of the other in the sauna it was Pin Yathay. As soon as we were seated on the scrubbed bench I put some question or other to him. I forget what it was, but it certainly had nothing to do with dollars. I am not as lacking in subtlety as that. But Pin was on his guard. Or rather, he was anxious not to have to be on the guard. Arranging himself in the half-lotus position he gave me an impromptu lesson on the importance of emptying the mind. Then he closed his eyes, and for the next ten minutes neither of us said a word. Soon I was squirming in the heat. My companion remained perfectly still. He had retreated inside a Buddhist concentration. Indeed he seemed not to be breathing, and I briefly alarmed myself by imagining he was dead. In Cambodia his heart must have taken a fearful pounding, and conceivably it was not the brightest idea to have brought him to such a place.

But all was well. If anybody's heart had suffered it was mine. As we took refreshments in the rest-room afterwards it was several minutes before my pump stopped knocking against the walls of my rib-cage.

When I was sufficiently recovered I asked Pin whether his experiences in Cambodia had done anything to damage his faith. Most Christians, I said, faced with that kind of ordeal, would have given up their belief in God. Pin smiled, and shook his head. Definitely, he said, his faith had been improved. He asked me to remember that Buddhism is not in its core a belief in anything, rather it is a way of improving one's life. But what he did believe in were the concepts of karma and rebirth. What we do in this life will affect us in the next. Perhaps what had happened in Cambodia was because of the moral decline of the country over many hundreds of years. But also, what we do now, how we live now, will help us now.

Then I asked whether he still felt oppressed by his experiences. Did he, for example, suffer in his dreams? Were there nightmares? Again Pin shook his head. The exercise of writing his book had proved an effective therapy. He had no bad dreams any more, and he had put the Khmer Rouge firmly behind him. Now he was living partly in Manila, partly in France, with his third wife, another Cambodienne who had been in Paris at the time of the upheavals. She had given him three sons, who had replaced the children he had lost.

Finally I put my own predicament to him. I said to Pin Yathay that, after reading his book, Elizabeth Becker's and Someth May's, after reviewing the Cambodian tragedy, I had some difficulty in finding any excuse for my own work. But even before I had finished saying this Pin gave me his reply. He had grasped my drift perfectly. He knew just how I felt. But I wasn't to let it get on top of me. The essential thing, he intimated, was to live life as it presents itself – as one finds it oneself,

275

and not as other people find it, whatever their situations. My writer's block was a *malade imaginaire* and I should pay no further attention to it.

The things that happened in Cambodia, like some of the things that are happening in parts of Indonesia, are exceptional. That is what makes them tragic. Civilization does after all have something to offer, and perhaps it behoves us to record and celebrate lesser events. If I learned anything in the Solomons I learned that Clausewitz got it back to front. War is not a continuation of politics by other means. Politics is a continuation of war by other means. War, when it does occur, is always a slide down the evolutionary ladder.

*

At the appointed hour, and with my notebooks full, I flew from Honiara on Guadalcanal to Yandina on Mbanika, one of the Russell Islands. The flight took forty minutes. The diminutive aeroplane, which might have been assembled from the bits and pieces in my grandmother's kitchen drawer, landed in a puddle. The pilot declined to leave his seat. A typhoon, which two days before had devastated Vanuatu, a thousand miles to the south-east, was now limping toward the Solomons. We had courted a major upset among the clouds and understandably the man was anxious to return to base before the heavens broke conclusively. 'If I stay here,' he said, 'by lunchtime I won't have a plane left to go anywhere.'

I hadn't minded the tossing and the bumping. More or less I was on my way home. Once I got clear of the Solomons I had only Port Moresby, Manila, Taipei, Hong Kong, Bangkok and Amsterdam between me and London. A couple of days on the reefs up in New Georgia perhaps, and then – whoosh!

That night the weather made a noise like one of the longer programmes of an automatic washing machine. Squall. Silence. Wind. Silence. Squall. Silence. Wind. And then the besetting deadweight of tropical rain. This, I was assured, was the typhoon blowing itself out. But there was a little left in the beast yet. It was not about to lie down just like that.

But I wasn't quite finished either. Unbeknown to my host, the finance manager of the Lever Brothers' copra plantation, I had come to Yandina as a potential saboteur. I wanted to discover whether there was any truth to the story about the Australian who had invented a coconut dehusker.

Clearly if the maverick Aussie's revolutionary fanglement worked the Solomons were about to be hit by the biggest South Sea hurricane ever. At Yandina alone there were 4000 Melanesians dependent on the copra factory. If at a stroke the copra workers were all made redundant then the domestic economy would be pushed back as far it would go.

My self-appointed mission was to expose the scandal before it happened. Yet I was on uncomfortable ground. Mbanika was a private island. Levers had graciously invited me to Yandina on the assumption that I was merely a roaming travel-writer. More, they had laid on a copious supply of baked beans, tinned stew and welsh rarebit for my nourishment. Like a cur I was about to abuse their hospitality with a belch and a fart.

In the end face was saved on both sides. John, the finance manager, took me on a tour of the plantation, and I pretended to be frantically impressed until such time as I could raise the issue without seeming unduly impudent.

We were standing on Shark Point. Shark Point is a cliff off which a great quantity of US Army ordnance was dumped into the sea in 1946, on the principle that it was cheaper so to dispose of it than crate the goddam pile back 'cross the 'cific. Now the site was used to get rid of the entrails of slaughtered cattle. A small herd was maintained on the island so that, on Christian feastdays, everyone could enjoy fresh meat. When the viscera are tipped into the water sharks from many miles around gather to create what John described as a lively churn. Hence the name, Shark Point.

'Next time throw in a few coconuts,' I ventured slyly. 'Then the sharks can whip you up some beef-flavoured coconut milkshake.'

'Oh coconuts,' John snorted.

'Anything wrong with coconuts?' I probed.

John heaved a sigh that appeared to settle right in front of his face, for he jerked his head back as though it were being attacked by wasps.

'Everything. Copra prices are collapsed, and likely to remain so for a long while. Possibly for ever in fact. It's no longer cost effective to farm the things.'

'Then isn't the answer to reduce the costs? For example, if a proper mechanical dehusker could be found . . .'

John smiled.

'Don't make me laugh,' he said. 'On average someone comes along with a new machine once a year. Some of them even work, just about. But the trouble is they don't work fast enough. Melanesians are still much quicker, therefore more economical.'

'But what if . . .'

'Besides,' John continued, 'we've got a different solution. We're switching to cocoa and coffee. It'll give our workforce something to do.'

I looked out across the sea, which was strangely calm. Not one shark's fin broke the pale blue mirror. The storm, it seemed, was spent.

But it wasn't spent. It was merely recuperating before one last blast.

The following afternoon the *Iu Mi Nao*, the biggest of the passenger boats registered in the Solomons, was late; and even when it did appear, an angelic white speck between two smaller plantation islands on the horizon, John told me to sit down again.

'It'll be another hour at least. She's an old lady, but very deliberate. The time to move is when she cuts her engines, right here in front of us.'

Obediently I lay back in my cane chair. Soon I heard parties of Melanesians coming up the road behind us, while across the waters dug-out canoes began converging on the landing-stage just beyond the copra factory.

'Relax,' said John, intercepting my anxiety. 'It's the big event here. There's only one other vessel that calls in at all regularly.'

But eventually even John's patience broke. We slung my bags into his jeep and were there half an hour before we need have been. So were hundreds of other people. Russell Islanders, Malaitans, Gilbertese, and a few fat Polynesians milled about in a wholly uncharacteristic animation, their normally passive features riven by the prospect of the boat.

As with infinite sluggishness the *Iu Mi Nao* crept nearer, my heart sank. Out of the offing I saw her for what she was. Not the poetic sketch that adorns p. 164 of Gavin Young's *Slow Boats Home*, but 500 tons of heavily oxidized groaning metal.

Christ!

The shore-fasts thrown, there was a mad scramble for the gaping hole in the hull which served as the boat's portal. Through this unfriendly aperture I was propelled by those around me in such a manner that when I landed inside I landed on all fours.

I found my legs and turned, just in time to see my kit flying toward me.

'Upstairs!' John gesticulated. 'Get yourself upstairs!'

I made it to a companion and got myself upstairs. There I was politely directed to the first-class cabin at the 'fore by two Bellonan women chewing sugar cane. They did not remove the cane from their mouths when I addressed them, but their hand-signals were courteous and beautiful. One look inside the cabin, however, was enough to decide me against any indoor sailing. I would stay outside until the *Iu Mi Nao* reached Gizo, my destination. It was a nasty airless hole that would not have disgraced Rove prison. The only mitigating feature was a set of antique aircraft seats, incongruously covered with much worn blue velvetine. These, when I entered, were mostly occupied by sacks of rice and cardboard boxes tied up with string. My fellow-passengers preferred the floor, on which several mattresses were spread. There was also a large number of babies. Presumably these were the chief reason for travelling superiorly – as a kindness to other passengers.

Having parked my belongings in a dark corner I returned to the deck. Here all was a mess of beer-cans and fruit-skins. With difficulty I made it to the rail. The *Iu Mi Nao* was already pulling into the lagoon. The jetty was receding, but still crowded. Those not falling in the water were waving a long goodbye.

Once out of Yadina the boat altered course to north-west, with the larger high-hilled island of Pavuvu to port. Soon, behind Pavuvu, a staggering red-green-gold sunset began seeping across the sky. Then, portside again, a spate of smaller islands. Flat wooded reefers, disembodied clumps of pubic hair floating on the translucent sea. I wanted to laugh.

When the light faded a crewman touched me on the arm and pointed to the cabin. I looked around and saw that the deck had emptied.

'Thanks,' I said, 'but I'm fine right here.'

Five minutes later I was where I'd been told to be, and feeling unbearably close to my non-existent maker. The lovely sunset had abruptly revealed its hidden self. The storm came up faster than an Exocet. The swell was horrendous, and a driving rain had me soaked in seconds.

The cabin was scarcely a refuge. The stink was hellish, and so was the floor. Everybody had been or was being sick between the mattresses.

For a while I hid in the loo, a dark green steel-walled room that was really an enlarged canteen of the sort used by soldiers. Again I thought of Rove. But it was only when I realized I was not alone that I decided to give someone else a go. A giant rat, also green, was nibbling my sneaker laces.

The next ten hours were purely phantasmagoric. I tried going on deck again, but each time was firmly repelled by the elements. Removing a bundle of pineapples I curled up on a chair. I had just got myself into an astonishingly uncomfortable position when my larynx told me that if I moved another muscle I, too, would vomit. To compensate my brain went into a freespin. Before long Nicholas, a nice man claiming to be the purser, was crouching by my side, forcing conversation. He was from Tikopia, he said. Would I, when I got back to England, present his regards to Sir Raymond Firth? He had never met Sir Raymond, he said, but all the same he would certainly be glad if someone passed on his wishes. Then, before I was sure he existed, he had vanished.

On my other side – which, since I was squeezed up against the wall, in retrospect was odd – a man of about Firth's age was telling me that although the Great Game of Cricket would not be played Forever, there surely would be a Last Great Test when England would beat the Old Enemy resoundingly and the Final Tally of Wins and Losses would stand in England's Favour for the Rest of Time. But his voice, adopting the rhythm of the *Iu Mi Nao's* engine throbbing incessantly at a great distance below me, was so ineffably monotonous that I fell asleep. When I next looked at my watch it was one o'clock.

The cabin was empty, and everything had gone very still. The boat had dropped anchor precisely in the middle of nowhere. Or rather, on the edge of some Conradian immensity: for when I looked outside there was no land to be seen, no shore lights, but in every direction canoes were darting across the ink-black water like so many fleas.

Having taken on fresh passengers and discarded others the *Iu Mi Nao* chugged back into the storm. I returned to my seat and once again fell into a troubled doze. Three hours later it was the same again, only now we had found land. I stared down over starboard at a clearing that could have fitted three times onto a small-town theatre stage. A backdrop of outsized fronds had been run up by the props department, and the scene was lit by just two kerosene lamps. Beneath one of these, and beneath the still falling rain, a huddle of near-naked New Georgians examined their mail, endeavouring to decipher names and addresses before the words were washed away.

I rubbed my eyes as the ship's bell rang. Garsini (which I believe was the name of the landing) at once began retreating into the blackness. As the heavy pitch resumed I stumbled back to my makeshift berth and at once locked into another impossible position.

I now imagined I was a Japanese baby strapped to its mother's back.

This was no ordinary hallucination. It lasted well over an hour, and throughout that period it was inconceivable I could possess any other identity.

When I came properly to it was broad daylight and the *Iu Mi Nao* was ploughing along a wide green lane. On both banks large yellow logging machines from time to time lurched raucously out of the bush, looked at the passing vessel, and reversed into their secret hideouts.

I made my way up to the bridge and presented myself to the skipper, a short Guadalcanalian called Henry.

Henry was not at all surprised by my uninvited presence. He was a model of good humour, and willingly showed me his equipment.

'No, no radar,' he said, answering my question by pointing at his compass. 'We make do with this.'

'And charts?'

'Oh, you want to look at my charts. I see.'

Henry turned, unlocked a drawer and pulled them out, blowing off a quantity of dust in the process.

It didn't take an expert to see how perilous were the waters we had just traversed. But before I could comment on the miracle of Henry's seamanship – it was as though unassisted a blind person had walked across Paris in the rush hour – my eye was caught by the manufacturer's plate to the right of the wheel. Needless to say the *Iu Mi Nao* was made in Japan. Eight years ago she was on her way to the breaker's yard when the Coral Seas Shipping Company stepped in and bought her.

So I arrived in New Georgia, where I stayed two days in Gizo and two days in Munda, back the way I'd come. At Munda I met a Peace Corps worker who looked and spoke exactly like Rosemary Bush, one of the characters in the novel I had started writing and then abandoned in

Tretes. 'The flahs,' she said, staring at the horizon with a Martini in one hand, 'are worse than the shah-harks.' And then, for good measure, she said it again: 'The flahs ah worse than the shah-harks.' Otherwise much of my time I spent canoeing across the lagoons accompanied by a very pleasant Malaitan called Mr Lalao. Mr Lalao, a man just turned 50, would dive overboard whenever we passed the edge of the reef, usually without taking so much as a breath. He would stay down for what seemed an interminable age, and then resurface clutching a baby clam or a seaslug. The water was as clear as Gordon's Gin, and as warm as a bath. Soon I was joining him on his underwater forages.

Soon, too, I was swimming from coral island to coral island. Often I just rested on the surface, propelling myself gently forward by wriggling my toes, marvelling through my goggles at the Fabergé creations a few feet below me.

The high point was finding a blue starfish. Until that moment I simply hadn't known that blue starfish exist. And perhaps I'm still not convinced. What the blue starfish thought about me I don't know. Lying there, three fingers curled round the lip of a sandcovered shell, he would have noticed a large shadow pass across the seabed around him. Glancing up he would have observed a rather pale human being glide by, like an airship perhaps, a human being with slightly short legs, none too much hair on his head and a ridiculous smile on his face.

If, to the starfish, I looked like an idiot, that was because I felt like an idiot. A very happy idiot. The Solomons, far from destroying my health, as I feared would happen when I was reading Jack London the year before, had restored it. But only just. And I suspect that the large quantity of baked beans I ate on Mbanika was ultimately responsible for my recovery.

Within a short time of my arrival on Guadalcanal my stomach had once again broken down. Mrs Williams, Honiara's premier chemist, sold me a packet of Immodium. Further, she advised me not to eat a thing for twenty-four hours, but take soft liquids only. I followed her advice. I abstained from all solids. But I did not do what I should also have done and stay quietly indoors. Instead I rushed madly about in the heat, and finally paid the penalty.

George Anderson had engineered my invitation to a cocktail party given to honour the new US Ambassador to the region. Five minutes after arriving at the Honiara Hotel I was unceremoniously on my way out again. One sip of orange juice and I started keeling over. That awful moment just before a faint when the end really does begin to look very near. Faces spinning, blood pounding in the ears, pillars dissolving. Someone, I thought, had thrown a bucket of water over me. But it wasn't water, it was my own sweat.

'He's going,' I heard one voice say.

'Malaria,' said another.

'Definitely!' warbled a third.

George was at my side in a trice, and half-carried me to his car. He was also thinking out aloud. 'You might be our first case,' I heard him say. And he wasn't referring to malaria.

That galvanized me. I made a determined effort not to pass out and I didn't – mainly because I knew that if I did I'd never come to again.

'Well, this isn't going to do your image any good,' George continued as he climbed into the driver's seat beside me. 'Harold Robbins never faints.'

'Then perhaps I should,' I replied feebly and closed my eyes.

We got to the Mendana, where George left me propped against the long reception desk while he went off in search of Dr Edge.

Immediately I revived. The sweating stopped, and my brain rapidly normalized.

Out of breath George returned.

'It's okay,' he panted, 'Dr Edge is in his room and will be with you in a jiffy. How are you feeling?'

'Much better, thank you.'

George glared at me.

'Then for God's sake look as if you're ill!!'

Obviously I'd spoiled a first-class flap. Yet, with that remark of his, *you might be our first case*, George had created another. The Big Fear now took hold of me in a Big Way. Over the following days I did everything to take my mind off the possibility. Hence, in part, my determination to see as many people as possible. And in this respect Bill Guinan proved the perfect antidote. Rove took me completely out of myself. But whenever I was alone, whenever I returned to my room at the Mendana, I sat and brooded, consumed by paranoia. That damn gamma globulin! Stupidly, in my notebook, I even drew up a table of symptoms, or what I thought to be the symptoms, to assist me in a grim diagnosis. Thus, against 'Nightsweats', I found myself answering: Yes. Enervation? All the time. Confusion? Yes again. Rashes? None so far. Shortness of breath? Only when I smoke.

On these counts it was touch and go whether I had the roke or not. I could just about worm my way out of it. But when I considered my bowels the pendulum swung heavily, overwhelmingly against me. I'd had diarrhoea for close on three months, and as yet there was no sign of an abatement.

Mrs Williams's Immodium more or less held me together, but only for a week. After that I was on my own again. And at once the squitters returned.

'So that's it,' I concluded. 'What a huge waste life is!'

By the time I reached Yandina I was simply going through the motions, nothing else. I had this idea that if I could only make it back to England I could be hospitalized in comfort.

Eventually I did get back. I even trooped off to St Stephen's Hospital in Fulham and took the test.

The doctor who interviewed me was extremely suspicious. He couldn't understand why I thought I might have Aids. All gamma globulin, he said, was rigorously checked. So unless I had been up to something else . . .

At that point I lied. I described all the women in Bangkok I hadn't had as though I had had them, and, to egg the pudding, a dozen more in rural Java who were purely imaginary.

When I returned for the results a woman doctor put her hand on my shoulder, firmly closed the door of her consulting room, and asked me, in the nicest possible way, to have a seat.

'Well now . . .' she said, placing my file carefully in front of her. 'Let's have a look, shall we?'

'Oh God,' I thought, 'something has gone terribly wrong. I really have got it!' It was all a charade. She knew perfectly well what was inside the file.

The woman's expression paled a little as she read through the laboratory report. Then she looked up.

'You're quite well!' she said.

'Am I?'

'Yes, you are.'

I should have been more relieved and more thankful than I was, but the truth is I already knew I was well.

It happened on the *Iu Mi Nao*, something I omitted to mention. It was when I was in the john, the green canteen, in the middle of the storm. As I stood up to avoid the rat I glanced down into the bowl. To my astonishment I had produced a perfectly well-formed stool.

*

All along I've maintained that it's not the sights seen so much as the people encountered that intrigue me when I travel. But that one small sight I shall remember as long as I live. Not perhaps a very pretty image for a chap to carry around in his head, but salutary nonetheless. When I hear and read about Aids victims I find it impossible to ignore the suffering, mental as well as physical, that must be involved, just as, because I have spent time in S.E. Asia, I find it impossible to close my mind to the atrocities perpetrated in Cambodia or Irian Jaya. In both cases the people caught up in an untimely web of death seem to me, by any reasonable standard, to have been innocent and helpless. To condemn an individual because, let's say, he's gay is equivalent to condemning him for the colour of his skin, or his nationality.

After we had finished in the sauna I took Pin Yathay to an inexpensive and crowded Chinese restaurant in Soho. There we were obliged to share our table with two Japanese airline hostesses. These girls were particularly interested in my guest. Sharing my impression that he looked like a Japanese businessman they were convinced that he came from Tokyo. When it transpired he didn't we played the guessing game. Korean? No. Chinese? No, Indonesian? No. Thai? Wrong again. But you're getting warm, I said. The girls' faces went blank. Eventually Pin told them. Cambodia. One of the girls' faces lit up. She'd heard of Cambodia, she said. But that was all she had heard. Just the name.

Briefly I described what had taken place in that country. The airline hostesses were not impressed. On the contrary they seemed suddenly rather anxious to leave. A fairly typical Japanese reaction one would have to say. Misfortune contaminates, therefore the misfortunate should be avoided.

Perhaps Pin was a little bewildered by these people's ignorance and unconcern. On the other hand perhaps he regarded their ignorance and unconcern as welcome evidence that the evils of Pol Pot's regime are not universal. It was not, after all, in his character to issue hasty recriminations. At any rate, even when we said goodbye on the street afterwards he forebore to comment.